A PRACTITIONER'S HANDBOOK FOR INSTITUTIONAL EFFECTIVENESS AND STUDENT OUTCOMES ASSESSMENT IMPLEMENTATION

A PRACTITIONER'S HANDBOOK FOR INSTITUTIONAL EFFECTIVENESS AND STUDENT OUTCOMES ASSESSMENT IMPLEMENTATION

by **James O. Nichols**
Director, University Planning and
Institutional Research
The University of Mississippi

Resource Sections by

Sheri Blessing, *University of Kansas Medical Center*
Gale Bridger, *Louisiana State University, Shreveport*
Marilyn Brown, *University of Maryland, College Park*
Harriott Calhoun, *Jefferson State Junior College*
Mary Kinnick, *Portland State University*
Marsha Krotseng, *University of Hartford*
Gary Pike, *University of Tennessee, Knoxville*
Linda Pratt, *North Carolina Central University*
Donald Reichard, *University of North Carolina, Greensboro*
Brenda Rogers, *North Carolina Central University*
Bobby H. Sharp, *Appalachian State University*
R. Dan Walleri, *Mt. Hood Community College*
Lori Wolff, *The University of Mississippi*
Michael Yost, *Trinity University*

Agathon Press
New York

This is a substantially revised and expanded version of
Institutional Effectiveness and Outcomes Assessment Implementation on Campus:
A Practitioner's Handbook, Agathon Press, 1989.

© 1989, 1991 by Agathon Press
5648 Riverdale Avenue, #50
Bronx, NY 10471-2106

Library of Congress Cataloging-in-Publication Data

Nichols, James O. (James Oliver), 1941—
    A practitioner's handbook for institutional effectiveness and
student outcomes assessment / by James O. Nichols ; resource
sections by Sheri Blessing . . . [et al.].
        p.   cm.
    Rev. ed. of: Institutional effectiveness and outcomes assessment
implementation on campus. c1989.
    Includes bibliographical references and index.
    ISBN 0-87586-095-8 : $30.00
    1. Universities and colleges—United States—Evaluation.
2. Universities and colleges—United States—Accreditation.
I. Nichols, James O. (James Oliver), 1941–   Institutional
effectiveness and outcomes assessment implementation on campus.
II. Title.
LB2331.63.N54   1991   91-19200
378.73—dc20   CIP

Printed in U.S.A.

Contents

Preface and Acknowledgments   vii

CHAPTER ONE
Explaining the Handbook's Use in Institutional Effectiveness
and Outcomes Assessment Implementation   1

CHAPTER TWO
Overview of the Institutional Effectiveness
Implementation Plan: Its Assumptions, Basis,
and Execution   19

CHAPTER THREE
Building the Necessary Foundation for Institutional
Effectiveness: The First Year   31

Resource Sections

Developing the Expanded Statement of Institutional
Purpose (Michael Yost)   39

Attitudinal Surveys in Institutional Effectiveness
(Gale Bridger and Lori Wolff)   55

Cognitive Assessment Instruments: Availability and
Utilization (Marsha V. Krotseng and Gary R. Pike)   76

Assessment of Behavioral Change and Performance
(Mary R. Kinnick and R. Dan Walleri)   104

Assessment-Related Information from Institutional
Data Systems (Bobby H. Sharp and Sheri Blessing)   130

CHAPTER FOUR
Detailed Design at the Departmental Level   149

Resource Sections

Statements of Outcomes/Objectives and Assessment at
the Departmental Level (Linda Pratt)   155

Setting and Evaluating Intended Educational
(Instructional) Outcomes (Brenda Rogers)   168

Setting and Evaluating Objectives and Outcomes in
Nonacademic Units (Marilyn K. Brown and
Donald J. Reichard)   188

CHAPTER FIVE
Initial Implementation   209

CHAPTER SIX
Establishment of the Annual Institutional Effectiveness Cycle   219

Resource Section
Implementing Institutional Effectiveness at Two-Year
Colleges (Harriott Calhoun)   228

CHAPTER SEVEN
Maintaining Institutional Effectiveness Operations Over an
Extended Period of Time   239

APPENDIX A
Our University Expanded Statement of Institutional Purpose   245

APPENDIX B
Example Expanded Statement of Institutional Purpose for
Your Community College   257

APPENDIX C
Examples of Linkage Between Expanded Statement
of Institutional Purpose, Departmental/Program Intended
Outcomes/Objectives, and Assessment Criteria
and Procedures   261

APPENDIX D
Outline of Twelve-Month Sequence of Events for
Preparation of Expanded Statement of Institutional Purpose   275

APPENDIX E
Executive Summary Academic and Administrative
Program Review Procedure—Northwestern University   281

Index   287

Preface and Acknowledgments

When the first edition of this book was published in 1989 under the title *Institutional Effectiveness and Outcomes Assessment Implementation on Campus: A Practitioner's Handbook*, it was clear that assessment of student outcomes and institutional effectiveness was already a significant movement in higher education. Since then, the movement has grown in influence, as evidenced by the increasing interest of the federal government, the activities of regional and professional accrediting associations, and the concerns expressed by governors and state legislatures. Nevertheless, because this is still a relatively new trend, many institutions that are considering implementing a program of institutional effectiveness and student outcomes assessment are faced with the problem of how to put these relatively theoretical concepts into clearly manageable procedural form.

As we suggested in the Preface to the first edition of this book, the search for an implementation model is complicated by several factors. Institutions with national reputations in student outcomes or institutional effectiveness are often described as (a) unique, (b) being led by a Chief Executive Officer with a particularly keen interest in the subject, or (c) financially benefiting from implementation through their state funding formula and therefore able to invest heavily in the implementation process itself. Because these institutions are unique, their models of implementation seem irreplicable, which leaves more traditional two-year and four-year institutions "reinventing the wheel" of outcomes assessment or institutional effectiveness implementation.

The search for an implementation model or plan is further complicated by the difficulty of adapting another institution's actions to the campus environment and the position of a number of accrediting associations. Institutional effectiveness or outcomes assessment, more than many of the processes in higher education, must be tuned to each more than many of the processes in higher education, must be tuned to each particular campus environment. Trying to "plug in" procedures used at another institution can be dangerous.

Regional and professional accrediting associations, under the guidance of the Council on Postsecondary Accreditation, have been among the leaders in the spread of outcomes assessment or institutional effectiveness implementation. However, these accrediting bodies, while willing to set institutional criteria for implementation results, have been in most cases understandably reluctant to specify **how** these mandates are to be met for fear of being accused of being "prescriptive" regarding internal institutional operations.

It became apparent in the summer of 1987 that (a) the national movement toward institutional effectiveness was continuing to gain momentum, (b) there were a number of institutions that were beginning implementation, and (c) the absence of a generalized model or plan for implementation was causing wasteful and potentially hazardous duplication of effort in designing implementation processes on many different campuses. At that time, the undersigned primary author and a number of colleagues who had led successful outcomes assessment implementation on their own campuses, played major roles in the authorship of accrediting association documents concerning outcomes assessment or institutional effectiveness, pilot-tested accreditation association requirements concerning the subject, served on accreditation teams with individual responsibility for outcomes assessment, consulted widely in the field, or were then actively involved in implementation activities decided to pool their knowledge and experience in an effort to propose a general model or plan for implementation of institutional effectiveness and outcomes assessment.

It was determined that the implementation plan or model to be delineated in the first edition of this book should:

- Outline a general sequence of events leading toward genuine and comprehensive campus implementation of institutional effectiveness or outcomes assessment.
- Be adaptable to virtually every type of institutional circumstance.
- Require as small an amount of additional funding as possible by the institution.
- Be supported by detailed review of practice or literature in the field at the critical points of implementation.

Several years later, it was apparent to the primary author and his colleagues that the original circumstances leading to the development of the initial publication still existed, but that rapid developments in the field could usefully be incorporated into a revised version. It was determined that in addition to the very substantial updating of a number of the original resource sections, this second edition would (a) be more "generic" in tone, (b) include more examples of and a specific Resource Section concerning implementation at two-year colleges, (c) also cover performance and behavioral means of assessment of intended instructional (educational) outcomes, and (d) address assessment in non-academic areas. When we had completed our updates and additions we realized that we had produced a work that was more than fifty percent larger than the original version.

The pages that follow were designed to meet the original criteria as well as those established for the second edition. *A Practitioner's Handbook* is divided into three basic sections. Chapters I and II explain the *Handbook's* use and offer an overview of the institutional effectiveness or outcomes assessment implementation plan. Chapters III through VII deal with the specific sequence of events or activities suggested during the course of four years in working toward comprehensive institutional implementation. These chapters are supported by nine Resource Sections covering in greater depth more specific technical aspects of implementation, including tests, surveys and other aspects of instrumentation that have advanced substantially even during the preparation of this edition. Finally, the third section of the *Handbook* offers examples at the institutional and departmental levels of institutional effectiveness implementation at the fictitious institutions, "Our University" and "Your Community College." Overall, the *Handbook* is intended to provide the practical guidance needed for implementation as well as specific examples of that implementation.

It is important to understand that the field continues to grow rapidly, and with each passing year the experience base of institutions that have successfully implemented outcomes assessment or institutional effectiveness operations increases at a faster rate. Accordingly no publication in this area can remain completely definitive over a period of years. Nevertheless, we have attempted to provide substantially more information than was available at the time of the first edition and trust this new version will be a useful tool for its intended audience.

Acknowledgments

I am indebted to the Resource Section authors whose biographical sketches follow collectively and individually for the quality and promptness of their submissions as well as for their suggestions guiding the general refinement of the *Practitioner's Handbook*:

Sheri Blessing is a Research Analyst with the University of Kansas Medical Center. Her primary responsibilities include external reporting and data collection, including the use of automated data systems. Previously, she worked with Institutional Research at East Carolina University. She is currently working on her Ph.D. in Higher Education Administration at the University of Kansas.

Gale W. Bridger is Associate Professor of Education and Associate Vice Chancellor for Academic Affairs at Louisiana State University (LSUS) in Shreveport. She serves as chief planning and evaluation officer for the university and coordinates the institutional research function. In 1981–82, Dr. Bridger was instrumental in establishing LSUS as a pilot institution for the Criteria (while still in draft stage) of the Southern Association's College Commission. Her institution has adopted a performance plan that includes a multiple effectiveness measures, all coordinated through her office. She is a Past President of the Louisiana Association for Institutional Research and has served on a number of SACS visiting committees with primary responsibility for Criterion III: Institutional Effectiveness. Most recently, she has served on a task force to develop training materials for SACS visiting committee members. She earned her doctorate in secondary education at The University of Mississippi in May 1974.

Marilyn K. Brown has been Director of Institutional Studies at the University of Maryland at College Park since 1979. She earned her Ph.D. in higher and adult education at the University of Maryland in 1990. She was a member of the campus committee that developed and implemented the UMCP Academic Support Unit Review Process and has been a participant in numerous reviews on campus. Active in both the Association for Institutional Research and the Southern Association for Institutional Research, she has presented papers, served on panels, chaired the Local Arrangement Committee for the Baltimore AIR Forum, served on and chaired the Academic Affairs and Faculty Issues Track for the Forum, and served on the Nominating Committee. She is currently Secretary of SAIR.

Harriott D. Calhoun is Director of Institutional Research at Jefferson State Community College in Birmingham, Alabama. She is an active member of Southeastern Association for Community College Research, National Council of Research and Planning, Association for Institutional Research, and Alabama Association for Institutional Research. She is very involved at her college in institutional planning, in defining and assessing student learning outcomes, and in assessing institutional effectiveness. She earned bachelor's and master's degrees in sociology and received the Ph.D. in higher education administration from the University of Alabama.

Mary K. Kinnick is Professor of Education at Portland State University in Portland, Oregon and Coordinator of the program in Postsecondary, Adult, and Continuing Education. Her teaching and scholarship focus is on assessment and evaluation in higher education and she participates in the organizational leadership core of the doctoral program in Educational Leadership. She earned her Ph.D. in higher education at the University of Colorado, and she is a former Director of Institutional Research at Portland State University. She has served as President of the Pacific Northwest Association for Institutional Research and Planning (PNAIRP) and as a member-at-large on the AIR Executive Committee. Her publications include a chapter on "Increasing the Use of Student Outcomes Information" in Peter Ewell's (ed.) *New Directions for Institutional Research* monograph (no. 47, 1985), "Assessing Educational Outcomes."

Marsha V. Krotseng is Assistant Director of Planning and Institutional Research at the University of Hartford. She has actively studied assessment, institutional effectiveness, enrollment management, faculty, and institutional advancement issues at that institution and in her previous role as Institutional Research Associate and Assistant Professor of Higher Education at the University of Mississippi. Her responsibilities have included the development of attitudinal survey instruments for both graduating students and alumni. Active in the Association for Institutional Research, she is currently a member of the publications board. She also serves on the editorial advisory board for *Educational Studies*, engages in consulting on institutional effectiveness and executive information systems, and has presented numerous papers at regional and national conferences. Dr. Krotseng holds a doctorate in higher education from the College of William and Mary.

Linda K. Pratt holds a Ph.D. in psychology from Texas Christian University. As the Associate Vice-Chancellor for Academic Affairs for Research, Evaluation and Planning at North Carolina Central University in Durham, N.C., she coordinates and monitors the planning system and oversees institutional research and academic evaluation activities. Previously she served at the National Laboratory for Higher Education, where she wrote more than a dozen technical reports. Former President of the Southern Association for Institutional Research, she has also been active in the Association for Institutional Research, serving on the Professional Development Committee and the Nominating Committee and chairing the Workshop Committee. As a professor of psychology, she teaches and advises graduate students.

Donald J. Reichard has been Director of the Office of Institutional Research at the University of North Carolina at Greensboro since 1974. From 1970 to 1974, he was a Research Associate with the Southern Regional Education Board. His Ph.D. in higher education is from Michigan State University. In 1986–87, he served as President of The Association for Institutional Research. The title of his Presidential General Session Address at the 1987 AIR Forum in Kansas City (with Theodore J. Marchese) was "Assessment, Accreditation, and Institutional Effectiveness: Implications for Our Profession."

Brenda Hyde Rogers earned a Ph.D. in psychology from North Carolina State University where she holds an adjunct appointment and teaches tests and measurement. She served as Assistant Director of Institutional Research at North Carolina State University from 1982 to 1987 and is currently the Associate Director of the Office of Research, Evaluation and Planning at North Carolina Central University in Durham, N.C. She directed one of the seven student outcomes projects sponsored by NCHEMS/Kellogg and has written numerous papers and reports on student performance and institutional effectiveness that have been presented at national, regional and state conferences. She is currently president of the Southern Association for Institutional Research and a member of the Nominating Committee of the Association for Institutional Research.

Bobby H. Sharp is Director Of Institutional Research at Appalachian State University in Boone, North Carolina, where he also holds an academic appointment in the Department of Leadership and Higher Education. He earned a Ph.D. in Consumer Economics from Virginia Tech and holds other graduate degrees from the University of Kentucky and Duke University. His prior institutional research positions have included Associate Director of University Planning and Institutional Research at the University of Mississippi and Director of Institutional Research at the Mississippi University for Women. His research interests include decision support systems and modeling.

R. Dan Walleri received his Ph.D. in Political Science from the University of Hawaii in 1976. He has been at Mt. Hood Community College since 1978 and is currently Director of Research, Planning, and Administrative Computing. Mt. Hood is the national headquarters for the Consortium for Institutional Effectiveness and Student Success in the Community College, which is affiliated with the American Association for Community and Junior Colleges (AACJC). Dan is currently president of the National Council for Research and Planning (a council of the AACJC), a past-president of the Pacific Northwest Association for Institutional Research and Planning, and is an active member of the Association for Institutional Research. He has authored or co-authored articles on student outcomes, assessment, and institutional effectiveness.

Lori A. Wolff is an Institutional Research Associate and Adjunct Assistant Professor of Educational Research and Statistics at the University of Mississippi. She is a member of both the Association for Institutional Research and the Southern Association for Institutional Research (SAIR). She received a Ph.D. in higher education from Saint Louis University and undergraduate and masters degrees from Creighton University. While at Ole Miss, Dr. Wolff has co-authored articles and papers in the area of institutional effectiveness and outcomes assessment with Dr. James O. Nichols, including a paper concerning "The Status of Institutional Effectiveness at Institutions of Higher Education Within the Southern Association of Colleges and Schools," which won an award for best paper at the 1990 SAIR conference.

Michael Yost, Jr., has been at Trinity University, San Antonio, Texas, since 1971, and is currently Assistant to the President, Director of Institutional Research, and a tenured professor. He has earned bachelor's and master's degrees in the sciences and a doctorate in research design, methodology and applied statistics. Dr. Yost is experienced in the development, implementation and evaluation of educational and institutional programs, statistical analysis, and computer applications. He has published more than 150 articles and chapters dealing with methodological and statistical applications. He has also made numerous professional presentations in the United States and in Europe and is presently a consultant to several universities and a number of corporations and law firms.

In addition to these Resource Section authors, there is another group of individuals without whose work this publication would have been impossible. These are the staff within the Office of University Planning and Institutional Research (UPIR) at the University of Mississippi. They include Ms. Harolyn Merritt, who spent countless hours assisting in preparation of the manuscript, as well as Ms. Katherine Adams and Ms. Donna Walker, who were of invaluable assistance in editing the work. In addition, Dr. Marsha Krotseng, the co-author of one of the Resource Sections and a former staff member in UPIR, prepared the subject index. Finally, if the following document is readable and free of grammatical, spelling, punctuation, and similar errors, a major reason will be the contribution of Dr. Sharon Sharp, who served as copy editor for the document. Sharon's close scrutiny improved all our work markedly.

Institutional effectiveness and outcomes assessment implementation is as dynamic a field as there currently is in higher education. Suggested practices today, in the light of further experience and improved instrumentation, are being improved almost overnight. Nonetheless, this second edition of the *Practitioner's Handbook* represents the most current and up-to- date material and suggestions available to a number of us in the field. It is respectfully offered for your consideration and use.

December 1990
James O. Nichols
Oxford, Mississippi

Endorsement of this publication has neither been sought nor received from any professional or regional accrediting association.

JAMES O. NICHOLS has been Director of University Planning and Institutional Research and Adjunct Assistant Professor of Higher Education at the University of Mississippi since 1979. He has been active in the field of institutional research and planning at a series of progressively more comprehensive institutions since 1971 and during that time served in leadership capacities in state, regional, and national professional associations.

During the past four years, he has played a substantive role in the publication of regional accrediting association guidance regarding specific responsibility for assessment of institutional effectiveness; presented international, national, regional, and state level workshops on institutional effectiveness implementation; and served as a consultant to more than 30 institutions regarding outcomes assessment and institutional effectiveness implementation. He received his Ph.D. in higher education from the University of Toledo in 1971 and since that time has made numerous contributions to the literature of higher education and to the programs of many professional meetings. His other major professional interests relate to college and university fiscal planning.

CHAPTER ONE

Explaining the Handbook's Use in Institutional Effectiveness and Outcomes Assessment Implementation

What can be expected from this publication?

The purpose of this *Handbook* is to provide a "cookbook" for the individual or group of persons on a college or university campus who have been given responsibility by the institution's chief executive officer (CEO) for implementation of institutional effectiveness or outcomes assessment activities. As any good cook will admit, there is more than one way to prepare a stew, and that adage also holds true regarding institutional effectiveness and outcomes assessment activities. Presented in this *Handbook* is one recipe that the author and his associates recommend as a starting point for implementation (cooking) activities. Individual cooks (practitioners) on each campus will naturally want to season or adapt this recipe to the taste (environment) of their own clientele (campus). There is no implication that the methodology proposed is the only manner through which such activities should be implemented.

How does this *Handbook* relate to other recent publications in the field?

This document is different in a number of ways from others that have been published in the field. First, it focuses almost exclusively on the *how* of institutional effectiveness or outcomes assessment rather than the *why*. For a variety of reasons—ranging from the perceived intrinsic value of the assessment of student educational outcomes (as a means for refinement of the educational process) to the more pragmatic reality of external forces (accrediting agency, state governmental agencies, etc.) requiring such actions—institutions across the country have already answered the why question and are now seeking to determine how best to implement such assessment procedures. If your institution has not answered the why question in a clearly affirmative manner (for one reason or another), close this publication and devote your time to an activity that promises to be more productive. Unless an institution is clearly committed to institutional effectiveness or outcomes assessment at the beginning of implementation, much energy will be expended with little genuine hope for meaningful impact on actual campus operations.

Second, this document attempts to be decidedly more practical than theoretical in its approach to the subject. Even when describing *how*, professional educators frequently slip into the glories of the cognitive and affective domains and other educational jargon. This document will touch on such concepts strictly in laypersons' terms and move quickly to the more pragmatic means through which these concepts may be implemented on each campus.

This is a *handbook* rather than a scholarly work. In the body of the text, only sufficient references to credit primary sources will be found. However, in the resource sections amplifying the body of the text, sufficient references to provide additional guidance concerning the various subjects are provided. For those interested in pursuing the subject of institutional effectiveness and outcomes assessment past the level of this document into a more scholarly treatment, the publication *Assessment in Accreditation* (1989), by John Folger and John Harris, is recommended as a further primary source.

The *Handbook* is directed at the level of the practitioner rather than the chief executive officer (CEO). Although the support of the chief executive officer is absolutely essential to successful implementation, that support should have been gained in answering, "Why do this?" Also, the content of this document will be more detailed than one can reasonably expect a CEO to take time to digest. Undoubtedly, the practitioner or group whom the chief executive officer has appointed to implement such activities will want to brief the CEO or explain to him or her the general outline of the implementation plan developed; however, this explanation should remain quite general unless requested otherwise or necessary to insure the CEO's support.

Other than the CEO and the individual or group charged with responsibility for coordination and support of institutional effectiveness, departmental chairpersons are the most important parties in implementation. To assist departmental chairpersons in their endeavors, a companion work to the *Handbook*, the *Departmental Guide to Student Outcomes Assessment and Institutional Effectiveness* (Nichols, 1991), has been recently published. The *Departmental Guide* shares many of the subjects included in the *Handbook* and utilizes several of the examples from this publication. However, the *Departmental Guide* is about one-fifth the size of the *Handbook* so that it can be quickly reviewed by busy departmental administrators.

Finally, this *Handbook* describes a set of procedures for implementing **institutional effectiveness**, a concept that includes the assessment of student outcomes. However, institutional effectiveness extends beyond that important activity by placing the assessment of student outcomes as the focal point of an institution's commitment toward accomplishment of its statement of purpose.

The "assessment" movement sweeping through much of higher education is frequently focused at the departmental level solely within the academic components of an institution. These departmental outcomes assessment activities often seek to determine what students are learning in an effort to improve instructional methods or curricula. On some campuses, the results of the assessment of student outcomes or learning are compared to a departmental or program statement of expected or intended educational (instructional) outcomes. Although such assessment activities are laudable in their own right, in many instances they lack institutional-level commitment, and their continuation over an extended period of time may be questionable.

Institutional effectiveness, as described in more detail later in this chapter, raises the unit of analysis to the institutional level and incorporates assessment activities throughout the institution's instructional, research, and public service functions as well as its administrative and educational support components. Extension of the unit of analysis to the institutional level is accomplished by linkage of departmental statements of intended educational (instructional), research, and service outcomes, as well as administrative objectives, with an expanded statement of institutional purpose or mission. Verification that the institution's statement of purpose is being accomplished can be ascertained only through assessment results, which indicate that departmental/program intended outcomes (educational, research, and service) or objectives (administrative) are being accomplished. In this process, all components of the institution have a direct or indirect role to play in supporting or furthering accomplishment of the statement of purpose.

In summary, this document can be described as

1. Focusing primarily on the *how* in assessment and assuming that the question *why* has been answered;
2. Emphasizing the practical implementation of institutional effectiveness activities;
3. Constituting a handbook rather than a scholarly work;
4. Being intended for the practitioner-level user;
5. Describing a long-term program of genuine implementation, rather than a "quick fix";
6. Including student outcomes assessment within an overall program of institutional effectiveness.

National Development of the Assessment (Institutional Effectiveness) Movement

The movement toward assessment (and then institutional effectiveness) on a national basis began in the early 1980s when various national commissions or committees completed a series of studies, which included the following:

To Strengthen Quality in Higher Education: Summary Recommendations of the National Commission on Higher Education Issues (1982)

A Nation at Risk: The Imperative for Educational Reform (Bennett, 1983)

To Reclaim a Legacy: A Report on the Humanities in Higher Education (Bennett, 1984)

Involvement in Learning: Realizing the Potential of American Higher Education (NIE, 1984)

Each of these national commissions or committees called for a renaissance in American higher education and the development of "excellence," particularly in undergraduate education. Most of these studies also included some reference to assessment of undergraduate learning as a component of a program for enhancement of students' achievement.

By the mid-1980s, this call for an assessment of educational accomplishments, originally intended within the context of an overall improvement in higher education at the undergraduate level, had become separate and served as the centerpiece for the federal government's higher education policy under then Secretary of Education William Bennett. Addressing the American Council on Education in 1985, Bennett ("Bennett calls," 1985) indicated that "colleges should state their goals, measure their success in meeting those goals, and make the results available to everyone . . . If institutions don't assess their own performance, others—either states or commercial outfits—will most likely do it for them" (p. 25). This federal emphasis on assessment by Bennett culminated, at the close of the Reagan administration, in a change in the federal regulations through which the federal government recognizes the Council on Postsecondary Accreditation (COPA). The essence of the change in accreditation policy that related to institutional effectiveness or outcomes assessment is as follows (*Federal Register*, 1987, p. 173):

CHANGES IN FEDERAL ACCREDITATION POLICY

Part 602—Secretary's Procedures and Criteria for Recognition of Accrediting Agencies

§602.17—Focus on Educational Effectiveness

The Secretary determines whether an accrediting agency, in making its accrediting decisions, systematically obtains and considers substantial and accurate information on the educational effectiveness of postsecondary educational institutions or programs, especially as measured by student achievement, by—

(A) Determining whether an educational institution or program maintains clearly specified educational objectives consistent with its mission . . . ;

(B) Verifying that satisfaction of certificate and degree requirements by all students . . . who have demonstrated educational achievement as assessed and documented through appropriate measures;

(C) Determining that institutions or programs document the educational achievements of their students . . . in verifiable and consistent ways, such as evaluation of senior theses, review of student portfolios, general educational assessments (e.g., standardized test results), graduate or professional school test results, graduate or professional school placements, job placement rates, licensing examination results, employer evaluations, and other recognized measures.

(D) Determining the extent to which institutions or programs systematically apply the information obtained through the measures described in Paragraph (C) of this section to foster enhanced student achievement.

During the Bush administration, the momentum generated by former Secretary of Education William Bennett has until recently been neither intensified nor diminished; however, several recent events have indicated a change in this relative apathy on the part of the federal government. In December 1989, speaking in Atlanta at the annual meeting of the Southern Association of Colleges and Schools (SACS), Dr. Leonard Haines, Assistant Secretary of the Office of Post-secondary Education in the U.S. Department of Education, stated that the concept of institutional effectiveness was being seriously considered for inclusion in the reauthorization of the Higher Education Act in 1991. In January 1990, then Secretary of Education Lauro F. Cavazos (1990) listed the following goals for higher education by the year 2000:

- The gap in degree completion rates at both the associate and baccalaureate levels between black and Hispanic students, on the one hand, and white and Asian students, on the other, should be narrowed.
- Fifty percent of all bachelor's degree recipients should be able to demonstrate proficiency in a language other than English.
- All associate's and bachelor's degree recipients should be able to demonstrate proficiency in college-level math and science.
- All graduating students should be able to write coherent, grammatically correct papers and display a basic knowledge of world history, geography, and culture appropriate to their degree level.
- The number of U.S. college graduates completing doctoral programs in the basic arts, mathematics, sciences, engineering, and technological disciplines should be increased by 25%, with the number of women, blacks, American Indians, and Hispanics in this group increased by 50%.
- All students leaving colleges and universities should possess higher-order critical-thinking and problem-solving skills needed to contribute productively to the economic and political life of the nation.

It is of considerable interest to note both the substance of these goals and the performance, results, or outcomes manner in which they were set forth.

Adding their voice to the call for increased assessment activities in higher education were the members of the National Governors' Association. In their report entitled *Time for Results: The Governors' 1991 Report on Education* (National Governors' Association, 1986), the governors called for all colleges and universities to develop comprehensive programs to measure student learning.

This action of the governors is being echoed by legislators and state governing boards. In 1990, Ewell, Finney, and Lenth found that 84% of state governing/coordinating boards either have identifiable assessment initiatives in place or have plans for immediate adoption of such initiatives. These findings updated the results of a 1987 survey, which revealed "a basic change in attitude about the role of state boards, one that would not have been found even a few years ago." Continued the researchers, "Governors and legislators have placed the quality of undergraduate education and student learning squarely on the state agenda. The state boards aim to keep it there" (Boyer et al., 1987, p. 11).

Actions by state legislatures have varied widely in both form and substance. Some states, such as Virginia (Virginia General Assembly, 1987), have asked public institutions to report what assessment activities are taking place and have provided incentive funding to support such activities. Other states, such as South Carolina (South Carolina Commission, 1989), have taken much more prescriptive approaches by identifying specific effectiveness measures upon which institutions are to report.

How has the higher education community responded to this pressure?

The primary response of the higher education community has been through that mechanism designed and established to perform the "quality assurance" role in higher education: regional and professional accrediting associations. The basis for this response had been established many years earlier in practice and codified in the *Policy Statement on the Role and Value of Accreditation* adopted by the Council on Postsecondary Accreditation (COPA, 1982). These broad criteria of an institutional accrediting body, as shown in Figure 1, provide a natural framework into which institutional effectiveness and outcomes assessment concepts can be placed.

To provide further guidance, COPA, which coordinates the activities of virtually all accrediting agencies, issued a special report in 1986 entitled *Educational Quality and Accreditation*. This report dealt more specifically with the need for each institution to "demonstrate that it is accomplishing its purposes" (COPA, 1986, p. 7). This report recommends that educational institutions and programs "sharpen statements of mission and objectives to identify intended educational out-

Figure 1

Common Components of Institutional (Regional) Accreditation

The Accreditation of an Institution by an institutional accrediting body certifies to the general criteria that the institution:

a. Has appropriate purposes;

b. Has the resources needed to accomplish its purposes;

c. Can demonstrate that it is accomplishing its purposes;

d. Can give reason to believe that it will continue to accomplish its purposes.

COPA, 1982

comes" and "develop additional effective means of assessing learning outcomes and results" (p. 7).

Even before this guidance from COPA, many regional (institutional) and professional (programmatic) accrediting agencies included some form or requirement for assessment activities as described in *Educational Quality and Accreditation*. However, renewed emphasis on outcomes assessment and substantive changes in accreditation processes among regional and professional accrediting associations have sprung from COPA's guidance (North Central Association of Colleges and Schools, 1990; Middle States Association of Colleges and Schools, 1990; New England Association of Schools and Colleges, 1990) as well as from public pressure as voiced by federal and state officials.

The growth of assessment or institutional effectiveness implementation on campuses across the country since the late 1980s has been remarkable. Elaine El-Khawas (1990) reported in *Campus Trends 1990* that 8 in every 10 chief executive or chief academic officers responding to her survey indicated some assessment activity then taking place on their campus, and 8 in every 10 reported that in several years some form of comprehensive assessment program would be implemented on their campus. Among those assessment activities that El-Khawas (1989) reported on a year earlier as then being in place or planned were the following:

Assessment Activities Regarding	% with Activities in Place	% with Action Planned
Basic College- Level Skills	65	19
Knowledge in General Education	25	36
Knowledge in Major	26	31
Higher-Order Skills:		
Critical Thinking	14	46
Quantitative Problem Solving	18	42
Oral Communication	21	39
Writing	47	27
Changes in Student Attitudes/Values	17	34
Long-Term Outcomes of Graduates	25	44

The Difference Between "Institutional Effectiveness" and "Outcomes Assessment"

Among the earliest national leaders responding to the call for increased assessment activities was the Commission on Colleges of the Southern Association of Colleges and Schools (SACS), which in 1985 passed a major change in its accrediting procedures in which outcomes assessment (or in SACS's terms, "institutional effectiveness") was identified on an equal basis with institutional processes in the commission's *Criteria for Accreditation*. SACS consciously chose the term *institutional effectiveness* both to avoid the term *outcomes*, which many member institutions felt had become jargon-laden and had acquired undesirable connotations of "measuring everything that moves," and to indicate that the concept described was broader than assessment activities solely within an institution's academic departments.

The author and his associates have also chosen to utilize the term *institutional effectiveness* for the *Handbook*. This choice has been based on the belief that while student outcomes assessment should be the central and most visible focus of the assessment movement, the longer-term success of that movement is contingent upon its integration and support at the institutional level on each campus. In addition, the term *institutional effectiveness* is more descriptive and inclusive of the identification of institutional and departmental programmatic intentions than is the term *outcomes assessment*.

Although substantial diversity in the approaches to and extent of student outcomes assessment requirements by the various institutional (regional) accrediting associations remains, ample evidence exists (see sources cited earlier) that such bodies are in the process of refining and expanding their criteria regarding this subject. As this reformulation or reconceptualization takes place, it is entirely possible (some would say probable) that these products will tie in both the existing requirements for "appropriate purposes" and a "demonstration" that each institution is accomplishing its "purposes" with not only assessment, but also use of the assessment results to resemble the Institutional Effectiveness Paradigm originated by the primary author of this document and shown in Figure 2. In the meantime, to implement this paradigm genuinely and completely, each institution in every institutional (regional) accrediting associations should fully meet three of the four criteria required by COPA (see Figure 1) and show strong evidence of having "the resources needed to accomplish its purposes."

What then are the common components of institutional effectiveness or outcomes assessment?

Although regional and professional accreditation requirements differ in terms of semantics, most call for those components identified by COPA:

1. A sharpened statement of institutional mission and objectives
2. Identification of intended departmental/programmatic outcomes or results

Figure 2
THE INSTITUTIONAL EFFECTIVENESS PARADIGM*

Expanded Statement of Purpose

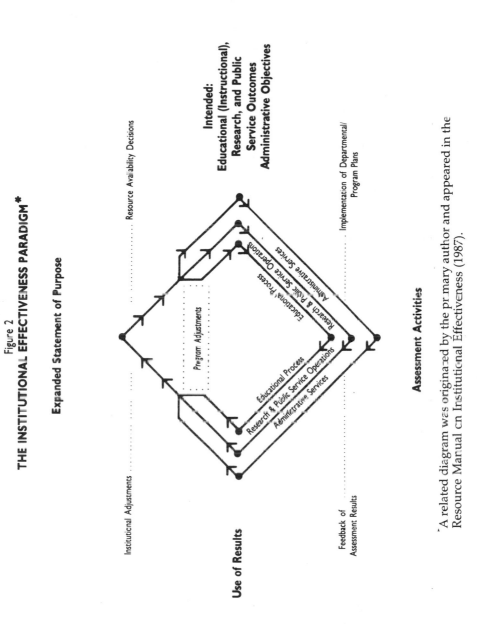

Intended:
Educational (Instructional),
Research, and Public
Service **Outcomes**
Administrative Objectives

Resource Availability Decisions

Implementation of Departmental/
Program Plans

Institutional Adjustments

Program Adjustments

Research & Public Service Operations
Administrative Services
Educational Process

Educational Process
Research & Public Service Operations
Administrative Services

Assessment Activities

Use of Results

Feedback of
Assessment Results

*A related diagram was originated by the primary author and appeared in the
Resource Manual on Institutional Effectiveness (1987).

3. Establishment of effective means of assessing the accomplishment outcomes and results

Added to this, implicitly, is the use of the assessment results to improve the function of the institution or program.

The Institutional Effectiveness Paradigm

How then should an institution go about integrating these three institutional effectiveness components into its ongoing academic and administrative operations so that they become a part of its fabric? What assistance does the literature and practice in the field of higher education administration offer? What current practices can be adapted to incorporate these components? One answer to these questions is graphically portrayed in Figure 2, the **Institutional Effectiveness Paradigm**, and is described in the following explanation.

This paradigm depicts activities that have been proposed, fostered, and occasionally practiced by many authors and institutions for a number of years. It is an important adaptation of the rational planning model that has existed and been discussed in the literature during the past. Skeptics will quickly ask, Why this rational model when we know that campuses are essentially political entities and often act irrationally? The answer is that its elements precisely fit those components required by COPA and inherent in most accreditation processes. Others will then ask, How is *this* version of rational planning different from those that have been proposed and implemented, only to fail, before? The primary differences in implementation of this paradigm are its focus on assessment of results (as opposed to processes and resource requirements) and the fact that representatives of our peers, and indirectly the public, are going to visit our campus periodically to see if the components of institutional effectiveness are indeed being practiced as well as they are professed to be.

The critical elements of the Institutional Effectiveness Paradigm displayed in Figure 2, whose implementation is the subject of this *Handbook*, are as follows:

1. Establishment of an Expanded Statement of Institutional Purpose
2. Identification of Intended Educational (Instructional), Research, and Service Outcomes/Administrative Objectives
3. Assessment of the Extent to which the Intended Outcomes and Objectives Are Being Accomplished

4. Adjustment of the Institution's Purpose, Intended Outcomes/Objectives, or Activities Based on Assessment Findings

In recent years, regional accreditation has focused on accomplishment of the institution's "statement of purpose" or mission. Yet, today, the purpose or mission statements of many institutions are virtually interchangeable. Why is this the case? There are many reasons, but two are most apparent. First, accreditation procedures, up until this time, have been primarily episodic. Every 10 years, the institution's mission or statement of purpose has been studied by a faculty committee, reworded (usually retaining the same lack of substance), presented to the visiting committee, and afterward promptly filed and forgotten for another 10 years. Second, such disregard for the influence of the statement of purpose was possible because of the assumption (some would call it a "leap of faith") that if the institution could demonstrate adequate educational and administrative processes and financial resources, then surely it must be accomplishing its purpose. There exist numerous additional reasons, and the result has been the singular lack of meaning or importance to actual institutional functioning that characterizes most current statements of institutional purpose.

Institutional effectiveness (and outcomes assessment) is changing the role of the statement of purpose. Instead of "assuming" their accomplishments, institutions are being challenged to demonstrate their overall effectiveness through assessment of departmental/program outcomes and objectives linked closely to the institution's statement of purpose. This requirement changes the mission or statement of purpose from a shelf-document with little practical use to the basis for institutional action that it was intended to be. In order to provide a useful basis for institutional effectiveness assessment, most existing statements of purpose must be substantially expanded and maintained to reflect institutional intentions. Further, a working relationship between the revised statement of purpose and the intended outcomes and objectives at departmental and program levels must be established.

Expansion and refinement of the institutional statement of purpose are described in more detail in Chapter 3 as an essential early element of implementing institutional effectiveness. A separate resource section within that chapter offers further guidance concerning means for establishment of such an "Expanded Statement of Institutional Purpose." In addition, Appendix A contains an example of a statement for a four-year college and Appendix B for a two-year institution.

Many aspects of an institution's expanded statement of purpose will require no additional funding, only adjustment of institutional policies. In the case of those components of the expanded statement of purpose that do require increased funding, the institution will be required to set its priorities among what will assuredly be more components and proposals than funds available to support them.

Actual implementation of the institution's expanded statement of purpose will, in most instances, take place at the departmental and program levels through the identification of intended outcomes and objectives linked closely to the expanded statement of purpose and focusing on the institution's intended impact on its constituents or external environment. This intent will primarily consist of institutional assertions concerning its role regarding instruction, research, and public service. These institutional statements of intentions will principally be implemented by the institution's academic units through identification of their own intended educational (instructional), research, and public service outcomes.

The institution's administrative departments also have a vital, if less direct or obvious, role to play in institutional effectiveness. Some expanded institutional statements of purpose will undoubtedly contain specific references to necessary administrative and educational support services (computer, library, counseling, etc.) as being essential to support of the institution's educational, research, and public service outcomes. In such cases, the institution's administrative departments will play a direct role and set objectives clearly related to the expanded statement of purpose. At other institutions, administrative units will not be as directly linked to the expanded statement of purpose but should establish objectives that they believe provide an administrative or physical environment conducive to accomplishment of the institution's expanded statement of purpose.

The formulation of statements of intended outcomes and objectives and assessment of their accomplishments are described in Chapter 4 and its resource sections, entitled "Designing Assessment at the Departmental Level," "Setting and Evaluating Intended Educational (Instructional) Outcomes," and "Setting and Evaluating Objectives in Nonacademic Units." Appendix C contains examples of a number of such statements of intended outcomes or objectives linked with the example expanded statements of purpose contained in Appendixes A and B. Once the expanded institutional statement of purpose and departmental statements of intended outcomes and administrative objectives are in place, the institution (primarily through its departments) will implement activities to accomplish these ends. Without much question, the single aspect of institutional effectiveness that has gained the highest level of public visibility is *assessment*. It is important to note that assessment, within the paradigm described, (a) occurs after establishment of the expanded statement of purpose and its supporting departmental or program statements of intended outcomes or administrative objectives, (b) is focused on ascertaining the extent of accomplishment of those outcomes and objectives identified, and (c) does not attempt to assess every aspect of an institution's operations. Probably the most unnoticed—yet in the opinion of some, most important—elements of institutional effectiveness operations are the feedback or reporting of assessment findings and the use of such findings in adjusting institutional and departmental actions. This use includes potential adjustment of the expanded institutional statement of purpose, modification to departmental/program statements of intended outcomes and administrative objectives, and changes in departmental operations designed to accomplish the purposes intended.

The paradigm described and illustrated in Figure 2 is neither complex nor unfamiliar. The primary difference from earlier paradigms of this type lies in its focus on results rather than processes or resources. Thus, implementation of this paradigm and institutional effectiveness is of necessity ends, rather than means, oriented.

Implementation of the Institutional Effectiveness Paradigm

Although the Institutional Effectiveness Paradigm shown in Figure 2 relates the common institutional effectiveness or assessment requirements contained in most accreditation criteria or standards (see Figure 1) to the literature and practice in higher education, it is apparent that implementation of the entire paradigm in a short period of time is not feasible on most campuses. This is true for the following reasons:

1. There is a clear sequential relationship between a number of the components (first, purpose; then, intended results, etc.).
2. Implementation in a short period (if possible) would leave little time for the institution's ongoing educational, research, and public service functions.
3. The nature of college and university governance requires participation and input by various constituents whose actions are relatively resistant to hasty action.

4. The fiscal implications of implementation of the paradigm in a
   short period could well be prohibitive.

How then does one go about implementing the Institutional Effectiveness Paradigm? The answer lies with the considerable thought,
organization, and participation outlined in the next chapter and ex-
plained in the balance of this *Handbook*.

Scores of practitioners in various fields have observed as they have
attempted to translate theory into practice, Nobody ever said this was
going to be either easy or quick. Implementation of institutional effectiveness is no exception. Unlike Shakespeare's Macbeth, who ap-
proached his mission by musing, "If it were done when 'tis done,
then 'twere well / It were done quickly," those who implement institutional effectiveness should do so carefully and thoroughly or someone's corpse (career-wise) could be the result. The following suggested four-year sequence of events is designed to accomplish
substantive implementation of institutional effectiveness while offering a good chance for the survival of that individual or group there-
with charged.

References: Cited and Recommended

Bennett calls on colleges to assess their own performance, publish results.
  (1985, November 6). *Chronicle of Higher Education*, p. 25.
Bennett, W. (1983). *A Nation at risk: The imperative for educational reform*. Wash-
  ington, DC: Government Printing Office.
Bennett, W. (1984). *To reclaim a legacy: A report on the humanities in higher
  education*. Washington, DC: Government Printing Office.
Boyer, C., Ewell, P., Finney, J. E., & Mingle, J. R. (1987). Assessment and
  outcomes measurement: A view from the states. *AAHE Bulletin, 39*(7),
  8–12.
Cavazos presents higher ed goals. (1990, January 29). *Higher Education and
  National Affairs, 39*(2), 1.
Council on Postsecondary Accreditation (COPA). (1982). *Policy statement on
  the role and value of accreditation*. Washington, DC: Author.
Council on Postsecondary Accreditation (COPA). (1986). *Educational quality
  and accreditation: A call for diversity, continuity, and innovation*. Washington,
  DC: Author.
Criteria for accreditation: Commission on Colleges. (1985). Atlanta, GA: Southern
  Association of Colleges and Schools.
El-Khawas, E. (1989). *Campus trends, 1989*. (Higher Education Panel Report,
  No. 78). Washington, DC: American Council on Education.
El-Khawas, E. (1990). *Campus trends, 1990*. (Higher Education Panel Report,
  No. 80). Washington, DC: American Council on Education.

Ewell, P., Finney J., & Lenth, C. (1990). Filling in the mosaic: The emerging pattern of state-based assessment. *AAHE Bulletin*, 42(8), 3–5.

Farnsworth, S., & Thrash, P. (1990, February 1). Letter to Chief Executive Officers of Commission Institutions regarding assessment from North Central Association of Colleges and Schools.

Federal Register, Department of Education. (1987, September 8). *52 CFR part 602 and 602.17, Secretary's procedures and criteria for recognition of accrediting agencies; Focus on educational effectiveness*. Washington, DC: Government Printing Office.

Folger, J., & Harris, J. (1989). *Assessment in accreditation*. Atlanta, GA: Southern Association of Colleges and Schools.

Middle States Association of Schools and Colleges Commission on Higher Education. (1990, May 18). *A framework for outcomes assessment—Draft*. Philadelphia, PA: Author.

National Commission on Higher Education Issues. (1982). *To strengthen quality in higher education: Summary recommendations of the National Commission on Higher Education Issues*. Washington, DC: Government Printing Office.

National Governors' Association, Task Force on College Quality. (1986). *Time for results: The governors' 1991 report on education*. Washington, DC: Author.

National Institute of Education (NIE) Study Group on Excellence in American Higher Education. (1984). *Involvement in learning: Realizing the potential of American higher education*. Washington, DC: Government Printing Office.

New England Association of Schools and Colleges, Commission on Higher Education. (1990, July 16). Letter to Dr. James O. Nichols regarding institutional effectiveness and outcomes assessment in NEASC.

Nichols, J. (1991). *Departmental Guide to Student Outcomes Assessment and Institutional Effectiveness*. New York: Agathon Press.

Resource manual on institutional effectiveness. (1989). Atlanta, GA: Southern Association of Colleges and Schools.

South Carolina Commission on Higher Education. (1989). *Guidelines for institutional effectiveness*. Columbia, SC: Author.

Virginia General Assembly. (1987). *Senate Joint Resolution 125*. Richmond, VA: Author.

CHAPTER TWO

Overview of the Institutional Effectiveness Implementation Plan: Its Assumptions, Basis, and Execution

Assumptions and Management Decisions Supporting Plan Implementation

The *how* of institutional effectiveness and outcomes assessment is clearly the heart of this *Handbook*. However, it is important to understand the assumptions and basic management decisions that undergird the conduct of the implementation plan described later in this chapter. The implementation plan presented assumes the following:

1. *Institutional support for genuine implementation*—Nothing in this document provides a means through which to emphasize form rather than substance in institutional effectiveness implementation.
2. *Sensitivity of subject*—The most "sacred" activity in higher education is that which takes place behind the classroom door, and no effort should be made by the administration to dictate instructional process or content.
3. *Limited additional funding for institutional effectiveness implementation*—Implementation will cost time and money; however, the expenditure of both should be limited as much as possible.

Probably the most important initial plan management decision or realization in implementation of institutional effectiveness is the need to appoint a single individual to coordinate the process. Why is this the case? First, implementation of institutional effectiveness will be a considerable effort ultimately impacting most aspects of the institution, and the nature of the work required will call for coordination and logistical support across departments and between management levels. Second, implementation of institutional effectiveness is one project that, unlike class scheduling, registration of students, and the payroll, can be postponed unless there is an individual designated to continue moving (pushing) implementation toward culmination. A recent survey (Nichols & Wolff, 1990c) indicates that this appointment of a single individual to coordinate implementation is the most often cited factor facilitating successful implementation.

Who should be appointed to coordinate institutional effectiveness implementation? There is no best answer to this question that applies to all institutions. Three general sources for such leadership appear to be emerging on campuses:

1. Academician—Some institutions find that the credibility gained by appointment of an "interested" member of the faculty to head implementation is worthwhile, given the sensitivity of the subject.
2. Institutional researcher—Given the primarily quantitative nature of the assessment activity and the existence of an office with such expertise, a number of institutions have chosen to designate their institutional research officer to coordinate the implementation effort.
3. Institutional planner—Clearly the heart of institutional effectiveness is its relationship to campus planning efforts, and a number of institutions are choosing to emphasize the connection between institutional effectiveness and planning through appointment of a planning officer to coordinate the implementation effort.

Any of the type individuals just described can be successful in the coordinator's role, as long as there is recognition that it is this individual's responsibility to see that implementation across the institution is being accomplished and, if not, to ensure that the institution's leadership knows why not.

Although the coordinator selected will have central responsibility for implementation, exercise of that role will necessarily be through a team appointed for that purpose, and actual implementation will be the responsibility of the individuals in the institution's administrative and academic departments. There appear to be three institutional effectiveness roles emerging as part of the implementation team: the institutional planner, the departmental facilitator, and the assessment support person (Figure 3).

Figure 3

The Institutional Effectiveness Implementation Team

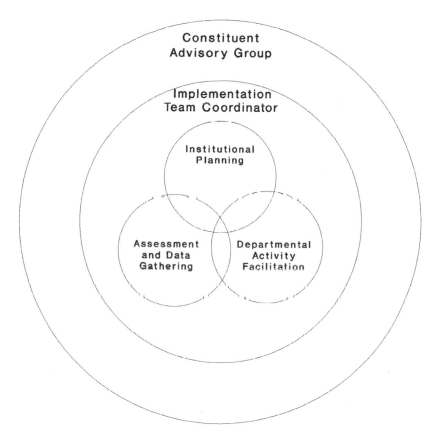

Chief Executive Officer

Constituent
Advisory Group

Implementation
Team Coordinator

Institutional
Planning

Assessment
and Data
Gathering

Departmental
Activity
Facilitation

The Institutional Effectiveness Paradigm begins and ends with planning and assessment of the success of its implementation. A key role emerging is that of coordinating and supporting the planning processes of an institution from the highest level through the academic and administrative departments on the campus. Most authorities in the field of college and university planning stress the importance of linking the ideas expressed in campus plans with the actions taken through fund allocation, and this link between planning and budgeting must be visibly maintained. However, on many campuses this linkage has grown to the point that planning has become little more than a useful form of budgeting. The planning required by institutional effectiveness, although related to budget planning as a means, is distinctly more ends oriented and calls for an additional outcomes or results focus to planning at many institutions.

Academic and administrative departments will undoubtedly require further explanation of the concept and assistance in implementation of institutional effectiveness. The role of departmental implementation facilitator requires an individual with patience, credibility, and knowledge of institutional effectiveness to work with individual departments. Although such an individual cannot be expected to direct implementation within each department, he or she should explain the concept personally to each department (as it relates to their discipline or function), suggest a general course of action that the individual department might take toward implementation, and outline assessment options that are open to the department and are centrally supported.

Although the establishment of intended outcomes and objectives and (to a lesser degree) the conduct of assessment to determine if the intended ends have been accomplished are departmental responsibilities, a clear need exists for a centralized assessment support entity. This functionary (on many campuses the Office of Institutional Research) can provide (a) the assessment expertise needed to assist departments, (b) the logistical means for most efficiently conducting standardized testing and distributing/processing attitudinal instruments, and (c) a centralized point or clearinghouse for assessment results. The organizational implications of such an assignment of responsibility to the institutional research component are reviewed in recent articles in *New Directions for Institutional Research* (Nichols & Wolff, 1990a) and *AIR Professional File* (Nichols & Wolff, 1990b).

Probably the second most-asked set of questions concerning institutional effectiveness (after how) relates to the cost and source of funding. Several basic points related to this subject need to be made:

1. There are clearly increased costs involved, both direct (out-of-pocket expenditures) and indirect (time).
2. The amount of additional direct cost incurred on each campus will depend on the institution's current activities (its existing level of expenditures for planning, institutional research, etc.), the nature of the assessment plan adopted, the size of the institution, and the extent to which the costs incurred are passed on to students through fees for testing. Hence, a cost estimate will be difficult until a number of policy issues are settled and an inventory of existing assessment assets conducted.
3. Many current institutional examples of successful outcomes assessment operations are the result of external grants for this purpose or state funding mechanisms (formulas) that have been altered to encourage and reward such activity. Regrettably, these sources will not be available to most institutions as they go about institutional effectiveness implementation.
4. Initial funding for implementation should be relatively open-ended, although thoroughly justified and carefully monitored.

Given the preceding comments, institutions are best advised to acknowledge two important points: First, implementation of institutional effectiveness will require additional expenditures for which they probably will not receive increased funding. Second, they should begin implementation activities by funding these from contingency or discretionary funds available at the highest levels of the institution until a number of policy-level decisions are made and historical cost data are available at the institution.

Overcoming campus inertia and encouraging institutional effectiveness implementation will take decisive action on the part of the institution's CEO and the establishment of incentives for departmental cooperation. The CEO must not only support implementation but also openly evidence that support. Most CEOs will make the expected verbal endorsement of institutional effectiveness implementation; however, it is their actions that will (or will not) convince those on the campus of their sincerity. Among the actions that a CEO may take to demonstrate visibly his or her support for implementation are

1. Taking an active (though not dominant) role in preparation of the Expanded Statement of Institutional Purpose;
2. Establishing his or her office's administrative objectives supporting the expanded statement of purpose;
3. Contributing to the formulation of his or her discipline's state-

ments of intended educational, research, or public service outcomes;
4. Referencing assessment results in public statements.

At the departmental level there also must be incentives toward
implementation. Probably the best incentive is the intrinsic value inherent in the concept of institutional effectiveness and the improvement of student learning. However, other more extrinsic (and some
would say material) means such as the following may be necessary:

1. Incorporation of institutional effectiveness implementation into
   the reward system (rank, tenure, etc.) for faculty
2. Provision of funding preferences within the institution to departments implementing institutional effectiveness
3. Increase of institutional visibility for those departments actively
   and effectively pursuing implementation

The Plan for Implementation of Institutional Effectiveness and Assessment Activities

Figure 4 contains a plan or sequence of activities for implementation of institutional effectiveness over a four-year period based on the
assumptions and plan management decisions reviewed earlier in this
chapter. Following the "Decision to Implement Institutional Effectiveness and Assessment Activities," events in the plan are portrayed as
developing simultaneously down separate, but closely related, plan-
ning/operational and assessment/evaluation activities tracks.

Building the Necessary Institutional Foundation

During the first year of implementation, most activity of a planning/
operational nature will be focused on "Establishment of an Expanded
Institutional Statement of Purpose" as a foundation for further activities. The "Implementation of Attitudinal Surveys" and the "Conduct
of an Inventory of Assessment Procedures" (as currently being employed at the institution or available to the institution) highlight the
assessment/evaluation activities during the first year of implementation, which can be described as **Building the Necessary Institutional
Foundation**. This first year of implementation activities is discussed

Figure 4

**A Four-Year Plan for Implementation of
Institutional Effectiveness and Assessment Activities
on a Campus**

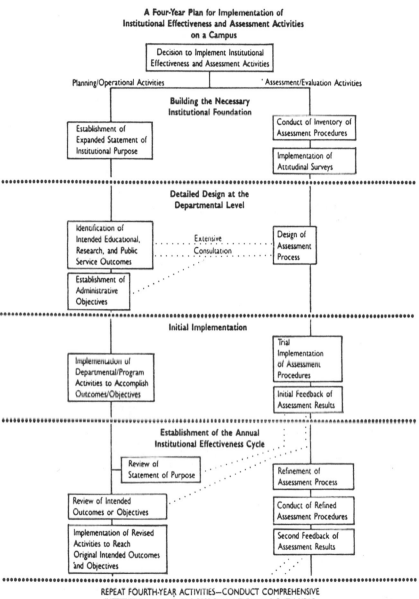

REPEAT FOURTH-YEAR ACTIVITIES—CONDUCT COMPREHENSIVE
INSTITUTIONAL AND PROCESS EVALUATION IN EIGHTH YEAR

• • • End of Implementation Year

in detail in Chapter 3, and four resource sections are provided to expand on the most important concepts contained in that chapter.

Detailed Design at the Departmental Level

The second year of implementation is characterized as **Detailed Design at the Departmental Level**, during which time the work accomplished the previous year at the institutional level will be extended to the departmental level. Planning/operational activities during the second year include the "Identification of Intended Educational, Research, and Public Services Outcomes" and the "Establishment of Administrative Objectives," both of which are closely linked with, and support accomplishment of, the expanded statement of purpose developed during the first year of implementation. These important statements of intended outcomes and objectives are closely coordinated with the "Design of the Assessment Process," through which accomplishment of these intentions will be evaluated. Second-year activities are described in Chapter 4, which includes three resource sections further explaining departmental outcomes/objectives and the design of an assessment process.

Initial Implementation

During the third year of implementation activities, the **Initial Implementation** of institutional effectiveness operations takes place. Based on their work during the previous year, the institution's components will be involved in "Implementation of Departmental/Program Activities to Accomplish Intended Outcomes/Objectives." The primary events during this third year will be the "Trial Implementation of Assessment Procedures," as designed during the previous year, and the "Initial Feedback of Assessment Results," as described in Chapter 5.

Establishment of the Annual Institutional Effectiveness Cycle

Establishment of the Annual Institutional Effectiveness Cycle is brought about in the fourth year of implementation activities and is described in Chapter 6. In that year, and each succeeding year, planning and operational activities will include "Review of the Institutional Statement of Purpose," "Revision of Intended Outcomes or Objectives," and/or "Implementation of Revised Activities to Reach Original Intended Outcomes and Objectives." Likewise, during each year in the annual cycle, "Refinement of the Assessment Process," "Conduct of Refined Assessment Procedures," and "Feedback of Assessment Results" will take place. An additional resource section dealing with implementation in the two-year college (included as part of Chapter 4) has been added to this edition.

Why can't institutional effectiveness be implemented faster?

Some institutions, based on their existing planning and institutional research activities, may be able to shorten the institutional effectiveness implementation plan by 6 months to a year. However, because most existing planning and institutional research functions are designed to support process-type decisions (budgeting, class scheduling, etc.), rather than assessment, the majority of institutions will require the full amount of time to complete implementation. The primary reasons for the lengthy period of time required for implementation are related to the assumptions regarding implementation enumerated earlier in this chapter.

Genuine implementation of institutional effectiveness will change the way many institutions operate. A change of this magnitude cannot be brought about in a short period without creating massive resistance to not only the substance of the change but also the rapidity of the process of change.

In the academic area, institutional effectiveness deals with the most sensitive prerogatives of the faculty—those related to control of the curriculum and the classroom. Although there is absolutely no intention for institutional effectiveness to infringe on these prerogatives, an attempt to rush or force implementation may very well be viewed as such by many faculty. Faculty participation in curriculum design and assessment of the accomplishment of intended outcomes is essential to successful implementation of institutional effectiveness. One immutable law of college and university administration is that you can't rush the faculty without meeting more resistance than it's worth.

Acceleration of the process of implementing institutional effectiveness would require more personnel commitment (although over a shorter period) and higher out-of-pocket costs than most institutions can tolerate. Most institutions of higher learning do not have extra personnel who can readily be diverted to developmental tasks such as implementation of institutional effectiveness. Implementation will require a considerable amount of time on the part of various committees and most certainly within the academic and administrative departments as they identify intended outcomes and objectives as well as the means for their assessment. Frankly, there is a limited amount of "extra" service that faculty can be asked to assume over a short period, in addition to teaching, research, and service. However, extended over the longer period of the proposed plan, this level of involvement is distinctly feasible.

Likewise, rapid escalation of direct out-of-pocket expenditures to support institutional effectiveness will not be feasible at most institutions. Rather, gradual escalation of funding to meet documented needs for activities will be found both more feasible and more acceptable to others on the campus over the longer period of time suggested.

If genuine institutional effectiveness implementation were either easy or quick, more successful examples would be available. On the other hand, careful, well-planned implementation stands a far greater chance for substantive success and continuation over a period of years.

What will be the greatest problems encountered in executing the proposed institutional effectiveness implementation plan?

The problems will, of course, vary from campus to campus, but three of the most likely are (a) gaining the genuine commitment of the institution's administrators, (b) dealing with faculty resistance, and (c) maintaining momentum during the extended period of implementation.

Although verbal commitment (i.e., lip service) to institutional effectiveness implementation will come relatively easily from most administrators, follow-through into sustained support demonstrated by their actions may be another matter. For those not truly committed to the intrinsic value of institutional effectiveness, the key to their sustained support may lie in the extent to which they each become personally identified with the implementation effort and cannot afford to have it fail without reflection upon themselves.

Faculty resistance will arise during the implementation process. Indeed, the recent survey by Nichols and Wolff (1990c) indicates that "indifference or resistance on the part of faculty" is the most often cited factor impeding institutional effectiveness implementation. Such resistance will take forms varying from open resistance from faculty stating that nothing they intend to accomplish is subject to "measurement," to more serious passive resistance which may be found in departments that refuse to implement. In both cases, patience is the key to successful implementation. When gently pressed, even the most vocal faculty member must admit that *some* of the things his or her discipline intends to accomplish are ascertainable or observable over time. From that admission, the reluctant faculty member will often gradually accept institutional effectiveness implementation rather than risk a loss of credibility with his or her colleagues as a reasonable member of the community of scholars.

The department that passively resists implementation is a more serious problem, yet one that also is subject to being overcome with patience. Short of a change in leadership, which ultimately may be necessary, probably the best course of action is the structuring of the individual and departmental reward systems to make it abundantly clear that cooperation in implementation is in the best interest of those involved.

Probably the single greatest problem likely to be experienced with the implementation plan proposed is the maintenance of campus commitment and momentum over the four-year period. On those campuses motivated toward implementation of institutional effectiveness to satisfy accreditation requirements, the leverage provided by this activity will help to sustain momentum. On other campuses it will be necessary to arrange events, activities, announcements, and so forth that emphasize how important institutional effectiveness implementation remains, what has been accomplished to date, what the current activities are, and where those support final implementation.

Summary

In this chapter, the essential components and the sequence of events for the proposed plan for implementation of institutional effectiveness have been very briefly outlined, as well as the assumptions upon which that plan is based and the plan management decisions that will need to be made. Finally, problems that the practitioner is likely to encounter during implementation have been identified. In the next several chapters, more detailed explanations of activities proposed during each year of institutional effectiveness implementation are presented.

References: Cited and Recommended

Nichols, J. O., & Wolff, L. A. (1990a). Organizing for assessment. In J. B. Presley (Ed.), *Organizing for effective institutional research* (pp. 81–92). New Directions for Institutional Research, no. 66, *XVII*(2). San Francisco: Jossey-Bass.

Nichols, J. O., & Wolff, L. A. (1990b). *The role of institutional research in implementing institutional effectiveness or outcomes assessment.* AIR Professional File, no. 37.

Nichols, J. O., & Wolff, L. A. (1990c, October 11). *The status of institutional effectiveness at institutions of higher education within the Southern Association of Colleges and Schools (SACS): Findings of visitation teams, extent of implementation, and factors facilitating/impeding implementation.* Contributed paper at the 1990 meeting of the Southern Association for Institutional Research, Ft. Lauderdale, FL.

CHAPTER THREE

Building the Necessary Institutional-Level Foundation for Institutional Effectiveness: The First Year

Following the institution's initial "Decision to Implement Institutional Effectiveness and Assessment Activities," the first year of implementation activities will be focused on accomplishing the necessary homework to support the balance of the effort during the following 3 years. The first year's work, as shown in Figure 5, is based on the assumptions that

1. There has been a visible and genuine campus commitment to institutional effectiveness implementation;
2. Adequate, though not unlimited, resources have been made available to begin implementation;
3. An individual has been named to assume leadership for coordination of overall institutional effectiveness implementation;
4. Team members with responsibility for institutional planning, departmental activity facilitation, and assessment (data gathering) have also been identified, along with an appropriate advisory group composed of representatives of a cross section of campus constituencies (see Figure 3, p. 21);
5. Basic institutional process-oriented data (enrollment, teaching loads, average salary, etc.) designed to support ongoing decision making at the institution are available.

Figure 5

The First Year of a Four-Year Plan for Implementation of Institutional Effectiveness and Assessment Activities on a Campus

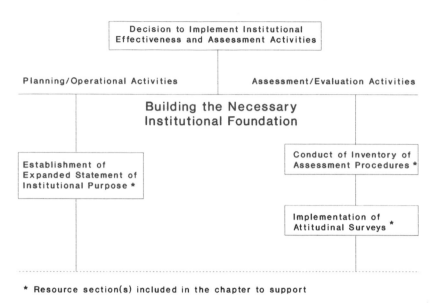

┌─────────────────────────────────────┐
│ Decision to Implement Institutional │
│ Effectiveness and Assessment Activities │
└─────────────────────────────────────┘

Planning/Operational Activities   Assessment/Evaluation Activities

Building the Necessary Institutional Foundation

┌─────────────────────────┐   ┌─────────────────────────┐
│ Establishment of   │   │ Conduct of Inventory of │
│ Expanded Statement of   │   │ Assessment Procedures * │
│ Institutional Purpose * │   └─────────────────────────┘
└─────────────────────────┘
                                      ┌─────────────────────────┐
                                      │ Implementation of   │
                                      │ Attitudinal Surveys *   │
                                      └─────────────────────────┘

* Resource section(s) included in the chapter to support

Within the first year, and in each of the succeeding years, implementation activities will be conducted along the separate, but related, planning/operational and assessment/evaluation activities tracks illustrated in Figures 4 and 5.

Planning/Operational Activities

Planning/operational activities undertaken during the first year of implementation include adaptation of the generic implementation plan provided in this *Handbook* to the specific institution and the formulation of an expanded institutional mission statement.

Figure 4, "A Four-Year Plan for Implementation of Institutional Effectiveness and Assessment Activities on Campus" (see page 25) contains a depiction of the generalized or generic approach to implementation that forms the basis of this *Handbook*. However, it is important to realize that this approach will need to be adapted to specific institutional circumstances. Based on their current situation, some institutions may be able to compress somewhat the process of implementation because of the prior existence of certain components (e.g., an enhanced or expanded mission statement) on their campus. Other institutions will find it necessary to extend the process or commit additional resources to offset initial deficiencies (e.g., lack of basic process-oriented institutional data). The implementation plan depicted in Figure 4 should be modified to incorporate institution-specific terms, adjustments in estimated times, and specific dates by which activities should be completed on each campus. If implementation is in response to accreditation requirements, the institution will also want to ensure that the specific jargon (*outcomes, expected educational results,* etc.) utilized by the accrediting association is also included in the adaptation.

The primary task along the planning/operational activities track during the first year of implementation is "Establishment of an Expanded Statement of Institutional Purpose." This is one of the single most important actions in implementation of institutional effectiveness operations. As stated in Chapter 1, the key difference between outcomes assessment for its own sake and institutional effectiveness is the purposeful manner in which assessment is focused on intended departmental/program outcomes or objectives linked to the Expanded Statement of Institutional Purpose in institutional effectiveness. This linkage is illustrated in Figure 6, and an understanding of it is essential to the concept of institutional effectiveness.

The Expanded Statement of Institutional Purpose is, then, the beginning and the end of the Institutional Effectiveness Paradigm shown in Figure 2 (page 11). It provides the sense of direction or institutional intention that is supported by the statements of "Intended Educational, Research, and Public Service Outcomes" and "Administrative Objectives" identified by the academic and administrative departments. Ultimately, it is the extent to which these intended departmental/program outcomes or objectives have been reached that is reflective of accomplishment of the Expanded Statement of Institutional Purpose.

The term *Expanded Statement of Institutional Purpose* has been chosen for two reasons. First, implementation of institutional effectiveness and outcomes assessment operations greatly expands and enhances the role of the document(s) as a guide to institutional priorities and operations. Second, the actual composition of the statement of purpose currently in existence at most institutions will need to be reviewed and substantially expanded. Many terms can be utilized to

Figure 6

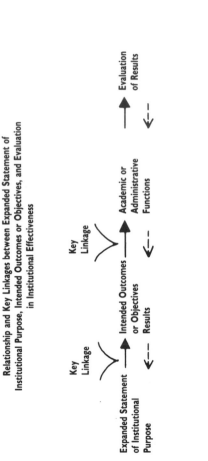

Relationship and Key Linkages between Expanded Statement of
Institutional Purpose, Intended Outcomes or Objectives, and Evaluation
in Institutional Effectiveness

identify and structure such a statement (*mission, role and scope, purpose, goals, philosophy,* etc.), but the important concept to grasp is that the document(s) serving as the campus's Expanded Statement of Institutional Purpose should provide a clear and unequivocal statement of institutional-level intentions for the future so that departmental/program statements of intentions may be directly linked to support such institutional-level intentions.

Given the importance of the Expanded Statement of Institutional Purpose, how does an institution go about establishment or expansion of its statement of purpose? The answers are clearly as numerous as the institutions that must accomplish this delicate task. However, in the resource section entitled "Developing the Expanded Statement of Institutional Purpose," beginning on page 39, the author reviews the past and future roles of such statements, indicates desirable characteristics of such statements, and discusses the possible role of strategic planning in this effort. Finally, Appendixes A and B contain examples of an Expanded Statement of Institutional Purpose for a four-year and two-year institution, and both examples offer sufficient substance for use as a basis for institutional effectiveness operations on either type campus. Appendix D offers a sequence of events that (subject to institutional adaptation) can lead to establishement of the Expanded Statement of Institutional Purpose within 12 months.

Assessment/Evaluation Activities

Two major activities regarding assessment/evaluation should take place during the initial year of implementation: (a) the conduct of an inventory of existing and available assessment procedures and (b) the implementation of attitudinal surveys.

The "Conduct of an Inventory of Assessment Procedures" is clearly the place to begin along this track and will undoubtedly produce surprising results on most campuses. Among these surprising results will be the realization of how much assessment activity is already taking place in many of the institution's academic departments. Although the quality of the assessment-related activities found to be taking place will vary widely, there will probably be instances of truly excellent assessment activities already in place that can be utilized as examples to the rest of the institution's academic departments.

What are some of the types of assessment/evaluation activities that may already exist on your campus? You may find activities such as the following:

1. Entrance examinations—Although such examinations are not designed specifically to measure achievement at your institution, they are useful in establishing the level of academic competency of your entering students, from which your own accomplishments can be judged.
2. Standardized and locally prepared tests of graduating students—Although your institution may not require such testing of student knowledge (cognitive learning), some academic departments continue to administer or require such examinations. At least one national testing firm (the Educational Testing Service) provides summary data regarding test scores to the institutions from which those students who took the examination reported receiving their degrees. In a separate resource section entitled "Cognitive Assessment Instruments: Availability and Utilization," beginning on page 76, the advantages, disadvantages, and costs of both locally designed and standardized cognitive examinations are reviewed.
3. Licensure examinations—Among the best end-of-program assessment procedures, already widely implemented in various disciplines, are licensure-type examinations such as those in accountancy, nursing, and law.
4. Performance examinations of graduating students—Many academic departments will be found to have a rich history of performance examinations regarding acquired motor skills, such as painting and music, in which students are required to demonstrate their proficiency prior to graduation. Assessments of skills as well as of more long term changes in students are discussed in the resource section entitled "Assessment of Behavorial Change and Performance" in this chapter.
5. Departmental alumni follow-ups—Many departments attempt to stay in touch with their graduates and have received comments regarding their programs from that source.
6. Existing institutional data systems—Among the most frequently overlooked sources of assessment information is the institution's automated data system. Although most such data systems are likely to be designed for support of transactional (registration, fee payment, payroll, etc.) activities or, at best, process-type decision support (teaching loads, average salaries, space utilization, etc.), their potential for support of assessment is considerable. A resource section concerning this subject and entitled "Assessment-Related Information from Institutional Data Systems" is provided in this chapter and begins on page 130.

The process of conducting this initial inventory of existing and available assessment mechanisms should result in a comprehensive directory of existing assessment procedures and results. It should also result in a similar listing and analysis by discipline of those nationally available procedures (primarily standardized tests) that are not currently utilized on the campus.

The other major assessment/evaluation activity undertaken during the first year of implementation should be "Implementation of Attitudinal Surveys." The attitudes of an institution's constituents, including current and former students, employers, and the general public, are one important barometer of the extent to which an institution's purpose is being communicated and how accomplishment of that purpose is perceived. Some institutions and individual departments may already be utilizing separate survey instruments. However, it is unlikely that such instruments are focused on soliciting responses directly related to the accomplishment of the Expanded Statement of Institutional Purpose or linked to departmental/program intended outcomes or objectives. This first year is an ideal time to initiate implementation of a family of attitudinal surveys to be focused specifically on these subjects.

A resource section entitled "Attitudinal Surveys in Institutional Effectiveness" is provided for further exploration of this subject. It begins on page 55 and includes a discussion of (a) the types of attitudinal surveys, (b) various commercial instruments available for this purpose, (c) the local design or adaptation of attitudinal surveys, and (d) the benefits gained through centralizing the processing of such surveys while decentralizing the design process and emphasizing effective feedback of the results to the departmental/program level.

Complete implementation of attitudinal surveys will not be feasible until an Expanded Statement of Institutional Purpose and departmental/program statements of intended outcomes and objectives are finalized by the end of the first and second years of the implementation plan, respectively. However, most survey and feedback design work can be completed parallel to these actions. By the end of the first year, pilot testing of the instruments can be accomplished, and their phased implementation can be initiated.

Summary

By the close of the first year of implementation activities, the foundation should have been laid and the tools gathered for constructing institutional effectiveness operations on the campus. The document(s) serving as the Expanded Statement of Institutional Purpose should be in place to guide planning/operational activities throughout the next three years. The completed campus "Conduct of Inventory of Assessment Procedures" and initial "Implementation of Attitudinal Surveys" serve to initiate identification and use of the means for assessment. Each of these actions at the institutional level supports a change in the focus of implementation activities to the department/ program level in the second year of implementation of institutional effectiveness on the campus.

Developing the Expanded Statement of Institutional Purpose

Michael Yost

In the preceding chapter, the Expanded Statement of Institutional Purpose (ESIP) has been described as probably the most important part of assessing institutional effectiveness. This document or collection of documents is developed in sequential steps in much the same way as an architect develops the blueprint for a new building; and, as the blueprint gives direction to those who construct the building, the ESIP gives direction to those who develop the institutional effectiveness and assessment plans at a college or university.

In the pages that follow, we describe the content of the ESIP, give examples of the content, describe how to construct the ESIP, and explain the linkages between the content of the ESIP and the operation of the institution.

The ESIP should be thought of as being made up of two separate but related parts (Figure 7): the institutional mission statement and the institutional goals statement. The institutional mission statement is sometimes also referred to as the statement of purpose for an institution. Typically, this document is printed in the front of an institution's catalog or bulletin. Institutional goals, supporting or developed from the institutional mission, constitute the action plan for the institution. Collectively, these two documents give direction to the overall operation of the institution and clearly identify its intentions. Each of the regional accrediting agencies in the United States requires that institutions have a valid, up-to-date mission or purpose statement. As an initial part of the process of developing an institutional effectiveness program for an institution, this document must be evaluated and updated.

The process of assessing institutional effectiveness is based on the

Figure 7

Components of the Expanded Statement of Institutional Purpose (ESIP)

Mission – Broad Statement of Institutional Philosophy,
Role, Scope, Etc.

Institutional Goals – Institutional-Level Action Statements
that Implement, Support,
and Are Derived from the Mission

a . . . .
b . . . .

degree of accomplishment of the institution's stated purpose as reflected in its mission or purpose statement. Because the institution is
encouraged to formulate departmental/program statements of intentions consistent with the institution's purpose, great clarity and specificity are needed in the statements of institutional intentions contained in the ESIP. Although an institutional mission statement need
not reach an operational level of detail, it should include substance
sufficient to provide a clear framework for subsequent statements of
institutional goals, which, in turn, would provide a clear sense of
direction for the institution's departmental statements. The ultimate

determination of effectiveness is the relationship of the statement of purpose and the accomplishment of institutional goals.

Let us begin this process by examining the parts of an institutional mission statement. To facilitate in this presentation, an example ESIP and an institutional mission or purpose statement have been developed for an institution referred to as "Our University." These documents are located in Appendix A, and portions will be cited as needed in the text of this resource section.

First, let's look at the length and inclusiveness of the statement. As stated earlier, the institutional mission statement is usually included as the first major topic in the catalog or bulletin of an institution. As a part of the research in preparing to write this chapter, statements of purpose or institutional intentions from many institutions were reviewed. Typically, this document was found to be between one and three single-spaced, typed pages in length. The institutional mission statement usually begins with a statement such as the following:

> Our University is an independent, nonsectarian, coeducational institution, in the tradition of the liberal arts and sciences. Seeking to be faithful to the ideals of its heritage, Our University is committed, in all of its policies and practices, to the unrestricted and rigorous pursuit of truth, to the certainty of values in human life, and to a respect for differing points of view.

This opening statement provides a brief history and philosophy of the institution, and states whether it is privately or publicly supported, whether it is coeducational or single sex, and what the institution represents. This portion of the mission statement for Our University is somewhat shorter than it is for most institutions.

Another part of the institutional mission statement describes the type of students that the institution enrolls and the geographic area (service area of the institution) from which they come.

> . . . to provide an outstanding education for a relatively small number of talented and highly motivated students from a diversity of geographic, ethnic, and socioeconomic backgrounds.

The first part of this statement describes the clientele (highly motivated, talented, with diverse ethnic and socioeconomic backgrounds), the size of the institution (relatively small), and the geographic area that the institution seeks to serve (diverse geographic backgrounds). This statement would have been written very differently if Our University had been an institution supported by city, county, or state funds with restricted geographic service boundaries. The next section of the mission statement deals with the faculty.

> To achieve this end, we recruit and retain outstanding faculty members who are dedicated to the art of teaching and advising; to the search for and dissemination of truth through scholarship, research and creative endeavor; and to service to the University and the larger community.

This statement describes all of the major activities engaged in by faculty members. These include teaching, advising, research (or creative activities), dissemination of information, and service. Although this statement does not place more emphasis on one of these areas than another, this is not always true at all institutions.

The academic environment is described in the next statement.

> We also seek to provide a supportive and challenging environment in which students can realize the full potential of their abilities and come to understand their responsibility of service in the human community.

This type of academic environment is appropriate for an institution that emphasizes the liberal arts and sciences. However, if Our University had contained an engineering school or had been an occupationally oriented institution, this statement could have been written very differently, as illustrated in Appendix B.

Because the major business of colleges and universities is to educate students, the description of the curriculum is one of the key elements of the institutional mission.

> The principal focus of Our University's curricular programs is undergraduate education in the liberal arts and sciences, combined with a number of preprofessional fields. Relations between the liberal arts and the preprofessional fields are carefully nurtured to provide mutually reinforcing intellectual experiences for students and faculty. Our University also offers master's and doctoral degree programs in selected professional areas that will prepare individuals for positions of leadership in their chosen careers.

For a relatively small institution with a tightly focused curriculum, this statement can be very concise and relatively short. As the curriculum becomes more diverse, the amount of explanation required in the mission statement is greatly expanded. Two points in the example are noteworthy. First, the statement clearly defines the "principal focus" of the curriculum and, second, it states the relationship between the programs. These are both important ingredients of the institutional mission statement.

All public institutions and the majority of private institutions have a sense of responsibility for providing some level of service to the community in which they are located. This service can take the form of faculty/staff participation in community events or non-university-sponsored events that take place on the university campus. In any event, if an institution does assume a public service role, it should be described in the institutional mission statement.

> In addition, recognizing its responsibility to the larger community, Our University provides a variety of carefully selected programs of continuing education and cultural enrichment.

Although some of the faculty at almost all institutions engage in research or other creative academic endeavors, not all institutions assume the responsibility of developing and maintaining a research program. Typically, small institutions do not have research programs and large institutions do. Much of the decision as to whether or not to have such a program is a function of faculty, staff, equipment, space, and funding. In the event that an institution assumes a research function, it also should appear as a part of the institutional mission statement.

> Finally, Our University recognizes its responsibility in maintaining a position of excellence and leadership in research.

It is difficult to believe that the administration and staff of an institution would exclude any individual from enrollment or employment because of sex, race, religion, or national origin. Along with the moral issues associated with discrimination are the many state and federal laws forbidding it. Because many individuals (students and employees) read the institutional mission statement, it is wise to include the institution's nondiscrimination statement in the mission statement.

> In its recruitment and retention of members of the university community, Our University, consistent with its academic and institutional heritage, maintains an openness to all qualified persons.

This sample nondiscrimination statement is a shortened form of the legal version published by the federal government.

Because the institutional mission or purpose statement defines the most fundamental criteria for assessing institutional effectiveness, it serves several important functions. It (a) provides guidance for administrative decisions regarding the overall direction of the institution through the Statement of Institutional Goals; (b) provides direction to each of the colleges, divisions, and departments of the institution, creating an umbrella under which those units may plan, operate, and evaluate their programs; and (c) establishes a general blueprint for the development of a process for assessing and improving institutional effectiveness. For these reasons, it is impossible to overstate the value and usefulness of mission statements as statements of purpose that articulate the institution's commitment to important outcomes for students.

Developing the Institutional Mission Statement

Given the importance attached to the institutional mission statement, a significant task for each institution is to conduct the research needed to formulate that critical document. The potential approaches are, of course, as numerous as the institutions that must undertake the task. Assuming a broad perspective, much of the current literature in the field of higher education describes the general process of deriving the institutional mission statement as an outcome of "strategic planning." Numerous writers (Cope, 1981; Keller, 1983; Shirley, 1982, 1983) have provided descriptions of the process, and although procedures suggested vary widely, these authorities appear to agree on a number of important concepts. Strategic planning is an ends-oriented approach to planning that seeks to answer the questions What is the business of the institution? and How does the institution fit into an educational picture of the city, region, state, or country? It focuses on assessment of the institution's internal strengths and weaknesses and the institution's fit with or niche in the external educational environment. Although various techniques may be used, the result of this assessment is identification of environmental opportunities that are a good match for the strengths of the institution. An assessment of the institution's internal strengths and weaknesses is a major component of strategic planning. Whether this assessment is informal or formal, oral or written, focused more on strengths or more on weaknesses, the findings are critical in planning for the future.

The result of strategic planning is a clear sense of institutional direction resulting from conscious decisions about the role of the institution. The ongoing objective is the creation of a match among environmental opportunities, institutional values, and strengths, coupled with resources available to support action in high-priority areas.

Now, let's consider an example of the application of strategic planning to Our University. Suppose that Our University had survived for nearly 100 years as a relatively small, private institution that had not undergone a great deal of change or reform. Suppose, further, that the institution was well endowed, and that it had a local and regional reputation of being a "good" institution, but one that did not appear to have any outstanding academic programs. The physical plant was in good condition, the budget was balanced, and enrollment was stable and at an acceptable level. The members of the board of trustees, after hiring a new president, decided that the mission of the institution should be reviewed and evaluated and, if necessary, changed.

At this point in time, the data required to support the evaluation of the existing mission (and possibly to support the development of a new mission) were gathered. Historic data indicated that the existing mission statement had not been evaluated since the last regional self-study, and at that time there was only a cursory review of the mission statement. Also, since the last review of the mission statement, there had been several changes in the administrative structure of the institution and several academic programs had been implemented that did not appear to fit within the existing mission statement and the curriculum as a whole. In the previous 10 years the institution had become a disjointed collection of academic units. The new president suggested that a study be conducted to determine whether it would be feasible for the "principal focus of Our University's curricular programs to be undergraduate education in the liberal arts and sciences, combined with a number of preprofessional fields."

With this potential mission in mind, studies of internal strengths and weaknesses and external market constraints were undertaken. An examination of the external market constraints indicated that the nearest institution with this type of curricular offering was almost 500 miles away; high school students in the city and region were traveling outside of the region to attend schools with this type of curricular offering; on a national basis, there was an increase in the enrollment in this type of institution; and noted experts in education were recommending that students acquire a liberal arts education. The assessment of internal strengths indicated that the new mission could be pursued in light of sufficient liberal arts curricular offerings in basic academic areas; talent and diversity in the faculty; and classroom, laboratory, and residence hall space; financial reserves; library resources; and faculty/staff support. The assessment of internal weaknesses indicated that selected graduate and undergraduate academic programs would need to be strengthened, and others phased out; selected classrooms and laboratories would need to be modified; selected academic programs would need to be initiated; faculty would need to be given opportunities for retraining; and university funds would have to be reallocated. When all of the positive and negative internal and external factors were assessed collectively, this portion of the new institutional mission statement was enthusiastically accepted by the governing board, the faculty, and the staff. At this point, the meaning of the mission had to be more clearly defined in terms of institutional goals; and following this, the operational plan for achieving the mission had to be developed and implemented in the individual departments and programs of the institution.

This example is but a brief sketch of the assessment and strategic planning needed to develop a small portion of a mission statement for an institution. A large amount of other data would have to be gathered and a tremendous number of judgments would have to be made in order to develop a new mission statement.

Staffing and timing are both critical components in conducting the research needed to support the strategic planning and the development of an institutional mission statement. The rule of thumb for staffing and participation is to have broad-based involvement and representation of both faculty and administrators. If a subcommittee working structure is used, then both faculty and administrators should be on each subcommittee. Also, faculty and administrators should both be used to chair subcommittees. Some institutions may also choose to involve students and staff in this process. Broad-based involvement and representation help ensure that the end product (the mission statement) will represent individuals at all levels within the institution and that these individuals (and hopefully those whom they represent) will assume ownership and identification with the mission statement.

Although a mission statement is seldom more than one to three pages long, a great deal of time is required for its development. Initially, decisions have to be made regarding what data and information need to be gathered. Once gathered, they must be reviewed and analyzed by the committee before a draft of the mission statement can be developed. It also takes a great deal of discussion and writing to develop what the committee considers to be the appropriate wording of the mission statement. Finally, getting approval of the document by the governing body of the institution, faculty, and administration will usually require the development of several revisions of the mission statement before it is acceptable to the members in each of these groups. At least 6 months are required to develop, write, and gain an acceptance of an institutional mission statement. Many institutions spend an entire academic year in the development of this document. One of the greatest challenges faced during the period of public review is retaining sufficient substance to provide a clear sense of institutional direction, rather than appeasing all aspects of the institution with a mission statement that is acceptable to all because it lacks any substance.

Obviously, there are many approaches that can be used to develop a new mission statement. Whatever an institution's approach, it is important to remember that the institutional mission statement forms the blueprint for identification of institutional goals and intended departmental and program statements of outcomes and objectives. This document, the institutional mission statement, also provides the ultimate basis for the evaluation of institutional effectiveness.

Developing Institutional Goals

The institutional mission statement should be worded so that persons reading it have no doubt as to the overall direction and orientation of the institution. However, this document does not articulate the mission of the institution at a level of detail that will support the development of a set of departmental/program priorities for action.

If we return to the blueprint analogy, the mission statement is analogous to the initial plot-plan an architect develops for a new university. An initial plot-plan lays out which buildings and roads will be in which location without describing in great detail the internal structure of each of the buildings. Just as an architect develops more elaborate plans that accompany the plot- plan and describe each building in detail, the faculty and administration must add more specificity to the mission statement. As the architect develops detailed plans that a builder uses to construct the buildings, the faculty and administration must add detail to their mission statement so that operational plans in the institution's departments/programs can be developed.

The development of institutional goals to accompany a mission statement is analogous to the development of the overall plan for the building from an initial plot-plan. Initially, an architect develops an overall plan for a building, and later he or she develops the many detailed drawings needed by the craftsmen who will build it. Institutional goals remain relatively general in nature, but they articulate the direction given to key concepts within the institution that identify what is to be accomplished. As a chief architect would give an initial or rough plan for a building to one of his or her colleagues who is going to develop the final plan, institutional goals should be developed and published within an institution to give direction to the development of operational plans and intended outcomes or objectives at all levels within the institution.

Who should develop the institutional goals? The personnel mix required to develop these goals is identical to that needed to develop the institutional mission. Broad-based involvement of faculty and administrators (and possibly students and staff) is a requirement. It is critical that each of these groups agrees to the validity of the goals, believes these goals represent both its own best interests and those of the institution as a whole, and accepts the need to work toward accomplishment of the goals. Without broad-based involvement and acceptance of the institutional mission and goals, the results of strategic planning will go unused, the institution will not grow and develop, and there will be no way to assess institutional effectiveness.

A great deal of data are gathered and used in the process of developing the mission statement. Along with the analysis of the data, there will be debate as to the relevance and meaning of the data to the institution. Because the goals form a document that is one level of specificity greater than the mission statement, all of the information gathered in the earlier endeavor will apply to the development of the goals.

In the development of the mission statement, some of the questions asked are as follows:

Should we do _____ ?

Can we move in "that" direction?

Are we capable of doing _____ ?

What will be the consequences of _____ ?

What implications does this have for _____ ?

Can we add _____ ?

What will be the effect of _____ ?

The questions asked in developing the institution's goals are very different from these. Because the decision to move the institution in a particular direction(s) has already been made during development of the mission statement, the questions change from *Should we?* to *How much?* Some of the questions asked are the following:

How much should we increase by _____[date]?

What administrative or academic organization will best accomplish _____ ?

What level of funding will be required to reach _____ by _____[date]?

What level of enrollment (or staffing) must we reach in order to _____ ?

What changes in the physical plant must be made by _____ [date] in order to _____ ?

The answers to these and other similar questions will result in the development of a valid set of goals for an institution.

There are several parameters that must be understood—and set—before an institution can begin to develop its institutional goals. The questions to be asked are

1. What structure will be used in organizing and sequencing the goals?
2. What time frame(s) and level of specificity will be used in the writing of the goals?
3. What level of the operation of the institution will warrant development of goals?

Each of these questions should be answered in detail before goals are written.

Although goals are typically written one at a time, the writers must have thought their way through some organizational structure before they begin. Without an organizational structure, it is easy to overlook important concepts and difficult to arrange the goals for presentation once they have been developed. The sample goals in Appendix A follow a modification of the overall administrative organization of Our University. In this document, there are goals established and approved at the institutional level for each of the major administrative subdivisions of the institution. For the most part, the goals for each administrative subdivision are ones that can be pursued more or less independently by the staff in that subdivision. Those goals that seem to cut across or require the joint effort of two or more administrative subdivisions appear in the first section of this statement. Because all of the subdivisions work to support the academic, research, and service missions of the institution, goals are developed for all of the administrative subdivisions. This implies that all of these subdivisions should participate in institutional effectiveness assessment. A different, more programmatic structure for the Expanded Statement of Institutional Purpose is illustrated in Appendix B.

Whenever mission or goals statements are developed at an institution, they are built on assumptions that are relevant at the time those goals statements are developed. Because the purpose of this entire endeavor is to assess institutional effectiveness, it is essential that the assumptions upon which those goals have been developed be included. It is amazing how quickly institutions forget (or selectively modify) their original assumptions. If the assumptions are not recorded, it will be impossible to assess institutional effectiveness validly in the future.

Well-written institutional goals contain two major ingredients. First, they include a description of some well-defined or measurable/accessible end result. Examples of these types of statements include the following:

Enrollment will reach _____ .

Admissions will achieve an acceptance rate of _____ .

Five new academic programs will _____ .

The business office will implement systems that will _____ .

The development office will reach an alumni giving rate of _____ .

Student services will have programs that will _____ .

The library will have holdings of _____ .

Financial aid will reach a support rate of _____ .

Some of the goals specify or state that a specific number, percentage, or rate be reached, whereas others state that something of an operational nature will be accomplished. Both are equally important and valid goals. Also, note that the concepts stated in these goals are very broad and inclusive.

If these statements are written very specifically or narrowly, then they become departmental or program objectives or outcomes, not goals. Keep in mind that the purpose of developing the mission and goals statements is to develop documents that, when distributed on campus, can give others direction and assistance as they develop the outcomes and objectives they will operationalize. If the goals become too specific, they infringe on the work and professional responsibility of others. Also, if goals statements are written too specifically, then an inordinately large number of them must be developed. From an assessment point of view, an excessive number of goals create personnel, time, and cost problems.

The second ingredient of a goals statement is the time frame. In the examples of goals given earlier, the end result was stated, but the reader was never told when it would occur. There was no way of telling whether it would occur next semester, next year, or in five years. It is important that the time required to achieve the intended action be stated as a part of each goal. Just as some changes within an institution are easier to make than others, it takes more time to achieve one goal than another. Changes in academic programs sometimes take as much as 4 years, major changes in budget allocations can usually be made in 2 years, changes in admissions ratios can be made in 1 year, and changes in institutional investment strategies can be made in several months. Obviously, the time frame used in a goals statement must fit the aspect of the institution to which it applies. It is even possible to use longitudinal time frames in developing goals. For example, a reasonable goal of this type might be as follows: The student retention/graduation rate will increase by 1% in each of the next 5 years and reach 70% by 19___. There are many options open to the creative persons or groups who develop mission and goals statements.

What aspects or subdivisions of an institution warrant the development of institutional goals? The answer is that since no one major aspect or subdivision of the institution is independent of the others, they all warrant the development of goals. However, when an institution chooses to evaluate and change its mission, some aspects or subdivisions tend to become more critical than others. If, for example, an institution chose to pursue academic excellence, then the quality of entering students, the quality of the faculty, the curriculum, and finances needed to support the endeavor would become key concepts of the plan for change. If these are the key concepts, then admissions, faculty recruiting, faculty development, curriculum council, financial aid, the development office, budget allocations, and so forth would become the key institutional operations within the plan for change.

Assuming that this logic is valid and that the list of key concepts and institutional operations is complete, then the Mission and Goals Committee should pay special attention to developing the institutional goals to accompany what they consider to be the key to the plan for change. This approach will focus the attention of the institution on the key concepts and help avoid the development of an excessive number of goals. It is critical that all of the key concepts in the planned change be covered by a goal, but it is just as important that an institution not write so many goals that it is overburdened with their sheer number. Balance and inclusiveness are critical when it comes to developing the proper types and number of institutional goals.

Whereas the mission statement is typically 1 to 3 pages in length, the institutional goals statement is typically 5 to 10 pages in length. Larger, more complex institutions tend to have longer institutional goals statements than do smaller institutions. At most institutions, it takes far less time to develop the institutional goals statement than it does to gather data, do the strategic planning, and develop the mission statement. It is conceivable that the goals statement can be developed in as little as 3 months. As with the mission statement, approval for the institutional goals statement should be obtained from the governing board of the institution, the faculty, and the administration.

Summary

When the institutional mission and goals statements are completed, they will provide direction for operational planning within all levels of the institution and, in turn, will give direction to the majority of the activities and efforts within the institution. These two documents comprise the Expanded Statement of Institutional Purpose, which, in conjunction with the more operational plans of the departments/programs, acts as the evaluation blueprint in assessing institutional effectiveness.

Figure 8 is a graphic summary of the text discussion. Institutions are administratively organized from the top down; as a result, goals, objectives, and assessments are also frequently organized in the same way (see Figure 8). Some obvious exceptions to this approach exist within almost all institutions (particularly at larger ones), but it is not necessary to discuss them at this point. The goals, objectives, and assessments are hierarchically organized from *top to bottom* within an organization, with the activities near the top of the organization being

Figure 8

Organization of Institutional Goals
and Department/Program Outcomes or Objectives
and Assessment

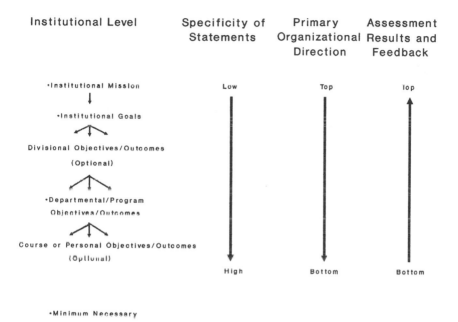

Institutional Level	Specificity of Statements	Primary Organizational Direction	Assessment Results and Feedback

very broad, general, and inclusive and the activities near the bottom being very task- or activity-specific. It is important that the reader see the necessity of maintaining key linkages between organizational levels within such a structure. Whereas the organizational structure has a top-to-bottom organization, the feedback of information is organized on a bottom-to-top basis. Think of the assessment process as one of *merging* the more specific assessments at the lower academic/ administrative levels into assessments at successively higher levels within the organization. Assessment at any level within an institution becomes a summary of the assessment of the areas within and immediately below that level.

With all of this rhetoric, the reader needs to keep one major concept in mind: Assessment is not done solely for its own sake. Institutions assess to improve their operation or effectiveness. Assessment should be tied to operations so that the information obtained from the assessment can be used for improvement and to validate the Expanded Statement of Institutional Purpose.

References: Cited and Recommended

Caruthers, J. K., & Lott, G. B. (1981). *Mission review: Foundation for strategic planning*. Boulder, CO: National Center for Higher Education Management Systems.

Chaffee, E. E. (1985). The concept of strategy: From business to higher education. *Annual Handbook of Higher Education, 1*, 133–172.

Cope, R. (1981). *Strategic planning, management and decision making*. Washington, DC: American Association for Higher Education.

Dutton, J. L., Fahey, L., & Narayanan, V. K. (1983). Toward understanding strategic issue diagnosis. *Strategic Management Journal, 4*, 307–323.

Ewell, P. T. (Ed.). (1985). *Assessing educational outcomes*. New directions for institutional research, no. 47. San Francisco: Jossey-Bass.

Keller, G. (1983). *Academic strategy: The management revolution in American higher education*. Baltimore, MD: Johns Hopkins University Press.

Kotler, P., & Murphy, P. E. (1981). Strategic planning for higher education. *Journal of Higher Education, 52*, 470–489.

Shirley, R. C. (1982). Limiting the scope of strategy: A decision based approach. *Academy of Management Review, 7*(2), 37–46.

Shirley, R. C. (1983). Identifying the levels of strategy for a college or university. *Long Range Planning, 16*(3), 92–98.

Attitudinal Surveys in Institutional Effectiveness

Gale Bridger and Lori Wolff

> O wad some Pow'r the giftie gie us
> To see oursels as ithers see us!
> It wad frae mony a blunder free us,
> And foolish notion.
> —*Robert Burns*, "To a Louse"

Surveys designed to measure the attitudes of an institution's various constituents provide important insights into the way others perceive the institution—its purpose, programs, and performance. These attitudinal surveys take many forms, address a range of publics, and generate a wealth of information to be ploughed back into the planning/evaluative process. If not carefully selected, administered, and utilized, they may also simply generate reams of paper that lie fallow on the shelf in some institutional researcher's office. To assist those who wish to begin a survey program, this resource section includes

1. A review of the survey instruments that are available commercially;
2. A consideration of the usefulness of contracted services;
3. An examination of the value of instruments developed in-house.

Pertinent to this discussion are these topics:

1. The identification of the kinds of information that can be acquired most effectively with survey techniques
2. The constituent groups who may best provide the information sought
3. The campus groups (e.g., central administration, student services, academic departments) that may benefit from the information so generated

Finally, having considered these points of selection and application, the section will provide some practical steps for conducting the surveys and disseminating the information for its effective use.

Commercially Available Surveys

The following agencies offer a full range of survey services that have been subjected to careful testing over a number of years to provide valid, reliable attitudinal data from several population groups:

1. The American College Testing Program (ACT) offers the ACT Evaluation/Survey Service (ESS).
2. The College Board in cosponsorship with the National Center for Higher Education Management Systems (NCHEMS) has available the Student Outcomes Information Service (SOIS).
3. The Educational Testing Service offers a family of instruments including Institutional Goals Inventory (IGI), Institutional Functioning Inventory (IFI), Student Reactions to College (SRC), and Program Self-Assessment Service (PSAS).
4. A fourth survey, the oldest and perhaps most widely known, targets one population only and is included here although it is not in the truest sense commercial. The Cooperative Institutional Research Program (CIRP) of the University of California, Los Angeles, and the American Council on Education maintains longitudinal data on American higher education and conducts annually the CIRP survey of entering freshmen.

American College Testing Program

The American College Testing Program Evaluation/Survey Service (ACT/ESS) now offers 12 survey instruments for use by colleges and universities. Each is an optical-scan instrument containing two or four pages of questions designed to permit a general evaluation of an institution's programs and services. Local personnel are afforded the option of designing 20 to 30 additional questions for inclusion in each survey. ACT also offers a catalog of additional items, which institutions may select from in lieu of writing their own questions. In addition, each instrument provides space for the participant to write comments or suggestions. Since 1979, over a million ESS instruments have been administered at more than 750 institutions. This extensive use of the ACT materials has made possible normative data for comparative studies as well as an opportunity for longitudinal studies within institutions. A brief description of each instrument follows.

The College Student Needs Assessment Survey is used to explore the educational and personal needs of enrolled college students and examine their career and life goals. This four-page questionnaire is comprised of five sections:

1. Background information—provides basic demographic data and information for subgroup selection for analysis of the student's responses
2. Career and life goals—gathers information on college major, occupational choice, and relative importance of various goals (both career and personal)
3. Educational and personal needs—asks the student to indicate need for a "lot of help" to "no help" in the areas of career development, educational planning, intellectual skills development, and life skills development
4. (and 5.) Additional questions, comments, and suggestions

The Adult Learner Needs Assessment Survey can be used to examine the education-related needs of adult learners and includes in its four pages items relating to the following:

1. Background—particularly as related to previous educational experience, family, and employment
2. Educational plans and preferences—with emphasis on the special needs of the adult, such as scheduling, location, and format of classes
3. Personal and educational needs—includes life skills development, educational planning, and association with others
4. (and 5.) Additional questions, comments, and suggestions

The Alumni Survey is useful in ascertaining the impact of the institution on its graduates. Four-page surveys are available for two-year and four-year institutions and provide information in the following sections:

1. Background information—tailored to the two-year or four-year graduate

2. Continuing education—provides extensive information on formal education since graduation/departure
3. Educational/college experiences—gauges the alumnus's perception of the value and impact of his or her education in areas such as quality of life, skills development, and independent living
4. Employment history—provides valuable information for alumni and placement offices as well as for various academic program planners
5. (and 6.–7.) Additional questions, mailing addresses, and comments and suggestions—provide additional information that may be useful locally

The Entering Student Survey, a four-page form consisting of five sections, is used to obtain information on the entering student's background, interests, and perception of the institution.

1. Background information
2. Educational plans and preferences—Unlike in the ACT Profile, responses come only from entering college freshmen, not from people in their junior year in high school.
3. College impressions—asks the student to rate the importance of various items in his or her decision to attend the school. The student also is asked to indicate agreement or disagreement with various descriptors providing a perception of the institution as held by entering students.
4. (and 5.) Additional questions, comments, and suggestions

The Student Opinion Survey, with two-year and four-year forms, is used to examine the perception held by enrolled, continuing students of their college's services and environment. The two-year form also includes items to explore the student's reasons for selecting the college and his or her overall impression of the school.

1. Background information
2. Use of and level of satisfaction with various campus services and programs
3. Level of satisfaction with the college environment in the following areas: academic, admissions, rules and regulations, facilities, registration, and general
4. Additional questions, comments, and suggestions

The Survey of Academic Advising is used to obtain information regarding student impressions of academic advising services. The four-page form includes the following:

1. Background information
2. Advising information—including frequency of advisor-and-advisee contacts and the period of time the student has been assigned to the current advisor
3. Academic advising needs—in which the student identifies topics discussed with the advisor and expresses his or her level of satisfaction with the advisor's assistance
4. Additional questions, comments, and suggestions

The Survey of Current Activities and Plans is designed for applicants to the institution who chose *not* to enroll. The survey requests the following:

1. Background information
2. Impressions of the college
3. Educational plans and activities
4. Employment plans
5. Additional questions, comments, and suggestions

The Survey of Postsecondary Plans is used with high school students to identify their occupational and educational plans after high school graduation. This survey also asks for the students' impressions of the particular institution conducting the survey and offers space for additional questions and for comments and suggestions. Information from the first part of this survey is not unlike that in the ACT Profile.

The Withdrawing/Nonreturning Student Survey is produced in both a two-page (short form) and four-page format. In both the student who chooses to leave college before completing a degree is asked to provide background information and to indicate reasons for leaving. These reasons are grouped in the following categories:

1. Personal (health, moving, marriage, social, etc.)
2. Academic (suspension, instructional quality, not challenged, etc.)
3. Institutional (scheduling problems, inadequate advising, programs or facilities, etc.)
4. Financial (availability of work or financial aid)
5. Employment (conflict between work and school, etc.)

Both forms also provide space for comments and suggestions. The long form, in addition, asks for the student to rate his or her satisfaction with various institutional services and characteristics.

ACT offers a variety of flexible services, and institutions may elect simply to purchase one or more of the survey instruments or to contract for a full range of mailing, scoring, and reporting services.

Student Outcomes Information Service

The Student Outcomes Information Service (SOIS), cosponsored by the College Board and the National Center for Higher Education Management Systems, is in many respects like the ACT/ESS. The questionnaires focus on six different points during and after college:

1. Entering student
2. Continuing student
3. Program completer and graduating student
4. Former student
5. Recent alumnus
6. Three- to five-year follow-up

The questionnaires, offered in formats for both two-year and four-year institutions, provide background demographics; survey educational experiences, plans, and goals; identify need for, use of, and satisfaction with institutional services; and give perceptions and impressions of the institution as held by the various survey populations.

Perhaps the most significant difference between the SOIS and ACT families of surveys is the coordinated, research-oriented approach of the SOIS, which is supported by a carefully written handbook, *Student Outcomes Questionnaires: An Implementation Handbook* (2nd ed., 1983), by Peter T. Ewell.

Ewell takes the novice practitioner through the process step by step and carefully points out tricks and essential steps to help guarantee successful, usable survey results. As with ACT, data processing and questionnaire analyses are available. Annual summaries of information from participating institutions are also made available.

Educational Testing Service

The Educational Testing Service (ETS) College and University Programs offer a different array of survey instruments focusing primarily on program planning and evaluation. The following components of the Institutional Research Program for Higher Education (IRPHE) are available from ETS:

1. Institutional Goals Inventory (IGI)
2. Community College Goals Inventory (CCGI)
3. Small College Goals Inventory (SCGI)
4. Program Self-Assessment Service (PSAS)
5. Graduate Program Self-Assessment Service (GPSA)
6. Student Reactions to College (SRC)
7. Institutional Functioning Inventory (IFI)
8. Student Instructional Report (SIR)

The goals inventories (IGI, CCGI, and SCGI) differ in content and focus in addressing the concerns of the three different types of institutions (i.e., university or large college, community college, and small college). In format, however, they are alike—each has 90 statements of possible institutional goals, and participants are asked to indicate their opinions of the importance of each statement in terms of both what exists and what they would *like to see exist*, providing a future orientation as well as a look at the present. The inventory is appropriate for use by students, faculty, and administrators, thus offering the opportunity to gain perceptions of the institution's goals and purpose. A Canadian IGI in both French and English and a Spanish/English IGI are available, as is a Canadian CCGI in English only.

The Program Self-Assessment Service (PSAS) consists of a set of questionnaires that address areas such as curriculum, program purposes, departmental procedures, faculty activity, student accomplishment, and the general environment for work and learning. The PSAS assumes that the perceptions and assessment of those most directly involved with any department or program can contribute to an improved quality and functioning of the area surveyed. Thus, the service offers three assessment questionnaires: for faculty, students who major in the department or program, and recent graduates of the program. Responses provide a profile of the targeted program or department and can assist in the program review process by identifying areas of strength and those areas that need attention.

The Graduate Program Self-Assessment Service (GPSAS) is the parent of the previously described PSAS. GPSA is cosponsored by the Graduate Record Examination Board and the Council of Graduate Schools in the United States. Instruments have been developed for both master's and doctoral level programs and address the parallel constituent groups identified in the PSAS discussion, i.e., students enrolled in the program, faculty, and recent graduates. Survey questions provide information on 16 areas of program characteristics including environment for learning, scholarly excellence, teaching quality, faculty concern for students, curriculum, departmental procedures, resources (such as library and laboratories), faculty work environment, student accomplishments, and others.

The Student Reactions to College (SRC) survey is used to solicit opinions from enrolled students about their college experience: instruction, counseling, out-of-class activities, administrative affairs, and so forth. The 150-item questionnaire is grouped into 19 areas of interest and provides information about students' needs and concerns. There are separate forms for community colleges (SRC–2) and for four-year colleges and universities (SRC–4).

The Institutional Functioning Inventory (IFI) is helpful to faculty, students, and administrators who wish to assess administrative policies, teaching practices, and academic and extracurricular programs. The questionnaire consists of 132 items; students surveyed respond only to items 1 through 72. The IFI grew out of a study of institutional vitality supported by the Kettering Foundation; and comparative data are available for public universities, four-year state colleges, private liberal arts colleges, community colleges, and private junior colleges.

The Student Instructional Report (SIR) is a brief, objective questionnaire that helps instructors gain information about students' reactions to their courses. The questionnaire offers students the opportunity to comment anonymously on their courses and instruction. Six factors are covered:

1. Course organization and planning
2. Faculty–student interaction
3. Communication
4. Course difficulty and work load
5. Textbooks and readings
6. Tests and/or examinations

The SIR is not intended to replace regular student–faculty communication. It does provide an additional means by which instructors may examine their teaching performance.

Extensive comparative data are available through ETS based on SIR administrations in the United States and Canada. The questionnaire is available in Spanish and in a Canadian version in both French and English.

All of the ETS instruments offer space for optional local items, and like ACT and College Board/NCHEMS, the services of basic data processing and reporting are available. Special services and professional assistance may be negotiated as well.

Cooperative Institutional Research Program

The Student Information Form (SIF) used in the Cooperative Institutional Research Program (CIRP) contains standard biographic and demographic data-gathering items, which have been regularly included for each entering freshman class. It also contains research-oriented attitudinal questions, which are modified from time to time. The SIF includes a wide-ranging set of questions, including items dealing with students' personal habits, reasons for attending college, political views, and others. The report, generated by the optical-scanned responses and provided to the institution, gives responses in percentages for the institution and comparative data for all institutions in the participant institution's category.

Contracted Services

Most management consultant services and marketing consultants are capable of developing and conducting surveys of the public to determine perceptions about a given institution's reputation, purposes, and programs. A number of agencies now market themselves primarily to the higher education community. Because these are organizations in a highly competitive market, individual groups will not be identified here. However, there are some advantages to contracting for survey services:

1. The contract is usually for a turnkey process (i.e., it includes tailoring the survey to the specific needs of the client, gathering and processing the data, and presenting and interpreting the results to appropriate groups).
2. The contractual process may be regarded more favorably by those surveyed because it is individualized and carries the identity of the contracting institution.
3. The contractor may provide on-site consultants who may lend added credibility to the process and the findings through discussion with others.

An excellent example of the best contractual arrangements is that offered by NCHEMS through its Institutional Performance Survey (IPS). The focus of the IPS is comprehensive measurement of the institution through questions regarding effectiveness, leadership and decision styles, and institutional culture and environment. Although the instrument used is standard, the total survey-and-consultant process is tailored to the needs of the campus. Because the survey is standard, the total cost is significantly lower than what could be anticipated from an individually designed survey.

Some disadvantages of contracted services should be noted:

1. An institution may expect the contract cost to run as high as $30,000 to $40,000.
2. The resultant data will not have the benefits of comparability to normative data or summary data from other institutions of the same level or type.
3. The time required for the full development of such services may be counterproductive.

These disadvantages, however, may be negated when the institution's needs are determined to be met best by a specially designed survey.

Frequently, for example, institutions are interested in gaining through telephone sampling or similar marketing techniques reputational kinds of information or community needs assessment data. Such services contracted by local sampling and marketing agencies may be quite successful and not unduly expensive. This approach should, in fact, be selected if (a) available commercial instruments do not meet the institution's identified need, (b) the expertise of labor force is not available in-house, or (c) the contracted arrangement can provide the data required in a cost-effective and timely manner.

Locally Developed Surveys

Locally developed (or in-house) surveys take time and expertise to design. On most campuses the responsibility for designing such instruments may fall on either the staff of the institutional research office or faculty members from a discipline such as education or one of the social sciences. One of the primary reasons for using surveys developed locally, as opposed to those purchased through off-campus vendors, is cost-effectiveness; locally developed surveys are simply cheaper. Regardless of the dollars potentially saved, one should keep in mind the caution from H. R. Kells in *Self-Study Processes* (1980) that "a poorly designed instrument, used at the wrong moment with an unreceptive audience, will yield little or no useful information and it may damage the sense of community and morale at the institution involved" (p. 69). On the other hand, designing and utilizing locally developed survey instruments can be a most effective way for the institution not only to gain a sense of ownership for the entire assessment and evaluation process but also to bring a personalized touch to it.

In decisions about the use of locally developed instruments for an individual institution, one valuable resource is Peter Ewell's (1987b) presentation of a general set of pros and cons regarding the use of either standardized or locally developed instruments. This set, although it refers specifically to tests, is applicable to assessment or survey instruments. The complete outline of the pros and cons is provided in the resource section entitled "Cognitive Assessment Instruments: Availability and Utilization," beginning on page 86; thus, it will not be repeated in this section, but the list should be consulted when making the decision regarding whether or not to use locally developed instruments. Perhaps the most important of the advantages of using locally developed instruments is that the instrument can be designed to reflect the specific curriculum or program at the institution that is being assessed or evaluated. A locally designed survey instrument "improves the fit between the questionnaire content and the institution's concerns" (Stevenson, 1985, p. 5). Kells in *Self Study Processes* (1980) also emphasizes that if an institution uses locally developed surveys, the instrument must be matched to the special circumstances of the institution to enable the goals of the assessment process to be achieved. Rhode Island College, for example, administered its own entering student questionnaire to provide data for individualized learning plans for its students, showing how instruments designed by university personnel can hit the mark when special needs, goals, or circumstances arise. Such in-house surveys allow the institution to collect and analyze information "that people [at the institution] care about so as to answer unique questions about a program," (Dennison & Bunda, 1989, p. 51).

Designing and using locally developed instruments in this way causes the university to work as a community. Even though the need for an assessment instrument may first be conceived in the office serving the institutional research or planning function, numerous campus departments or offices stand to gain from the survey process, and thus should play an essential role in the development of the survey instrument (Fisher, 1988). Peter Ewell in *Student Outcomes Questionnaires: An Implementation Handbook* (1983) also emphasizes the need for campus involvement (even though his publication deals primarily with a standardized set of questionnaires) by noting that such involvement "will help ensure better response rates and will ultimately facilitate effective use of the questionnaire results" (p. 17). As with virtually any process, involving more people can cause frustration, but it also can bring in different perspectives that may lead to new insights about the institution (Ewell, 1985).

A secondary benefit from the use of an instrument designed on campus is the institutional personalization that can be accomplished. Northeast Missouri State University, which has one of the foremost models for institutional effectiveness, exemplifies this personalization. Their set of instruments has included the frequent, prominent use of the institution's name on the survey's form. The use of an institutional symbol or logo gives the instrument a professional look and becomes a recognizable symbol that can be associated with the survey and its results (Fisher, 1988). This personalization may add to the ownership of the assessment process for those who develop the survey and may also encourage respondents to take the time and effort to answer the questionnaire.

If the decision is made to use a locally developed survey instrument, adherence to a general outline of procedures in design of the instrument may help expedite the process. The steps in the development of a localized instrument do not vary substantially from those an institution would pursue when using a standardized instrument and are presented in the following list.

Steps in Designing a Localized Survey Instrument

1. Have a meeting of those initiating or requesting the instrument and those chosen as being responsible for design of the instrument.
2. Make firm decisions at the institution with regard to who will cover the cost; handle the mailing, receiving, data entry, and statistical analysis; and oversee the publication of and access to the results.
3. Hold a meeting between those responsible for the design and those on campus whose offices might benefit from the survey

results. All involved at this point should be asked to provide suggestions for questionnaire items.

4. Now, and throughout the process, focus on choosing an institutional logo that will appear on the instrument and in any publication about the survey or its results. This adds to the personalization and ownership of the instrument.
5. Obtain from several off-campus vendors standardized instruments on the topic of interest.
6. Contact other institutions or a clearinghouse, if possible, to obtain locally developed instruments in the area to be surveyed.
7. Have all personnel involved with the survey—those responsible for the design and those who might benefit from the survey and its results—spend time reviewing the different standardized and localized instruments obtained.
8. Design a draft instrument.
9. Struggle through what may be several iterations of drafts and edits based on the voluminous suggestions from the faculty, staff, and administrators who play a role in the overall process.
10. Perhaps, execute a trial administration to volunteer students, staff, or faculty to test the instrument in draft form.
11. Through step 10, arrive at the final instrument design.
12. Once the final design is chosen, arrange to have it printed for mailing, either through the Printing Office at the institution or an off-campus vendor.
13. Lastly, follow through with the plans the institution has made regarding distribution, data entry, analysis, and publication of results.

In terms of the actual structure of the instrument, it might serve the institution well, as just mentioned, to first review several commercial standardized instruments. Doing so allows the institution to identify the general areas that would be appropriate to include for its particular assessment process. Another approach might be to seek out other locally developed instruments created at other institutions. These actions may allow the institution to make a smooth transition from a standardized instrument to one that is designed locally to meet the specific institution's needs, goals, and circumstances. A panel at the 1990 American Association for Higher Education (AAHE) Assessment Forum (Amiran et al., 1990) focused on the issue of "borrowing" locally developed instruments from other institutions. The panel and audience identified a need for a clearinghouse to facilitate collaboration between institutions. Perhaps such a clearinghouse may be available soon as a place for institutions to find and review other locally designed surveys.

Designing a survey instrument utilizing on-campus personnel, although cheaper in terms of out-of-pocket cost, will not be cheaper in terms of time. Undertaking an assessment process that involves the use of a locally developed instrument takes a great amount of commitment from those asked to be responsible for the design. The best advice for an institution is to weigh Ewell's pros and cons carefully and choose the type of instrument, be it standardized or locally developed, that is best for the circumstances of a given institution.

Characteristics of Survey Information

Survey information falls into two categories: (a) factual, demographic data and (b) opinions or perceptions. A caution about each category is in order here.

First, some demographic data are perhaps verifiable by checking other sources of, for example, student information. However, that process would be time-consuming and certainly not generally needed. The caution here is simply that responses to survey items may not be absolutely accurate. A participant may subtract or add years to his or her age; an alumnus may exaggerate income. Still, most respondents tend to answer honestly and accurately, and for the purposes of the survey the information has value.

A more significant caution regards the second category—opinions or perceptions. The institution's leadership must be certain to recognize that these results are just that—perceptions, not necessarily reality or fact. They may tell us a great deal about how we are viewed by others or by ourselves, but these must be taken alongside other kinds of data (quantitative, measurable information) to have a complete picture of the institution, its strengths and its shortcomings.

Survey Populations

By referring to the various surveys developed by the testing agencies and reviewed on the first pages of this section, we may immediately identify some of the survey populations whose opinions and perceptions we value. These include students, faculty, and alumni, and subgroups of those (e.g., entering students, nonreturning students, recent alumni, perhaps even tenured faculty). Other survey populations on campus might be administrators and nonteaching staff.

The general population in the institution's service area is an appropriate survey population for reputational-type surveys. Any group of individuals who uses or may use the institution's services or in some other way has contact with and knowledge of the institution is an appropriate survey population, depending on the kind of information sought.

Employers of the institution's graduates are another valuable survey group. This was one of the findings of a recent dissertation that dealt with the various components of educational quality (Martin, 1989). Employer satisfaction with graduates as a component of quality generated a consensus among the four groups surveyed (members of the board of trustees, members of the state legislature, university administrators and faculty, and alumni). This component was ranked first to fifth in overall importance by 25 of the 28 subgroups and was listed as a top-10 component of quality in the remaining subgroups.

The first question an institution may ask when considering attitudinal surveys is, What do we want to know? The second question is, Who can tell us best? Thus are populations chosen. Once chosen, good research practices must be followed in sampling the populations. Certainly, wherever possible, surveying the total group is helpful. (For example, faculty, administrators, or nonreturning students may be surveyed as a total group.)

Information Users

With surveys selected and information gathered from populations defined, let us not relegate the results to a shelf somewhere. Who will use the information? Each campus will have its own individualized list, but perhaps these suggested users may help in planning meetings for dissemination of information.

Information/Perceptions	*Users*
Student Services	Registrar
	Student Affairs Officers
	Counselors
	Activities Director
	Student Government Association
	Financial Aid Officer

Academic Programs	Academic Vice President
	Academic Deans
	Department Chairs
	Curriculum Committees
	Faculty
Facilities	Central Administration
	Physical Plant Director
	Building Managers
	Librarian
	Athletics/Intramural
	Sports Director
Administration	President
	Administrative Staff
	Vice Presidents

For most efficient use of the results, a comparison of a group's intended attitudinal outcomes or objectives with related data generated through survey processes will bring these relationships into focus. Groups may then proceed with action plans to test further the effectiveness of their programs and services or to revise those offerings. A sharply honed presentation related specifically to the user group in that group's language and frame of reference, in other words, is essential.

Design for Survey Implementation and Dissemination of Results

The implementation of a program of attitudinal surveys should be undertaken systematically with clear results in mind. Representatives from each of the potential user groups should be involved in the process, participating in the identification of survey populations and of kinds of information desired. The following sequence of activities should occur. The subpoints are given as examples and should trigger additional items specific to the institution's needs.

1. Identification of intended results for the survey activity, for example:
   a. To acquire additional personal and demographic information about various student, alumni, and other population groups

   b. To gain information for program improvement

   c. To obtain perceptions of institutional quality

   d. To inform external publics of the institutions

2. Selection of appropriate instruments, considering, for example:

   a. Available financial resources

   b. In-house expertise and data processing support

   c. Content of commercially available instruments

   d. Feasibility of longitudinal use

3. Establishment of a time schedule for administration:

   a. Entering students—each orientation period

   b. Continuing students—every third year? alternate years?

   c. Exiting/noncontinuing students—as a part of the exiting process

   d. Graduating seniors—as a part of the diploma application, graduation checkout, or similar activity

   e. Recent alumni—every year within 6 months of graduation

   f. Alumni follow-up—each year for graduates 5 years out or, perhaps, every other year or every third year for classes 3 to 5 years out

   g. Program-related questionnaire—at the time of program review, or, perhaps, every 5 years

   h. External publics—at 5- to 10-year intervals, particularly at times of mission review or as needed to identify new constituencies or new programs

4. Collection and interpretation of data, considering, for example:

   a. Contractual arrangements for mailing, processing, tabulating, and summarizing data

   b. Assignment of personnel and allocation of release time for these activities

   c. Establishment of types of reporting desired (i.e., means, percentages, comparisons, simple frequencies) by subgroups or aggregated only

5. Dissemination of information:

   a. Identification of key user groups

   b. Partitioning of data into manageable segments (not everything to everybody at one time)

   c. Scheduling of small-group sessions for presentation and interpretation of data

6. Follow-up sessions to review:

   a. Usefulness of information as catalyst for change or in reaffirmation of status quo, or for initiation of new programs and services

    b. Need for additional data

    c. Need for instrument redesign or continued use

    d. Longitudinal implementation of survey cycle

As one examines the preceding outline, a number of additional questions, items for inclusion, or cautions will come to mind. The cross fertilization of ideas and needs that surfaces in discussions with key user representatives as they deal with these additional items may be as valuable to the health of the institution as the resultant survey data.

Some key elements for that group to keep in mind to help ensure success for the program follow.

1. Avoid overcontact with survey populations. It is important that the same community leader, alumnus, or, for that matter, continuing students not be asked at too frequent (one year or less) intervals to participate in survey activities. The key to avoiding this problem is to establish a central office that, at the least, serves as a clearinghouse for all such activity and, at the most, conducts the gathering and dissemination of all such data. The oversurveying of populations is not cost-effective, gives fragmented information, and may well alienate the survey participant, thus yielding less dependable data and creating public relations problems for the institution.

   Alumni surveys are an easy prey to this problem. For example, the Placement Office conducts a career satisfaction survey, the Development Office asks many of the same questions in a survey designed to identify potential donors, and the graduate's academic department asks these questions to determine achievement of programmatic goals. One survey, centrally coordinated with participation by all these users in its development and in planning for dissemination of results, will develop much more positive relationships between the institution and its alumni.

2. Establish a plan for multiple contacts for mail surveys to increase response rate.

   a. A letter from the CEO or other key officer (the student's dean, perhaps, in the case of program-related surveys) explaining the need for the information and appealing to the person's loyalties as a member of the institutional community will convey the importance of the survey and place it in a positive light.

  b. Inclusion of a postage-paid return envelope is advisable, as is the mailing of surveys at forwarding-address-requested level of postage rather than at a lower rate.
  c. A follow-up postcard reminder is helpful. Of even greater effect is a personal phone call, which, in some cases, may be linked to calls for other purposes—recruitment calls to applicants, calls encouraging continuing students to preregister, or fund drive calls to alumni and community, for example.
  d. Some institutions have even included a dime or, perhaps, a pencil or pen with the school's name stamped on it or a small note pad. These add little to the cost and may be an additional enticement to the person being surveyed.

3. If work is being done in-house, be certain that the time, personnel, and facilities are adequate to the task. If these requirements are not met, the project is very likely to bog down. Appropriate follow-up cannot occur if data are not processed in a timely fashion, and any positive effect of the earlier activities is quickly lost if user groups cannot see the results of their earlier efforts and if the public surveyed sees no evidence of use of the results. It is sometimes much more cost-effective and profitable to the institution to forego some individualized information needs to take advantage of the efficiency of basic services offered by the various testing services.

4. Select segmented elements of data for presentation over a continuing period of time and be certain to follow up on their use. Peter Ewell, in *Assessment, Accountability, and Improvement: Managing the Contradiction* (1987a, p. 19), made this point emphatically: *"Don't show everything at once."* Ewell's point is to guarantee that the institution will continue to have new information to report and to demonstrate ongoing commitment. Accountability to our external constituencies may require this kind of juggling of information. Internal accountability, however, needs this segmentation of information for a different purpose: a user may focus on narrower areas for improvement and change, and that concentration of effort is more likely to result in a stronger institution than are attempts to address all areas simultaneously.

Summary

Patricia Hutchings, in *Six Stories: Implementing Successful Assessment* (1987), says, "In some ways the important point may be less *what* one does than the need to do *something*. Yes, everything will be imperfect, it's better on paper" (p. 13). Certainly, a plan for attitudinal surveys is a way to "do something" and offer constructive, useful results in the early stages of an assessment process.

The institution that takes the steps necessary to implement attitudinal surveys will indeed see itself as others see it, and it will, if the information is carefully used, free itself from many a blunder and foolish notion.

References: Cited and Recommended

The ACT evaluation/survey service, Specimen set [Instruments]. Iowa City, IA: American College Testing Program.

Amiran, M. R., Golden, A., & Wright, B. D. (1990, June 27–29). *Why reinvent the wheel? The gentle art of "borrowing" instruments*. Panel discussion at the fifth annual American Association for Higher Education Assessment Forum, Washington, DC.

Assessment Resource Center bibliography. (1987). Knoxville, TN: Assessment Resource Center, University of Tennessee.

Cavanagh, D., & Soellner, P. (1987). *The FIPSE value added grant for Rhode Island College*. Paper presented to the second National Conference on Assessment in Higher Education, Denver, CO.

Cooperative Institutional Research Institute. (1986). *The American freshman: National norms for fall 1986*. Los Angeles, CA: University of California.

Dennison, G. M., & Bunda, M. A. (1989). Assessment and academic judgements in higher education. In P. J. Gray (Ed.), *Achieving assessment goals using evaluation techniques*. New Directions for Higher Education, no. 67, XVII(3). San Francisco: Jossey-Bass.

ESS in action. (1987). Iowa City, IA: American College Testing Program.

ETS college and university programs. (n.d.). [Brochure]. Princeton, NJ: Educational Testing Service.

Ewell, P. T. (1983). *Student outcomes questionnaires: An implementation handbook* (2nd ed.). Boulder, CO: National Center for Higher Education Management Systems.

Ewell, P. T. (1984). *The self-regarding institution: Information for excellence*. Boulder, CO: National Center for Higher Education Management Systems.

Ewell, P. T. (1985). Some implications for practice. In P. T. Ewell (Ed.), *Assessing educational outcomes*. New Directions for Institutional Research, no. 47, XII(3). San Francisco: Jossey-Bass.

Ewell, P. T. (1987a). *Assessment, accountability, and improvement: Managing the contradiction*. Washington, DC: American Association for Higher Education Assessment Forum.

Ewell, P. T. (1987b). Establishing a campus-based assessment program. In D. F. Halpern (Ed.), *Student outcomes assessment: What institutions stand to gain*. New Directions for Higher Education, no. 59, XV(3). San Francisco: Jossey-Bass.

Fisher, M. B. (1988). Surveying your alumni. In G. S. Melchiori (Ed.), *Alumni research: Methods and applications.* New Directions for Institutional Research, no. 60, *XV*(4). San Francisco: Jossey-Bass.

Hutchings, P. (1987). *Six stories: Implementing successful assessment.* Washington, DC: American Association for Higher Education Assessment Forum.

Institutional performance survey [Instrument]. Boulder, CO: National Center for Higher Education Management Systems.

Kells, H. R. (1980). *Self-study processes: A guide for postsecondary institutions.* Washington, DC: American Council on Education.

Lenning, O. T., Beal, P., & Sauer, K. (1980). *Retention and attrition: Evidence for action and research.* Boulder, CO: National Center for Higher Education Management Systems.

Martin, L. (1989, December). *Perceptions of the importance of various components of educational quality in Mississippi public universities.* Unpublished doctoral dissertation, University of Mississippi. (University Microfilms no. 319591, catalog no. 9019274.)

McClain, C. J. (1987, Winter). Assessment produces degrees with integrity. *Educational Record, 68*(1), 47–52.

Resource manual on institutional effectiveness. (1987). Atlanta, GA: Commission on Colleges of the Southern Association of Colleges and Schools.

Section III. (1989). *Criteria for accreditation: Commission on colleges.* Atlanta, GA: Southern Association of Colleges and Schools.

Stevenson, M. R., Walleri, R. D., & Japely, S. M. (1985). Designing follow-up studies of graduates and former students. In P. T. Ewell (Ed.), *Assessing educational outcomes.* New Directions for Institutional Research, no. 47, *XII*(3). San Francisco: Jossey-Bass.

Student-outcomes questionnaires [Instruments]. Boulder, CO: National Center for Higher Education Management Systems.

Cognitive Assessment Instruments: Availability and Utilization

Marsha V. Krotseng and
Gary R. Pike

The current "ubiquity of tests has led some academics who know little about assessment to think the term *means* testing"—and testing alone (Marchese, 1987, p. 6). In fact, number 2 pencils and optically scanned forms comprise just one (albeit highly visible) element of the process—the act of cognitive assessment. Although the disputations characteristic of medieval universities and their offspring, the American colonial college, are no longer the order of the day, creative assessment options such as portfolios have grown increasingly common. Based on the systematic scheme represented by the Institutional Effectiveness Paradigm in Figure 2 (see page 11), individual institutions have adopted unique strategies for cognitive assessment in the realization that the only truly effective assessment will be tailored to their own culture and clientele.

Appropriate Assessment: Which One of the Above?

This resource section advances a wide array of cognitive assessment alternatives: standardized tests of both general knowledge and learning in the major field, locally developed instruments for assessing general and specialized knowledge, tests of critical thinking, and portfolios. The discussion extends beyond the design of such instruments to incorporate their appropriate application, capabilities, flexibility, advantages, and pitfalls.

Of the six goals that then U.S. Secretary of Education Lauro F.

Cavazos placed before the higher education community in early 1990, three directly address cognitive assessment:

- All associates and bachelor's degree recipients should be able to demonstrate proficiency in college-level math and science.
- All graduating students should be able to write coherent, grammatically correct papers and display a basic knowledge of world history, geography and culture appropriate to their degree level, and
- All students leaving colleges and universities should possess higher order critical thinking and problem-solving skills needed to contribute productively to the economic and political life of the nation. ("Cavazos presents," 1990, p. 1).

At the state level, members of the State Higher Education Executive Officers association have reported the growing use of student and institutional outcomes measures in evaluating educational effectiveness (SHEEO, 1990).

Thus, the critical question is not whether to saddle this assessment steed, but, rather, how to harness its full potential without being thrown. As the seasoned rider analyzes a thoroughbred's nature before leaving the gate, colleges and universities can similarly avoid a false start at cognitive assessment by scrutinizing the ever-expanding universe of available methods detailed in the following pages.

Two primary queries posed by Halpern (1987a) necessarily precede the selection of an appropriate instrument: "What do you want to know?" and "Why do you want to know it?" (p. 109). "Clear and succinct answers to these questions will [then] provide direction to the secondary questions, 'What should you measure?' and 'How should you measure it?'" (p. 109). In the present context, the reason for assessment is readily apparent—to analyze an institution's intended (and actual) educational outcomes. Comprising this path to institutional effectiveness or program improvement are such discrete stepping-stones as the determination of students' academic progress and the use of examinations as "gateways" to upper-division coursework or as benchmarks for budget decisions and accountability (Halpern, 1987b). Once an institution has set forth its Expanded Statement of Institutional Purpose and the supporting departmental/program statements of intended outcomes/objectives, the identification of proper instruments can proceed logically and smoothly. As Harris (1985) concluded, "You can compare your students to [others] nationally on standardized tests without having definite educational goals. . . . But without such goals, you can't be sure the tests reflect your curriculum" (p. 13).

Resnick and Goulden (1987) cited 13 basic methods of assessment of learning originally reported in an American Council on Education (ACE) survey of 450 college and university presidents and academic vice presidents:

1. College-level skills or minimum competency tests
2. Tests of general knowledge in the humanities and sciences
3. Comprehensive tests in a student's major
4. Tests of critical thinking
5. Tests of quantitative problem solving
6. Tests of oral communication
7. Tests of writing
8. Value-added measures of student gains while in college
9. Mathematics placement tests for entering students
10. English placement tests for entering students
11. Reading placement tests for entering students
12. Placement tests in other skills for entering students
13. Pre- and posttests for remedial courses

By 1989, basic skills testing was in place at 65% of all higher education institutions, and another 19% planned to institute such measures. Almost all public two-year institutions had programs to assess basic skills (El-Khawas, 1989). Beyond the basics, El-Khawas reports that half of all colleges and universities assess higher-order skills (e.g., writing) as an expected outcome of college study. Among the most widely evaluated and recommended means for assessing college's cognitive outcomes are the specific instruments highlighted in the following sections.

Assessment of General Knowledge

Emphasizing breadth across the curriculum rather than in-depth study, tests of general knowledge reveal the students' grasp of basic concepts and skills in the liberal arts (Hartle, 1985). Communication, computation, and critical thinking join elements from the social and natural sciences on both standardized and local instruments intended for this purpose.

Standardized Tests of General Knowledge

Since 1987, state mandates, accrediting associations, and revised campus policies have spurred tremendous growth in the number of institutions interested in assessing general education outcomes. Paralleling this development is the increased availability of instruments for measuring general learning. Prior to 1987 five tests were available for general education assessment: the ACT Assessment Program examinations, the College-Level Examination Program (CLEP) General Examinations, the College Outcome Measures Program (COMP) examination, the Graduate Record Examination (GRE) General Test, and the Scholastic Aptitude Test (SAT). Four new tests have been introduced since 1987: the Academic Profile, the College Basic Academic Subjects Examination (College BASE), the Collegiate Assessment of Academic Proficiency (CAAP), and the Education Assessment series.

All but one of the tests available prior to 1987 were initially designed for other purposes (e.g., undergraduate or graduate admissions considerations), not for evaluating general education programs. Although tests such as the ACT and SAT have been shown to predict initial undergraduate or graduate success, their relationship to coursework and experiences during the last two years of college is much less clear.

ACT Assessment. The ACT Assessment Program was designed as a battery of college entrance and placement examinations. The original ACT Assessment includes four tests requiring 30 to 50 minutes each: (1) English usage, (2) mathematics usage, (3) reading in the natural sciences, and (4) reading in social studies. A composite (total) score also is provided. Depending on the coefficients used, reliability estimates for the individual tests have ranged from .73 to .91. Alpha reliability for the composite score is reported to be .85.

Research has found that the ACT Assessment is capable of predicting subsequent performance in college, including cumulative grade point average and performance in specific classes (Munday, 1968; Richards, Holland, & Lutz, 1967). However, studies at Tennessee Technological University have failed to demonstrate a relationship between gains on the ACT Assessment exams and students' experiences in college (Dumont & Troelstrup, 1981).

Recently, the American College Testing Program introduced the Enhanced ACT Assessment exams. ACT provides concordance tables that translate composite, English, and mathematics scores on the original ACT Assessment exams into Enhanced ACT scores. Scores for social studies reading and natural sciences reading are not available for the Enhanced ACT Assessment because they have been replaced by the Reading and Science Reasoning tests. Data on the reliability and validity of Enhanced ACT scores for outcomes assessment are not available.

The ACT and Enhanced ACT Assessment examinations are published by the American College Testing Program, P.O. Box 168, Iowa City, IA 52243.

College Outcome Measures Program. Of the five tests developed prior to 1987, only the American College Testing Program's COMP exam was designed specifically to measure general education outcomes. The purpose of the COMP exam is to assess the knowledge and skills necessary for effective functioning in adult society (Forrest, 1982). Available as a 2.5-hour Objective Test of 60 multiple-choice items or a longer (4.5-hour) Composite Examination, the COMP exam provides a total score, three content subscores, and three process subscores (Forrest & Steele, 1982). The Composite Examination also contains measures of writing and speaking ability (Steele, 1979).

In the technical manual for the COMP exam, ACT staff report that the alpha reliability (internal consistency) of the total score is .84 for individuals (Forrest & Steele, 1982). Reliability estimates for the six subscores range from .63 to .68. Steele (1989) reports that the group means generalizability coefficient for total score is .96, assuming a sample size of 300 students. Generalizability coefficients for the six subscores range from .87 to .94 for samples of 300 students. Using Steele's data, Pike (1990) reports that the 95% confidence interval about universe score for total score is slightly more than ± 6 points for groups of 300 students.

The technical report for the COMP exam also contains several studies intended to provide evidence of the convergent and discriminant validity of the Objective Test. These studies generally reveal that scores on the COMP exam are related to patterns of coursework and other outcomes measures but generally unrelated to students' demographic characteristics (Forrest & Steele, 1982). Somewhat troubling, from the perspective of discriminant validity, is the fact that the best predictor of performance on the COMP exam is entering academic ability as measured by the ACT Assessment examination (Forrest & Steele, 1982).

Studies at several institutions have indicated that the COMP exam is highly sensitive to students' precollege characteristics and relatively insensitive to instructional effects (Davis & Murrell, 1989; Pike, 1989, 1990). In a study of college sophomores at 6 four-year and 8 two-year institutions in Washington State, the Council of Presidents and State Board for Community College Education (1989) reported that students' background characteristics are significantly related to total score and subscores on the Objective Test. The authors concluded that the COMP exam is basically a measure of aptitude or ability, and the test is relatively insensitive to educational effects.

Further information on the College Outcome Measures Program is available from the publisher, American College Testing Program, P.O. Box 168, Iowa City, IA 52243.

Collegiate Assessment of Academic Proficiency. The CAAP exam is intended to measure skills typically attained during the first 2 years of college. This test consists of five 40-minute modules that can be administered individually or in combination: (1) writing (either multiple-choice questions or a writing sample), (2) mathematics, (3) reading, (4) science reasoning, and (5) critical thinking (ACT, 1989). The first four modules parallel the tests in the Enhanced ACT Assessment.

KR-20 reliability (internal consistency) estimates for scores on four of the modules range from .76 to .93 (ACT, 1989). Reliability estimates are not available for the Science Reasoning test.

Two studies are currently under way to evaluate the concurrent and predictive validity of the CAAP exam. One study will examine the relationships between CAAP scores and end-of-sophomore-year grades. The second study will examine the accuracy of CAAP scores in predicting English and mathematics grades, as well as junior-year grade point average (ACT, 1989).

The publisher of the CAAP is the American College Testing Program, P.O. Box 168, Iowa City, IA 52243.

Scholastic Aptitude Test. Like the ACT Assessment exams, the Scholastic Aptitude Test was designed for use as a college entrance and placement examination. The SAT is comprised of two tests, verbal and quantitative, with a combined score also available. Research findings show that both the verbal and quantitative scores on the SAT are related to performance during the first 2 years of college (CEEB & ETS, 1988). Although the publishers of the SAT describe the exams as measures of problem-solving ability, studies have failed to demonstrate that the tests are sensitive to the effects of college coursework. Research by Ratcliff (1988) incorporates the SAT as a pretest in order to control for the effects of entering ability on posttest scores.

The Scholastic Aptitude Test is published by the Educational Testing Service, Princeton, NJ 08541.

College-Level Examination Program. The College-Level Examination Program (CLEP) General Examinations originally were designed to provide college credit for noncollege learning (CEEB, 1984). The General Examinations consist of five tests requiring 90 minutes each: (1) English composition, (2) humanities, (3) mathematics, (4) natural science, and (5) social science and history. Reliability estimates for the five tests range from .91 to .94 (CEEB, 1984).

Using experts in each content field, the CLEP development process has achieved high levels of content validity. In addition, research has linked performance on the CLEP exams to performance in introductory college courses (CEEB, 1986). Studies have not been conducted to evaluate the validity of the CLEP exams as program evaluation instruments.

Further details on these CLEP exams can be obtained from the College Entrance Examination Board, 45 Columbus Avenue, New York, NY 10023-6917.

Education Assessment Series. The Education Assessment Series (EAS) tests are modifications of the CLEP exams and are designed to provide information about student outcomes for program evaluation. The EAS consists of two tests intended to provide comprehensive nationally normed data in a relatively short administration time (45 minutes per module) and at a low cost. Because multiple forms of the tests will be available, institutions may administer the tests twice and examine changes in students' scores over the course of their college careers. The EAS was first pilot-tested in 1988, so data on the reliability and validity of the tests are still not available. However, additional information may be obtained by contacting the College Entrance Examination Board, 45 Columbus Avenue, New York, NY 10023-6917.

Graduate Record Examinations. A test usually given at the end of a student's undergraduate career, the Graduate Record Examinations (GRE) General Test has also been used to evaluate the effects of college curricula on student learning at several institutions (Ratcliff, 1988). The GRE General Test actually comprises three nationally normed tests designed to assess learned abilities that are not related to any particular field of study but that are related to skills necessary for successful graduate study (Adelman, 1985). Three scores are provided: verbal (antonyms, analogies, sentence completions, reading passages), quantitative (quantitative comparisons, mathematics, data interpretation), and analytical (analytical reasoning, logical reasoning) (Graduate Records Examinations Board, 1987). The full test is administered during a 3.5-hour period. Research on the General Test has revealed high levels of reliability for the three tests, ranging from .89 to .92 (Conrad, Trismen, & Miller, 1977).

In addition to scores on the three tests, it is possible to obtain nine item-type scores on the exam: (1) antonyms, (2) analogies, (3) sentence completions, (4) reading passages, (5) quantitative comparisons, (6) mathematics, (7) data interpretation, (8) analytical reasoning, and (9) logical reasoning (Wilson, 1985). Ratcliff (1988) has shown that clusters of undergraduate coursework can be formed that discriminate among performance on the nine item types. In addition, Wilson (1985) has reported that item-type scores are related to undergraduate performance and success in graduate school.

The publisher of the GRE is the Graduate Record Examinations Board, Educational Testing Service, CN 6000, Princeton, NJ 08541-6000.

Academic Profile. Of the four tests marketed since 1987, the Academic Profile is the oldest. Developed by the Educational Testing Service and the College Entrance Examinations Board to assess the effectiveness of general education programs, the Academic Profile is available in two forms: a short (1-hour) form designed to provide group data and a long (3-hour) form designed to provide data about individuals (ETS College & University Programs, 1987).

A norm-referenced total score and seven subscores (also norm referenced) are provided. Subscores include three content areas (humanities, natural science, and social science) and four skill areas (reading, writing, mathematics, and critical thinking). The newest form of the Academic Profile also provides proficiency scores in the areas of writing, mathematics, and reading/critical thinking (ETS, 1990). Research demonstrates that these proficiency scores can be used to evaluate student change over the course of a college career.

Because the Academic Profile has been in the pilot-testing phase, relatively little information is available regarding its reliability and validity. Recent publications do indicate that the most recent version of the Academic Profile will utilize scale scores (rather than percentage-correct scores), will have substantially lower intercorrelations among skill scores, and will have a short form that can be administered during one testing period of approximately 40 minutes.

Additional information concerning the Academic Profile can be obtained from Higher Education Assessment, ETS College and University Programs, Princeton, NJ 08541-0001.

College BASE. The College Basic Academic Subjects Examination is a criterion-referenced achievement test that can be used to evaluate individuals or programs. (National norms also are provided for comparative purposes.) One- and 3-hour versions of the test are available.

College BASE provides a composite score, four subject scores (English, mathematics, natural science, social studies), and three reasoning scores (interpretive, strategic, and adaptive reasoning) (Riverside Publishing Company, 1989). Subject scores are further subdivided into cluster scores and skill scores. For example, the mathematics score is composed of three cluster scores: (1) general mathematics, (2) algebra, and (3) geometry. The general mathematics cluster score contains skill scores for practical applications, properties and notations, and using statistics (Riverside Publishing Company, 1990).

The content of the test is based on recommendations of teams of reviewers for each subject area. Data on the reliability and validity of the College BASE are not yet available. However, a technical manual is in preparation. Currently, the exam is being used in Missouri for admission to teacher education programs, and it has been used by more than 25 institutions to evaluate their general education programs.

The College BASE examination is published by Riverside Publishing Company, 8420 Bryn Mawr Avenue, Chicago, IL 60631-3476.

Localized General Knowledge Alternatives

With increasing numbers of states and state higher education system offices mandating student outcomes assessment, these entities inevitably have fashioned their own substitutes for the familiar standardized route in search of instruments more closely paralleling a particular curriculum. According to ACE, fully 55% of all colleges and universities reported developing their own instruments for student assessment by 1989, a 10% rise from the previous year. Although many of these state-, system-, and institution-devised alternatives are not strictly local in the sense of being confined to a single place, they are more limited in scope and application and, hence, are referred to in this publication as "local instruments." Obviously, such general knowledge examinations can be better tailored to local circumstances and needs.

By Florida state statute, every community college and state university student must successfully complete all four tests of that state's College Level Academic Skills Project (CLASP). This examination is required for all community college associate degrees as well as for admission to upper-division status in all public universities. Developed by faculty from the Florida community colleges and state universities, CLASP is used to assess skills in both communication (reading, listening, writing, and speaking) and mathematics (algorithms, concepts, generalizations, and problem solving). Although this measure was specifically constructed for Florida institutions of higher learning, the Florida State Department of Education honors legitimate requests from individuals and institutions interested in the CLASP Technical Report and Test Administration Plan (Harris, 1985).

The New Jersey College Basic Skills Placement Test (NJCBSPT) is a series of five tests designed to meet the requirements of the assessment and evaluation program developed by the New Jersey Board of Higher Education. In addition to the five individual test scores (writing, reading comprehension, sentence sense, math computation, and elementary algebra), two composite scores can be derived from the language assessment parts of the test—one for Total English and the other for composition. This 168-item test is administered over a 3-hour period. Reliability estimates for the seven subscales range from .83 to .92. The content validity of the NJCBSPT was achieved by providing for constant review during test construction by a panel of experts from the New Jersey Basic Skills Council. Studies on the construct validity and predictive validity of the NJCBSPT are currently under way.

A well-known system-level requirement, the Regents' Testing Program of the University System of Georgia is administered to all rising juniors in the state's community colleges, four-year colleges, and universities. A prerequisite to graduation, the Regents' Program evaluates both reading comprehension and essay construction. The reading portion, a 1-hour test of 60 items, "consists of ten . . . passages, with five to eight questions on each, that test comprehension in terms of vocabulary, literal comprehension, inferential comprehension, and analysis" (Harris, 1985, p. 20). Review of the essay section involves multiple faculty evaluators (who have not taught the students) trained to use a consistent scoring procedure (Harris).

On the West Coast, the California State University System's Graduation Writing Assessment Requirement (GWAR) demands writing proficiency of all upper-division and graduate students. However, each of the 19 CSU campuses has implemented its own version of this requirement; whereas some campuses designate certain upper-division and graduate-level courses that entail "a large amount of writing," others "allow students to demonstrate proficiency on an actual writing test" (Harris, 1985, p. 20). As in Georgia and New Jersey, multiple faculty evaluations and a consistent grading procedure have proved integral to the process.

Finally, a few hardy institutions like Olivet Nazarene, dissatisfied with the standardized status quo, have assumed the whole burden of developing more satisfactory tests of general education for their students.

Standardized or Local?

Confronted with this complex assortment of instruments, college faculty members and administrators are well advised to consider their intended educational outcomes together with the strengths and weaknesses of standardized and locally developed examinations before committing to any particular program. Standardized instruments such as the COMP, ACT, GRE, and SAT obviously have weathered a number of prior applications and are readily available. More important, Ewell (1987) has described them as

1. Relatively easy to administer;
2. Acceptable in terms of faculty time invested, although costly if used in volume;
3. Generally less open to charges of subjectivity;
4. Nationally normed, allowing comparison across institutions.

On the other hand, standardized examinations suffer major disadvantages in that

1. They may or may not reflect the content of a specific institution's curriculum.
2. The results often are reported as a single performance score (or, at best, four to six subscores), obscuring both the laudable and the less healthy aspects of the curriculum.
3. Normative comparison scores may be inappropriate for general curriculum evaluation (e.g., GRE norms, compiled from those taking the test, may not be suitable for comparison with scores from an entire graduating class [Ewell, 1987]).

As suggested earlier, the attributes of state- and systemwide examinations alleviate several of these concerns. Specifically, such faculty-developed instruments will be

1. Tailored to the individual curriculum;
2. Available for more detailed analysis of results;
3. Amenable to a variety of formats including essays or task and problem-solving exercises;
4. Perceived as legitimate by faculty because at least key colleagues have played a role in the tests' design (Ewell, 1987).

But, neither are these examinations absent certain drawbacks. According to Ewell (1987), they

1. Reflect only the priorities of a particular institution or system and may, therefore, hold less external credibility;
2. Cannot be compared with results from other institutions or programs outside the system or state;
3. Can be costly to produce, especially in terms of that precious commodity—faculty time;
4. Will not necessarily be well constructed without special on-campus training or expertise.

Specialized Knowledge: Assessment in the Major Field

Historically, assessment of student learning in the major field has been an important topic in higher education (Banta & Schneider, 1988). "Comprehensive exams in the major fields or across fields, using essays and oral interrogation and modeled on English university practice, [were] common in American higher education through most of the nineteenth century" (Resnick & Goulden, 1987, p. 80). Indeed, descriptions of senior culminating experiences at Swarthmore and St. Johns have become almost legendary. For the majority of today's institutions, however, standardized examinations in the major field of study afford a practical alternative for assessing in depth understanding of a specific subject, commonly referred to as specialized knowledge.

Standardized Instruments

According to Harris (1985),

> If a department is primarily interested in assessment for program evaluation, it may not need to administer outside tests. Rather, it may be able to use the test results its students and graduates ordinarily provide in their application for graduate or professional education, or for licensure or certification. A post-graduation examination [such as the CPA] . . . will have obvious leverage on the department's faculty. Departments often develop "batting averages" out of such information. (p. 20)

If, instead, circumstances clearly call for outside measures, viable standardized alternatives are suggested in the following paragraphs. Given the tremendous number of tests that are currently available, this review covers only a limited number of measures in detail, focusing primarily on the disciplines of business, chemistry, and psychology. However, the same publishers produce similar tests for most other major fields as well.

Major Field Achievement Tests (Business). The Educational Testing Service provides 16 tests in specific academic disciplines. Of these, the most recently introduced test (April 1990) is in business. Subscores cover seven areas: (1) accounting, (2) economics, (3) finance, (4) legal and social issues, (5) marketing, (6) management, and (7) quantitative business analysis (ETS, 1990).

Unlike the other major field examinations, the Business Test is not based on the Graduate Record Examinations. (There is no GRE area test for business.) Instead, faculty from across the country participated in developing the Business Test, which is intended to measure material covered in a core curriculum (ETS, 1990). Institutions may add as many as 50 locally developed questions to the test to tailor it to their own core curriculum. Information on the reliability and validity of the Business Test is not currently available.

Major Field Achievement Test in Chemistry. The Major Field Achievement Test (MFAT) in Chemistry is a modification of the Graduate Record Examinations area test in chemistry. This test is much shorter than the GRE version and has a significantly lower level of item difficulty (ETS, 1990). Areas covered in the test include analytical, inorganic, organic, and physical chemistry (ETS, 1989). Only a total score is provided for this MFAT component. The reliability estimate for total score on the test is .91. National norms also are provided for the test.

Major Field Achievement Test in Psychology. Like the test in chemistry, the MFAT in psychology is a modification of the GRE area test in psychology. However, unlike the MFAT for chemistry, the psychology test yields a total score and two subscores: one for experimental psychology and the second for social psychology.

Reliability estimates are .91 for total score, .80 for experimental psychology, and .83 for social psychology (ETS, 1989). This MFAT draws on material from cognition and perception, comparative psychology, sensation, developmental psychology, clinical and abnormal psychology, social psychology, and measurement and methodology.

Information regarding these or any of the other Major Field Achievement Tests is available from the publisher, Higher Education Assessment (18-U), ETS College and University Programs, Princeton, NJ 08541-0001.

CLEP Subject Tests (General Chemistry). The College Entrance Examination Board has developed approximately 30 subject area tests, including a test in general chemistry. These tests are designed to provide college credit for noncollege learning.

Research on the General Chemistry exam indicates that the test exhibits adequate levels of reliability (approximately .89), and expert review by a test development committee has established its content validity (matched to introductory chemistry courses). In addition, studies have found that test scores are moderately correlated with grades in general chemistry courses.

The College Entrance Examination Board, 45 Columbus Avenue, New York, NY 10023-6917, publishes this and other CLEP subject examinations.

Graduate Record Examinations (General Chemistry). The Graduate Record Examinations Program (GRE) offers subject tests in 17 disciplines, including chemistry. Each of these tests yields a total score, and eight tests provide subscores (Conrad, Trisman, & Miller, 1977). Research indicates that all of the tests evidence acceptable levels of reliability (.82 to .96) (DeVore & McPeek, 1985). Reliability (internal consistency) is .86 for the chemistry examination.

Because the GRE subject tests are designed to predict performance in graduate school, norms are not available for college seniors, and subscores are not matched to patterns of undergraduate coursework. The Educational Testing Service is attempting to overcome these limitations by providing shorter versions of the subject tests, removing the most difficult items, providing norms for college seniors, and developing a flexible report format.

The GRE subject instruments are published by the Graduate Record Examinations Board, CN 6000, Educational Testing Service, Princeton, NJ 08541-6000.

Graduate Record Examination (Psychology). The Graduate Record Examinations Board also provides a subject-area test in psychology. Unlike the test in chemistry, the psychology test yields two subscores: experimental and social psychology (Conrad, Trisman, & Miller, 1977). Reliability estimates are .93 for total score, .87 for experimental psychology, and .85 for social psychology.

Further description of this examination is available from the Graduate Record Examinations Board, CN 6000, Educational Testing Service, Princeton, NJ 08541-6000.

AACSB Business Management Test. The American Assembly of Collegiate Schools of Business (AACSB) has commissioned the development of outcomes measures for evaluating the quality and effectiveness of business management programs. These measures include a paper-and-pencil test of knowledge in business and a series of assessment center exercises designed to test students' abilities in applying their knowledge.

The AACSB Business Management Test covers content in seven areas: (1) accounting, (2) business strategy, (3) finance, (4) organization theory, (5) marketing, (6) management information systems, and (7) quantitative analysis and operations research (AACSB, 1987). The AACSB (1987) reports that reliability estimates for the paper-and-pencil measures range from .79 to .86. Interrater reliability estimates for the assessment center exercises are not available.

Because the Business Management Test has been under development, extensive information on its validity is not available. Thus far, the only indication of the instrument's validity is based on the use of content experts in test development. Additional research on the validity of the tests is progressing.

The publisher of this subject-specific instrument is the America Assembly of Collegiate Schools of Business, 605 Old Ballas Road, Suite 220, St. Louis, MO 63141.

AICPA Achievement Test, Level II. The AICPA Accounting Testing Program has been developed by the American Institute of Certified Public Accountants (AICPA) to provide information for accounting educators and the accounting profession. Four tests are available through this program: (1) the Accounting Orientation Test; (2) the Accounting Aptitude Test; (3) the Achievement Test, Level I (for college sophomores); and (4) the Achievement Test, Level II (AICPA, 1987). Of these four tests, the Level II Achievement Test is most appropriate for assessment in the major at four-year institutions. The Level II Achievement Test is available in either 50-minute or 2-hour versions and covers five content areas: (1) financial accounting, (2) cost and managerial accounting, (3) auditing, (4) taxation, and (5) information systems.

The brochure from the publisher does not provide information concerning the reliability and validity of these exams. However, norms, in the form of percentile ranks, are available for all four AICPA tests. These norms are based on number of years spent studying accounting and are updated regularly (AICPA, 1987). Test fees are based on the number of answer sheets ordered.

These instruments may be obtained from the American Institute of Certified Public Accountants Project, The Psychological Corporation, 555 Academic Court, San Antonio, TX 78204.

ACS Test in General Chemistry. The General Chemistry examination developed by the American Chemical Society (ACS) is a confidential, norm-referenced test of the outcomes of instruction in general chemistry. According to the ACS (1985), research has shown the reliability (internal consistency) of the test to be .86. The ACS also reports that the content of the test has been drawn from information presented in introductory chemistry courses. Scores on the General Chemistry exam are moderately correlated with grades in introductory college chemistry courses.

Additional information may be secured by contacting the Examinations Committee, American Chemical Society, University of South Florida, Chemistry Room 112, Tampa, FL 33620.

National Teacher Examinations. State and local mandates for teacher education reform frequently have resulted in use of the National Teacher Examination (NTE) as a rite of professional passage into the elementary or secondary classroom. The NTE program offers 3 Core Battery Tests and 30 Specialty Area (subject-area) Tests, all of which are designed to provide measures of achievement for students in teacher education programs (NTE Policy Council, 1985). Reliability estimates are in the high .80s to low .90s for the Core Battery Tests as well as the Specialty Area Tests, and research has linked the content of the tests to the curricula of colleges and universities (NTE Policy Council, 1984). However, NTE score reports are not designed for program evaluation purposes, and modifications of the report format have not been undertaken.

The National Teacher Examination is published by the Educational Testing Service, CN 6051, Princeton, NJ 08541-6051.

As suggested earlier, a number of professional licensing and certification examinations routinely taken by students afford readily available outcomes measures. Prospective attorneys agonize until receiving official results of their state's bar examination; likewise, accounting majors anxiously approach the rigorous certified public accountants (CPA) examination. Physicians, nurses, psychologists, and other health care professionals also are subject to national and state licensing board requirements, such as the examination by the National League of Nursing. Departments and institutions keep close track of their graduates' performance on such measures, often vying with one another for the highest percentage of successful completions. Moreover, graduate schools of business, law, and medicine have access to students' entry scores on the GMAT, LSAT, and MCAT, respectively.

Locally Developed Alternatives

Locally constructed instruments aimed at program improvement through assessing the accomplishment of intended educational outcomes have arisen out of necessity—"in the absence of available standardized alternatives" (Ewell, 1987, p. 18). For instance, the University of Tennessee at Knoxville (UTK) combines some 45 faculty-developed instruments with the GRE's standardized tests to measure the competencies of various departmental majors. A number of publications by UTK's Center for Assessment Research and Development extensively discuss this nationally recognized assessment program, together with the process of test evolution.

Other locally designed examinations have emerged from "dissatisfaction with the match in content and coverage between available standardized tests and the curriculum" (Ewell, 1987, p. 18). Among the prime examples are an experimental sophomore-junior project at King's College (Pennsylvania) and pilot activities at Berea, Carson-Newman, and Mars Hill colleges testing institutionally prepared written and oral examinations for senior English, religion/philosophy, and political science majors (Weiner, 1987).

At Indiana University of Pennsylvania, an innovative program known as the Pre-Teacher Assessment Project employs trained teacher-evaluators to assess sophomore education majors on each of 13 skill dimensions: planning and organizing, monitoring, leadership, sensitivity, problem analysis, strategic decision making, tactical decision making, oral communication, oral presentation, written communication, innovativeness, tolerance for stress, and initiative. Among the vehicles for this evaluation are videotaped scenarios, teaching simulations, and organization of an educational fair (Orr, 1987).

Thus, the prevailing assessment mode has brought higher education full circle. As Ewell (1987) has pointed out, recent "pressures for enhanced assessment have stimulated colleges and universities to reexamine the senior comprehensive—in general education or, more commonly, in the major field—as an alternative to standardized testing" (p. 18). An integral component of the curriculum and, more significantly, the gateway to graduation, the traditional senior comprehensive examination "entailed objective demonstration of a student's mastery of core concepts and material . . . [and] application of these concepts to an extensive critical essay or problem-solving exercise" (p. 18). However, in contrast to the institutional effectiveness paradigm advanced in this *Handbook*, the "primary intent . . . was to determine what students knew and not to identify the strengths and weaknesses of the curriculum" (p. 18).

To Buy or Not to Buy?

Arguments favoring the use of standardized versus locally developed major subject tests echo those presented on pages 86 through

92. Nationally normed and less susceptible to charges of subjectivity, standardized examinations also may prove poor measures for a particular department's curriculum, and, thus, its intended educational outcomes. Although local examinations can easily be customized, they, in turn, consume faculty time and yield no external norms. Ultimately, the best advice is to carefully compare intended educational outcomes for the department or program with the material examined on each standardized test prior to reaching this crucial decision. And, there is no single "correct" solution. Whether the choice is to buy or to build a test, the appropriate answer can vary from field to field within an institution.

Assessment of Cognitive Development

Although most institutions tend to focus on the assessment of basic skills, general education, and learning in the major, many colleges and universities are becoming increasingly concerned with the assessment of higher-order thinking skills. As Mentkowski and Chickering (1987) have noted, "Many faculty are now working to teach and assess competence in critical thinking (e.g., problem-finding, problem-framing, and problem analysis with the marshalling of supportive evidence and argumentation) as a more enduring outcome of undergraduate education" (p. 153) By 1989, ACE found 14% of all higher education institutions already assessing critical thinking skills, with nearly half planning to introduce assessment of these skills. As with the assessment of other types of learning, a variety of instruments are available. Yet, assessment of cognitive development and critical thinking differs from other types of outcomes assessment in that production measures become much more prominent.

Standardized Tests

One difficulty with instruments currently available for assessing cognitive development is their high correlation with measures of general intelligence (Baird, 1988). As a consequence, many of the efforts to assess effectiveness of programs designed to enhance critical thinking have not produced any significant results (McMillan, 1987).

Analysis of Argument. The Analysis of Argument is a production measure designed to assess clarity and flexibility of students' thinking skills. After reading a passage representing a particular position on a controversial issue, students are asked to write a response disagreeing with the position taken in the passage. After 5 minutes they are told to write a second short essay supporting the original position (Stewart & Winter, 1977). The two essays are then scored using a 10-category scheme.

Because interrater agreement is a function of training, the authors do not provide estimates of reliability. However, Stewart and Winter (1977) report that studies have shown scores on the Analysis of Argument test to be significantly related to other measures of cognitive development and to students' educational experiences.

The author of this instrument is David G. Winter of the Department of Psychology, Wesleyan College, Middletown, CT 06457.

Erwin Scale of Intellectual Development. The Erwin Scale of Intellectual Development (SID) is an untimed instrument designed to measure intellectual development based on the Perry (1970) scheme. Three of Erwin's four subscales (dualism, relativism, and commitment) parallel Perry's categories of intellectual development (Erwin, 1983); the fourth subscale is empathy.

Research by Erwin (1983) indicates that all four subscales have acceptable levels of reliability (from .70 to .81). This research also shows that scores on the SID are significantly related to other measures of development, including measures of identity and involvement.

This 86-item intellectual development scale is named for its author, T. Dary Erwin of the Office of Student Assessment, James Madison University, Harrisonburg, VA 22801.

Measure of Epistemological Reflection. The Measure of Epistemological Reflection (MER) provides a bridge between recognition and production measures. Six stimuli corresponding to Perry's levels of development are presented to subjects, who are asked to justify the reasoning contained in each stimulus. Standardized scoring procedures provide a quantified measure of intellectual development (Baxter-Magolda & Porterfield, 1985).

Alpha reliability (internal consistency) estimates across stimuli may be as high as .76, and interrater reliability has ranged from .67 to .80, depending on the amount of training provided to the raters. Research also reveals support for the theory underlying the MER, indicating significant score differences for different education levels (1985).

This untimed measure was developed by Margaret Baxter-Magolda of the Department of Educational Leadership, Miami University, Miami, OH 45056.

Reflective Judgment Interview. Like the Measure of Epistemological Reflection, the Reflective Judgment Interview (RJI) provides a bridge between recognition and production measures. Requiring approximately 40 minutes to administer, the RJI consists of four dilemmas that are presented to students individually. Each dilemma is followed by a series of questions designed to identify the stage in Perry's scheme being used to deal with the dilemma (King & Kitchener, 1985). A subject's score is the average rating across the four dilemmas and across raters.

Based on research results, the Reflective Judgment Interview evidences acceptable levels of reliability (ranging from .73 to .78). In addition, the RJI has been found to be significantly correlated with other measures of critical thinking and to level of education (Kitchener & King, 1981).

The coauthors of this instrument are K. S. Kitchener, School of Education, University of Denver, Denver, CO, and P. M. King, Department of College Student Personnel, Bowling Green State University, Bowling Green, OH 43402.

Test of Thematic Analysis. The Test of Thematic Analysis assesses students' critical-thinking skills using a compare-and-contrast format. Students are given two sets of data and asked to describe (in writing) how these sets differ. This process requires approximately 30 minutes. The content of the essays is scored on a 9-point scale (Winter, 1977), yielding a total score; in addition, measures derived from human information processing research (differentiation, discrimination, and integration) can be used to evaluate the structure of the written responses (Schroder, Driver, & Streufert, 1967).

Studies have revealed high levels of interrater agreement for the Test of Thematic Analysis (Winter & McClelland, 1978), and scores have been found to be significantly correlated with both academic ability and coursework (Winter, McClelland, & Stewart, 1981). In addition, measures of the structural characteristics of students' essays have been found to be significantly related to other measures of critical thinking, as well as to educational experience (Winter & McClelland, 1978).

David G. Winter of the Department of Psychology, Wesleyan University, Middletown, CT 06457, authored this test of critical thinking.

Watson-Glaser Critical Thinking Appraisal. The Watson-Glaser Critical Thinking Appraisal (CTA) is a 100-item multiple-choice measure designed to assess students' critical-thinking abilities. In addition to a total score, five subscores are provided: (1) inference, (2) recognition of assumptions, (3) deduction, (4) interpretation, and (5) evaluation of arguments (Crites, 1965; Helmstadter, 1965).

Research indicates that the CTA is a reliable instrument. Total-score reliability estimates range from .85 to .87 (Crites, 1965; Helmstadter, 1965). Moreover, scores on the CTA are significantly related to students' college experiences and are predictive of performance in courses emphasizing critical thinking (Westbrook & Sellers, 1967; Wilson & Wagner, 1981).

The publisher of this 50-minute critical-thinking measure is Harcourt, Brace, and Jovanovich Publishers, 6277 Sea Harbor Drive, Orlando, FL 32821.

Portfolio Assessment

Clearly, cognitive assessment comprises much more than standardized and locally developed test instruments. Student portfolios have gained increasing acceptance and use over the past several years as a viable means of evaluating both general knowledge and learning in the major. Once confined primarily to the fine arts, today's portfolios appear in a variety of departments and can encompass a wide array of indicators, including writing samples, summaries of accomplishments, students' reflections on their college experience, videotapes, and speeches. Former AAHE Assessment Forum Director Pat Hutchings (1990) characterizes portfolio assessment as "a collection of student work done over time. Beyond that, the rule is variety—and appropriately so" (p. 6). According to Hutchings, new instances of portfolio use arise almost weekly—from the music department at Kean College to Spanish at the University of Virginia and entry-level placement at Miami University of Ohio (p. 6).

Applications of Portfolio Assessment.

The following brief illustrations drawn from Hutchings's (1990) work reflect the range of institutions—public and private, four-year and two-year—that have turned to some form of portfolio assessment alternative. The diversity of applications and materials incorporated in these portfolios is indeed striking.

Alverno College. Recognized as a pioneer in outcomes assessment, Alverno College has applied portfolio evaluation in the context of general education as well as in specific majors. Several approaches used in general education include an Academic Career and Resource Journal, a Communication Portfolio, and a General Performance Portfolio. Providing students with an introduction to portfolio assessment, the Academic Career and Resource Journal is used throughout each student's orientation course and includes assessment findings in beginning coursework and test results from learning and lifestyle inventories. The Communication Portfolio includes separate speaking and writing sections. Videotaped speeches and written feedback from general education and major courses, as well as from the Integrated Competence Seminar (described in a moment), are among materials maintained in the speaking portfolio. Samples of work from introductory writing classes and written self-assessments have become part of the writing portfolio; systematic collection of more advanced work may be undertaken in the future. The General Performance Portfolio focuses on social interaction skills and on the specific individual and collaborative skills that all students must demonstrate through grappling with crucial social issues in the Integrated Competence Seminar. The departments of English, natural sciences, and psychology also have employed portfolio assessment to enhance development among their respective majors.

Butler University (Indiana). The College of Business at Butler University employs portfolios to assess problem solving, communication styles and abilities, and metacognitive processing. Among the various indicators maintained are scores, student work samples, and student self-evaluations. Future portfolios may expand to include materials relevant to ethical, global, and interpersonal and intrapersonal development.

College of William and Mary. Faced with Virginia's statewide mandate requiring assessment of student learning, the College of William and Mary's foremost concern was to design useful measures for a student population that already scored well on standardized tests. Thus far, portfolios have proven quite successful for assessment in major fields such as philosophy and music. The college also has pilot-tested portfolio assessment of general educational objectives.

Dundalk Community College (Maryland). Dundalk Community College, a two-year institution, is pursuing portfolio use in assessing not only student writing but also development of an aesthetic sense and critical-thinking skills.

Kenyon College (Ohio). Each student in Kenyon College's history department must complete a portfolio containing two course-assigned papers, one revised and expanded research paper, and an autobiographical essay regarding his or her work as a historian. Two history department faculty evaluate this portfolio and conduct an oral interview with the student.

SUNY at Fredonia. Portfolios form part of a larger assessment of the

SUNY General College Program at Fredonia. Students compile materials from entrance through the senior year, including a final self-evaluation. The pedagogical intent is to heighten students' awareness of their own learning processes, encourage reflective thinking, and involve them in their own learning.

San Diego State University. Among the many programs employing portfolios at San Diego State University are classics, social work, and recreation. For 1,700 students in the teacher education program, portfolios track students' individual growth as learners, multicultural sensitivity, and insights from field experience. This information provides a basis for exit interviews conducted through core courses.

Pros and Cons of Portfolios. As Hutchings (1990) cautions, one "sure route to nowhere is to have assessment come forward as an 'add-on' activity unrelated to the regular work of faculty and students" (p. 6). Portfolio assessment allays this concern because it builds on papers, projects, and other assignments that students have completed for courses. Portfolios also provide deeper insight into students' progress, revealing not only the final outcomes—or ends—of 4, 5, or more "critical years" but also the means by which students have arrived at those outcomes. Thus, portfolio assessment can prove effective either as a stand-alone measure or as a supplement to the other cognitive measures just discussed. Further advantages associated with this form of assessment include its value in sparking conversation between faculty advisor and student, its practical utility for the faculty member asked to compose a letter of recommendation, and its circumvention of the misuses of and possible biases inherent in standardized tests. In providing a natural opportunity for students to make connections among their diverse subjects, portfolios can serve as a potent learning device.

On the other hand, this relatively new assessment technique is still being "debugged"—even by institutions that have employed it extensively. Portfolios are "difficult to make neat sense of" and, thus, do not always satisfy requirements of external audiences such as employers and graduate schools (Hutchings, 1990, p. 8). Some of their unwieldiness, however, can be surmounted with the incorporation of more traditional outcomes indicators (e.g., standardized test results). Portfolio review and evaluation can prove time-consuming as well, not only because each set of materials is unique but because individual student conferences generally are involved. Among their other disadvantages, portfolios present storage problems over time, may lead to duplication of materials when used to assess both general education and learning in the major field, and entail an initial period of development and acclimation for new faculty. Finally, it can be expensive to initiate and sustain portfolio assessment. Alverno College has addressed this last issue by having the unit that houses the materials pay directly for them; hence, the institution supplies materials maintained in the Assessment Center and departments, and students are responsible for their own copies as well as for their Academic and Resource Career Journals.

Toward Assessment of Learning with Proper Perspective

Gregory R. Anrig, president of the venerable Educational Testing Service, ironically has cautioned that although individual institutions may find ETS (and similar standardized) examinations "helpful," externally imposed tests actually may prove detrimental. He continues, "There is not a consensus about what the core of learning should be, making it difficult to develop *a quality test* [emphasis added] to be used for institutions in an entire state" (Anrig quoted in Jaschik, 1985, p. 16). Thus, experts would wager that institutions will not be fully satisfied with only one of the many assessment measures outlined in this *Handbook*. Alverno College, Northeast Missouri State University, and the University of Tennessee at Knoxville are just several of the institutions currently incorporating multiple methods—and doing so successfully. Within a particular field, combining multiple cognitive measures such as standardized and locally written examinations, oral examinations, portfolio analyses, and demonstrations yields a more thorough picture of effectiveness than using any single instrument.

Whatever the method(s) of assessment, Marchese (1987) has reminded us that the process invariably entails judgment by external parties—faculty members reviewing achievement across courses, outside examiners, or even the producers of standardized instruments. "Somebody beyond the agent of instruction [often an accrediting team] is asking the questions, What does it add up to? What was learned? Is that good enough?" (p. 7). Institutions, however, must move beyond these queries toward answers that enhance instruction and educational outcomes, and, ultimately, their effectiveness. As Marchese (1987) has noted, "Assessment per se guarantees nothing by way of improvement, no more than a thermometer cures a fever" (p. 8). Faculty and administrators who respond to the assessment siren with "a data-gathering effort only" have missed the whole point and set themselves up for the proverbial fall (Marchese). Yes, cognitive assessment does involve testing. But, evidence of an institution's true commitment to assessment does not emerge from an impressive slate of examinations alone; the real proof lies in its reply to the question Where do we go from here? In the oft-imitated song, Sam Cooke claims, "I don't know much about history . . . biology . . . a science book . . . or the French I took." Colleges and universities can easily verify such statements through testing. However, what they subsequently do with that information will determine their actual effectiveness. The first three letters in *cognitive* represent an important point about the assessment of learning: it is just one component of a much larger process; the other pieces of the paradigm ensure that the results will be analyzed and judiciously applied.

References: Cited and Recommended

Adleman, C. (1985). *The standardized test scores of college graduates, 1964–1982.* Washington, DC: Study Group on the Conditions of Excellence in American Higher Education.

American Assembly of Collegiate Schools of Business (AACSB). (1987). *Outcomes measurement project: Phase III report.* St. Louis, MO: Author.

American Chemical Society (ACS). (1985). *Norms for the ACS test in general chemistry.* Unpublished manuscript. Tampa, FL: Author.

American College Testing Program (ACT). (1989). *Report on the technical characteristics of CAAP.* Iowa City, IA: Author.

American Institute of Certified Public Accountants (AICPA). (1987). *AICPA accounting testing program.* San Antonio, TX: Psychological Corporation.

American Psychological Association. (1985). *Standards for educational and psychological testing.* Washington, DC: Author.

Baird, L. L. (1988). Diverse and subtle arts: Assessing the generic outcomes of higher education. In C. Adelman (Ed.), *Performance and judgment: Essays on principles and practice in the assessment of college student learning* (pp. 39–62). Washington, DC: Government Printing Office.

Banta, T. W., & Schneider, J. A. (1988). Using faculty-developed exit examinations to evaluate academic programs. *Journal of Higher Education, 59,* 69–83.

Baxter-Magolda, M., & Porterfield, W. D. (1985). A new approach to assess intellectual development on the Perry scheme. *Journal of College Student Personnel, 26,* 343–351.

Borg, W. R., & Gall, M. D. (1983). *Educational research.* New York: Longman.

Cavazos presents higher ed goals. (1990). *Higher Education and National Affairs, 39*(2), 1, 4.

College Entrance Examination Board (CEEB). (1984). *Technical manual overview.* Princeton, NJ: Educational Testing Service.

College Entrance Examination Board (CEEB). (1986). *Outcomes assessment in higher education.* Princeton, NJ: Educational Testing Service.

College Entrance Examination Board and Educational Testing Service (CEEB

& ETS). (1988). *Guide to the Scholastic Aptitude Test*. Princeton, NJ: Educational Testing Service.

Conrad, L., Trismen, D., & Miller, R. (1977). *Graduate Record Examinations technical manual*. Princeton, NJ: Educational Testing Service.

Council of Presidents and State Board for Community College Education. (1989). *The validity and usefulness of three national standardized tests for measuring the communication, computation, and critical thinking skills of Washington State college sophomores: General report*. Bellingham, WA: Western Washington University Office of Publications.

Crites, J. O. (1965). Test review. *Journal of Counseling Psychology, 12*, 328–330.

Curry, W., & Hager, E. (1987). Assessing general education: Trenton State College. In D. F. Halpern (Ed.), *Student outcomes assessment: What institutions stand to gain* (pp. 57–65). San Francisco: Jossey-Bass.

Davis, T. M., & Murrell, P. H. (1989). *Joint factor analysis of the College Student Experiences Questionnaire and the ACT COMP Objective Exam*. Unpublished manuscript, Memphis State University, Center for the Study of Higher Education, Memphis, TN.

DeVore, R., & McPeek, M. (1985). *Report of a study of the content of three advanced tests*. GRE Research Report no. 78-4R. Princeton, NJ: Educational Testing Service.

Dumont, R. G., & Troelstrup, R. L. (1981). Measures and predictors of educational growth with four years of college. *Research in Higher Education, 14*, 31–47.

Educational Testing Service (ETS). (1989). *Major field achievement tests: Comparative data guide*. Princeton, NJ: Author.

Educational Testing Service (ETS). (1990). *Higher education assessment newsletter*. Princeton, NJ: Author.

Educational Testing Service (ETS) College and University Programs. (1987). *The academic profile*. Princeton, NJ: ETS.

El-Khawas, E. (1989). *Campus trends, 1989*. Washington, DC: American Council on Education.

Erwin, T. D. (1983). The Scale of Intellectual Development: Measuring Perry's scheme. *Journal of College Student Personnel, 24*, 6–12.

Ewell, P. T. (1987). Establishing a campus-based assessment program. In D. F. Halpern (Ed.), *Student outcomes assessment: What institutions stand to gain* (pp. 9–24). San Francisco: Jossey-Bass.

Forrest, A. (1982). *Increasing student competence and persistence: The best case for general education*. Iowa City, IA: ACT National Center for the Advancement of Educational Practice.

Forrest, A., & Steele, J. M. (1982). *Defining and measuring general education knowledge and skills*. Iowa City, IA: American College Testing Program.

Graduate Record Examinations (GRE) Board. (1987). *GRE guide to the use of the Graduate Record Examinations Program*. Princeton, NJ: Educational Testing Service.

Halpern, D. F. (1987a). Recommendations and caveats. In D. F. Halpern (Ed.), *Student outcomes assessment: What institutions stand to gain* (pp. 109–111). San Francisco: Jossey-Bass.

Halpern, D. F. (1987b). Student outcomes assessment: Introduction and overview. In D. F. Halpern (Ed.), *Student outcomes assessment: What institutions stand to gain* (pp. 5–8). San Francisco: Jossey-Bass.

Harris, J. (1985). Assessing outcomes in higher education. In C. Adelman (Ed.), *Assessment in American education: Issues and contexts* (pp. 13–31). Washington, DC: Office of Educational Research and Improvement.

Hartle, T. W. (1985). The growing interest in measuring the educational achievement of college students. In C. Adelman (Ed.), *Assessment in American education: Issues and contexts* (pp. 1–11). Washington, DC: Office of Educational Research and Improvement.

Helmstadter, G. C. (1965). Watson-Glaser Critical Thinking Appraisal. *Journal of Educational Measurement, 2,* 254–256.

Hutchings, P. (1990). Learning over time: Portfolio assessment. *AAHE Bulletin, 42*(8), 6–8.

Jaschik, S. (1985, September 18). Public universities trying tests and surveys to measure what students learn. *Chronicle of Higher Education,* pp. 1, 16.

King, P. M., & Kitchener, K. S. (1985). *Reflective judgment theory and research: Insights into the process of knowing in the college years.* Paper presented at the annual meeting of the American Educational Research Association, Boston.

Kitchener, K. S., & King, P. M. (1981). Reflective judgment: Concepts of justification and their relationship to age and education. *Journal of Applied Development Psychology, 2,* 89–116.

Marchese, T. J. (1987). Third down, ten years to go. *AAHE Bulletin, 40*(4), 3–8.

McMillan, J. H. (1987). Enhancing college students' critical thinking: A review of studies. *Research in Higher Education, 26,* 3–30.

Mentkowski, M., & Chickering, A. W. (1987). Linking educators and researchers in setting a research agenda for undergraduate education. *Review of Higher Education, 11*(2), 137–160.

Munday, L. A. (1968). Correlations between ACT and other predictors of academic success in college. *College and University, 44,* 67–76.

National Teacher Examination (NTE) Policy Council. (1984). *A guide to the NTE Core Battery tests.* Princeton, NJ: Educational Testing Service.

National Teacher Examination (NTE) Policy Council. (1985). *Guidelines for proper use of NTE tests.* Princeton, NJ: Educational Testing Service.

Orr, J. (1987, September 29). Pre-teacher assessment: Plan to upgrade teaching quality. *Indiana (PA) Gazette,* p. 13.

Perry, W. G., Jr. (1970). *Forms of intellectual and ethical development in the college years.* New York: Holt, Rinehart & Winston.

Pike, G. R. (1989). Background, college experiences, and the ACT COMP exam: Using construct validity to evaluate assessment instruments. *Review of Higher Education, 13,* 91–117.

Pike, G. R. (1990). *Alternative scoring schemes for the ACT COMP exam: A research note.* Paper presented at the annual meeting of the American Educational Research Association, Boston.

Ratcliff, J. L. (1988). *Development of a cluster-analytic model for identifying coursework patterns associated with general learned abilities of college students.* Paper presented at the annual meeting of the American Educational Research Association, New Orleans.

Resnick, D. P., & Goulden, M. (1987). Assessment, curriculum, and expansion: A historical perspective. In D. F. Halpern (Ed.), *Student outcomes assessment: What institutions stand to gain* (pp. 77–88). San Francisco: Jossey-Bass.

Richards, J. M., Jr., Holland, J. L., & Lutz, S. W. (1967). Prediction of student accomplishment in college. *Journal of Educational Psychology, 58,* 343–355.

Riverside Publishing Company. (1989). *College BASE: Guide to test content.* Chicago: Author.

Riverside Publishing Company. (1990). *Preliminary summary of the College BASE technical manual.* Chicago: Riverside.

Schroder, H. M., Driver, M. J., & Streufert, S. (1967). *Human information processing.* New York: Holt, Rinehart & Winston.

State Higher Education Executive Officers (SHEEO). (1990). *State priorities in higher education: 1990.* Denver, CO: Author.

Steele, J. M. (1979). *Assessing speaking and writing proficiency via samples of behavior.* Paper presented at the annual meeting of the Central States Speech Association, St. Louis, MO.

Steele, J. M. (1989). *College Outcome Measures Program (COMP): A generalizability analysis of the COMP Objective Test (Form 9).* Unpublished manuscript, American College Testing Program, Iowa City, IA.

Stewart, A. J., & Winter, D. G. (1977). *Analysis of Argument: An empirically derived measure of intellectual flexibility.* Boston: McBer.

Weiner, J. R. (1987). *National directory: Assessment programs and projects.* Washington, DC: American Association of Higher Education Assessment Forum.

Westbrook, B. W., & Sellers, J. R. (1967). Critical thinking, intelligence, and vocabulary. *Educational and Psychological Measurement, 27,* 443–446.

Wilson, D. G., & Wagner, E. E. (1981). The Watson-Glaser Critical Thinking Appraisal as a predictor of performance in a critical thinking course. *Educational and Psychological Measurement, 41,* 1319–1322.

Wilson, K. M. (1985). *The relationship of GRE General Test item-type part scores to undergraduate grades.* GRE Research Report 81–22P. Princeton, NJ: Educational Testing Service.

Winter, D. G. (1977). *Thematic Analysis: An empirically derived measure of critical thinking.* Boston: McBer.

Winter, D. G., & McClelland, D. C. (1978). Thematic Analysis: An empirically derived measure of the effect of liberal arts education. *Journal of Educational Psychology, 70,* 8–16.

Winter, D. G., McClelland, D. C., & Stewart, A. J. (1981). *A new case for the liberal arts.* San Francisco: Jossey-Bass.

Assessment of Behavioral Change and Performance

Mary K. Kinnick and
R. Dan Walleri

What can you do or do better as a result of an educational experience? How much better or in what different ways can you perform a particular task or demonstrate a skill, be it cognitive (e.g., ethical analysis, study skills, test-taking skills), affective (e.g., empathizing, valuing), psychomotor (e.g., keyboarding, dancing with flexibility) or some combination? What do you do—how do you behave—as a result of your educational experience in ways that distinguish you from your noncollege cohorts, from those who experienced a different educational program, or from other subgroups of students? During your educational experience, how do you make use of your environment, and what do your experiences infer about outcomes?

Although admittedly oversimplified, these questions help frame the assessment arena of this resource section—using assessments of behavior and performance as indicators of institutional effectiveness. Other resource sections in this volume provide information about cognitive assessment instruments and attitudinal surveys, primarily focusing on assessing general and specialized knowledge and self-reported attitudes, beliefs, and values. This section focuses exclusively on methods and approaches designed to collect information directly and indirectly on behavior and on performance from sources other than paper-and-pencil cognitive and attitudinal instruments.

Illustrations, rather than an exhaustive listing and description of this kind of assessment, are provided. The section is designed to steer the reader toward written resource material, to identify red flags associated with this kind of assessment, and to promote creativity in identifying and implementing these kinds of assessment approaches and measures.

The authors accepted the challenge of writing this resource section for several reasons. First, some behaviors that institutions intend to—and most likely can and do—affect are neglected in our assessment practices. For instance, faculty at Portland Community College were asked to identify the kinds of student success they perceived as most important for their students (Gerber, 1990). Then they were asked to identify the kinds of information about student success they perceived as potentially most useful to them in planning their classes, curricula, programs, and services to students. In the set of top-10 "student success outcomes," 4 suggest the assessment of behavior or performance: (1) developing positive behaviors (e.g., initiative, honesty, self-discipline); (2) setting educational and career goals for themselves; (3) identifying educational or career goals relevant to their talents and abilities (i.e., self-assessment); and (4) achieving self-identified goals. Although these student success outcomes reflect the values of faculty at only one particular community college, they call attention to the need for approaches beyond paper-and-pencil cognitive tests and attitude surveys.

Second, the area of psychomotor skills is almost totally neglected in the literature and, to a large extent, in actual assessment practice. Student development in this area appears to be an implicit, rather than an explicit, goal of higher education. The explicit goal of developing psychomotor skills appears more in the elementary and secondary sectors of education. These observable skills, however, relate to success in many vocational, technical, and professional education programs and careers and are a part of numerous college offerings (Lenning, 1977).

Third, behavioral and performance assessment approaches may allow us to document some of the more potent and far-reaching effects of college on students. Howard Bowen's classic text *Investment in Learning* (1977) is a rich source of information on these potential effects and how they have been measured. Some of these outcomes include motivation to continue learning, citizenship, consumer behavior, employability, and job performance.

Social skills and interpersonal skills and behaviors such as intercultural communication, collaboration, conflict resolution, and team building are receiving more attention as valued outcomes of higher education. Behavioral and performance assessment approaches offer promise in documenting changes in these outcomes areas.

Getting Started: Critical Issues

The first step is to adopt a working definition of *behavior* and *performance*. The following definitions are used in this resource section (adapted from Carroll & Schneier, 1982, pp. 2–3):

> Behavior: refers to anything a person does . . . writing reports, solving mathematical problems on a computer, repairing machines, voting, getting a job, using the library, talking with faculty outside of class, etc.

Information on behavior may be collected in three distinct ways: by (1) direct observation, (2) self-report, and (3) unobtrusive measures such as physical traces, archives or records, simple observation, and contrived or hidden observation using video- or audiotapes (Webb, Campbell, Schwaartz, & Sechrest, 1966).

> Performance: refers to how well a person does something . . . how well reports are written, how well math problems are solved, how quickly and properly the machine is repaired, how good the painting is, etc.

Performance may refer to a process as well as a product. Level of performance may be judged using relative standards (i.e., comparisons of one's performance to that of others, of the performance of those in a control group versus those in an experimental group, or of one's own performance over time) or absolute standards (i.e., arbitrary or intuitive and value-based ones) (Clarkson, Neuburger, & Koroloff, 1977).

Assessing behavioral changes in students and using observation and judgment to assess performance raise a host of conceptual and methodological issues, especially when the identified behavioral and performance changes involve values and motivational factors. The problems associated with such assessment efforts include analysis of outcomes unrelated to an institution's mission, inadvertent measurement of one outcome when the intent was to measure something different, and drawing of unwarranted causal inferences.

A key point of departure in ensuring reliability and validity is the design stage. Here are seven important questions that should be answered before initiating an assessment program:

1. What are the valued outcomes, and which ones lend themselves to assessment using either behavioral data or direct appraisal of performance?

2. What criteria should be used to judge performance?
3. What, if any, are behavioral manifestations of the valued affective, cognitive, or psychomotor outcomes sought? Where can we make reasonable inferences from behavior to changes in cognition and affect?
4. What is the unit of analysis? the institution? a specific program or discipline? a particular class? all students? particular subgroups of students?
5. What will be the time frame? Assess while in college? after leaving college (and how long out—1, 5, or more years)? or both?
6. What approach and data sources will be used—qualitative, quantitative, or both? Rely on self-report, observation, or both? Who will judge performance?
7. Does the institution have the resources, expertise, and time to adopt a behavioral and/or a performance appraisal approach?

Somewhat unique to this area of assessment is the dichotomy of outcomes subsumed under "behavioral changes" and "performance." On the one hand, there are psychomotor skills, such as keyboarding, where the behavior is concrete and relatively simple to observe and measure; that is, the outcomes are fairly clear and quantifiable. On the other hand, there are behavioral changes purportedly influenced by the college experience that can serve as indicators of civic and moral development, referred to hereafter as "constructs."

Valued Outcomes and Performance

The first and foremost question to answer is, What behaviors fall within the domain of a particular college's Expanded Statement of Institutional Purpose (ESIP), program outcomes, or administrative objectives? In the case of psychomotor skills, few college catalogs list behaviors associated with these skills as explicit expectations of the college experience, even in the case of community colleges that offer a wide array of vocational programs. Psychomotor skills are certainly implicit in many academic and professional programs (e.g., speech, art, dentistry, nursing, dance), and assessment of student performance is directly or indirectly related to such skills.

Many colleges explicitly incorporate behavioral constructs, such as citizenship and leadership, as part of their ESIP, especially private colleges and colleges with a religious affiliation (Grandy, 1988). For many other colleges, such behaviors are undoubtedly implicit within their educational or cocurricular program.

Of particular concern in assessing construct behaviors is the consistency between institutional and student values. If the students do not share institutional values and act on this difference, a valid assessment program will demonstrate this incongruity and suggest that the college is failing in its efforts to produce desired outcomes.

Construct behaviors apply to all students but are not necessarily a consequence of a specific class, discipline, or other college experience. Assessment requires institutional consensus, which may be difficult to achieve, as in the determination of general education requirements. Even if consensus can be achieved on desired outcomes, the underlying values may be in conflict. These value conflicts can produce just the opposite from desired behaviors. As Grandy notes (1988, p. 156):

> What can happen is "reverse maturation." Students may question the values learned in childhood, and actually "grow" in the opposite direction from that intended by the college. It is generally a goal of college to teach students to question authority and think for themselves. Indeed, they will probably do that even if it is not an institutional goal. Thus, it should not come as a surprise that some students enter college being religious and respecting authority and leave with negative feelings towards religion and authority.

Assuming that the fostering of certain behaviors lies within the ESIP or statements of intentions at the department or program level, what constitutes demonstration of the behavior in measurable terms? What criteria will be used? Examples for psychomotor skills might include typing speed for a student in office occupations, or time to task completion (e.g., changing a transmission) for a student in automotive technology. Behavioral constructs, however, pose a whole range of measurement problems, as Grandy (1988, p. 141) has noted:

> Often we use words like "citizenship," "responsibility," "moral," and "ethical" without thinking much about what we mean. For purposes of assessment, and for program development as well, it can be useful to move away from those words and find more specific words that communicate more clearly. If a person develops "citizenship," does that mean that he always votes in national elections? Does that mean he is gainfully employed? Or does he simply have to stay out of jail?

Once a set of valued outcomes has been identified, a hard look should be taken at whether or not change in behavior or performance can reasonably be expected, given the extent to which students are able or encouraged to practice these behaviors and performances during the course, program, or institutionwide experience. To illustrate, consider the college that wants its students to produce written communications at the end of the college experience that meet a series of technical and artistic or creative standards. Let us suppose these criteria are not shared with the students, and few experiences are provided during the college years for them to produce papers and receive feedback. Why, then, should the college expect students to improve performance as a consequence of the college experience?

Once specific behaviors and performance areas have been identified, the challenge is to develop strategies by which the behaviors and performance skills can be systematically assessed and, more importantly, inferred as a consequence of the college experience. To what extent can the behaviors and skills be taught? How does one control for preexisting aptitude, behavior traits, maturation, and other effects independent of the college experience? Those planning the assessment should have some reasonable set of evidence that the behaviors and skills of interest can be affected by the college experience. This means becoming familiar with the available research literature on the effects of the college experience or aspects of it on specific behaviors or behavioral constructs of interest (e.g., leadership or service to community).

One final issue should be considered: When "behavior" is assessed, the main interest is in assessing "typical" or usual behavior, not behavior unique to the situation and moment (Harris, 1985). To what extent do observed behaviors in simulated experiences in the classroom generalize to behaviors that occur in other settings, in "real life"? Furthermore, even if change in behavior while attending college is observed, is it reasonable to assume that the behavior will generalize to noncollege settings and persist after college? Consideration of these questions should accompany discussions of the situations or circumstances under which behavioral data will be collected.

Unit of Analysis

Just as the type of indicators will vary with the behaviors under study, so will the unit of analysis. Many psychomotor skills are discipline or program specific. In this case, the assessment strategy is similar to that for any other competency, with the exception that demonstration of the competencies extends beyond paper-and-pencil operations. With the advent of computer technology, some psycho-motor skills, such as keyboarding, may be more generalizable across the curriculum.

Construct behaviors are less concrete and relate to the whole of the college experience or general education program (Baird, 1988; Grandy, 1988). Thus, the unit of analysis shifts from program or discipline to the individual student or groups of students in the assessment of construct behaviors.

Regardless of the unit of analysis chosen, it is unlikely that all students attending a particular institution will be involved in an assessment of behavioral change and performance. In some cases, students will be excluded by design, as when the assessment is based on a sample of students. In other cases, students may be excluded by the scope of the design, as when an institution's continuing education program is not included in the assessment effort.

In assessing behavioral change and performance, individual students or groups of students would normally be the unit of analysis. Program, discipline, and institutional effectiveness is assessed indirectly through inferences drawn from the assessment of students.

Time Frame

The time frame for assessment can be critical. Both psychomotor and construct behaviors can be measured during the college experience. However, desired outcomes should be validated through after-college experiences whenever possible. A student may demonstrate all the necessary task skills associated with an occupation or profession; but if he or she cannot retain a job due to poor social skills or a poor work attitude, the college's desired outcome has not been realized. Likewise, indicators of ethical behavior during college may not provide a test commensurate with subsequent life experiences.

Also, some behaviors and performances cannot be assessed adequately until the student has moved beyond the educational experience. Examples include career mobility, motivation to continue learning, and citizenship.

Approach and Data Sources

Both quantitative and qualitative approaches may be used in the assessment of behavioral changes. Prominent among them is the use of direct observations by assessors of a product, a work sample, or a performance. Assessing behavioral change is likely to involve a higher degree of subjective evaluation than assessing the cognitive domain through the use of standardized or locally developed tests. This, in turn, places even greater demands on ensuring reliable and valid measures, particularly ones with high inter- and intrarater reliability. Another major source of data will be students' self-reports of behavior and "running records" of student progress through the institution and behaviors after college (e.g., attendance patterns, employment status, transfer status).

Resources, Expertise, and Time

Adopting an assessment strategy, such as ethnography and case study, that involves direct and indirect (unobtrusive) observation of behavior has resource implications. The applicable approaches require special training and expertise, and data collection may be very time-consuming (with the exception of collecting self-reports of behavior by means of a survey). When first considering these approaches, institution or program staff and faculty must evaluate the resource implications and feasibility of such approaches. The existence of local graduate programs with opportunities for projects by graduate students and faculty may increase the feasibility of some of these approaches.

Assessment Strategies: Examples

This section reviews a variety of assessment strategies and the strengths and limitations of each. References to further information and resources available are provided.

Using What Is Available

As a first step, review by discipline or program area, especially for vocational, technical, and professional programs, external certification examinations or other external assessment exercises taken by graduates for entry into a specific occupation or profession. Do these examinations include the use of behavioral measures and/or observations of skill performance? For instance, a performance component of the National Teachers Examination might already be used to examine students before they enter a teacher education program and could be repeated upon their completion of the program.

A review should also be made of faculty members' means of assessing students'progress in courses and programs. To what extent and in what areas are practices such as the following being used: case analysis, simulation exercises, competency-based curricula, or portfolio development and assessment? Although these approaches may be used primarily to assess the progress and performance of individual students, over time they might become the source of information for assessing the performance of groups of students.

The use of externally normed assessment instruments offers savings of time and dollars as well as an increased awareness by faculty of what graduates are being expected to perform and at what levels of proficiency. One limitation is that for many areas, use of such instruments as pretests will not make sense because students will have had little or no experience performing an expected task (e.g., replacing a transmission, filling a tooth). Here, the institution may elect to compare its students with those in other programs and/or to compare the behavior and performance of new groups of graduates with those of previous ones.

Other limitations are that such examinations will not exist for many specific programs or will be primarily paper-and-pencil ones, will fail to cover specific kinds of performances and behaviors valued by the local faculty, or will not cover many valued outcomes of general education (either for the first 2 years of college or for the experience as a whole). For further references, see Conoley and Kramer, *The 10th Mental Measurements Yearbook* (1989), especially the section on the National Occupational Competency Testing Institute; also, check with state and national licensing boards for information on examination content and processes used for specific vocational/technical fields and the professions.

Student Flow and Tracking Systems

Inferring institutional effectiveness from observing the results of student attendance/enrollment tracking systems, or student flow, is more complicated than in the past. Assessment of performance in terms of student flow has traditionally focused on retention as measured through student tracking systems (or "running records," in the language of unobtrusive measurement). However, just as tracking has taken on greater importance (i.e., Can the institution retain students until they complete a degree or certificate?), the characteristics and enrollment behaviors of students have undergone fundamental change, making interpretation of student tracking results problematic at best.

Increasingly, a majority of postsecondary students are following nonlinear paths in the pursuit of educational and career goals. Creating a student tracking system on the basis of assumptions about students' intention to earn a degree or about the time to degree completion will produce assessment results that are incorrect or misleading in terms of student and institutional achievement. Inaccurate inferences will be drawn from data that track enrollment behavior. To limit such misinterpretation, students' self-reported motivation and goals should be incorporated within an institution's tracking system.

Updating existing student tracking systems or creating new ones that take into consideration motivation and goals can be accomplished by soliciting and monitoring students' declared intentions. By combining such data with other student characteristics (e.g., gender, ethnicity, socioeconomic class, high school performance, attitudes, values), researchers are beginning to employ student "typologies" in efforts to assess patterns of student flow (Richardson, 1990). The distribution of student types at an institution has significant implications for the delivery of student services and the instructional environment needed to ensure student success. Over time, the success of various subgroups of students in achieving their own original or updated goals could be assessed. For further information, see Ewell (1987), Richardson (1990), Terenzini (1987), Walleri (1990), and the resource section beginning on page 130.

Psychomotor Skill Assessment

The first challenge faced in assessing psychomotor skills is the paucity of specific research in this area. Lenning noted this in his 1977 review, and the problem remains. Nevertheless, psychomotor skills have been and still are an integral part of numerous college offerings (Lenning, 1977, pp. 61–62):

> It is certainly true that college courses in physical education, science (laboratory courses), music, drama, art, speech, and so forth, require primary emphasis on motor activity and coordination. Professional programs such as medicine, engineering, and architecture also emphasize this area. Furthermore, if an outcomes taxonomy is to cover all of postsecondary education, the vocational programs that enroll millions of students must also be considered. Most of these programs emphasize psychomotor skills such as perception, dexterity, and coordination.

The scarcity of formal assessment models, despite the importance of psychomotor skills across numerous disciplines and programs, derives, first, from assumptions within curriculum objectives. As discussed earlier, few institutions explicitly address these skills in their ESIP. Instead, psychomotor skills are treated either as unstated prerequisites or as inherent limitations that are only marginally affected by drill and practice. When explicitly addressed, such skills are more often considered in terms of accommodation, as in the admission of handicapped students to a program in compliance with Office of Civil Rights guidelines.

A second reason for the lack of "pure" assessment of psychomotor skills is that they are interrelated with cognitive and affective factors, which are the usual focus of assessment. The advent of computer technology is likely to accelerate this integration rather than differentiation. For example, one of the projects being funded through the National Center for Research in Vocational Education (1990, p.10)

> addresses the question of how machinists learn to use computer numerical control (CNC) technology. This technology was selected because it represents a prototype of changes in work which require an integration of traditional machining knowledge with the symbolic knowledge and logical skills involved in the new "informatics" that are affecting not just machining but many industrial occupations.

The research on cognitive and affective factors has tended to rely on standardized testing programs. Such an approach fails to address direct observation and performance assessment by faculty both within the context of assessment in general and psychomotor skills in particular. This situation has led Stiggins and Bridgeford (1986, p. 470) to conclude:

> If measurement researchers continue to emphasize only those tests that serve large-scale assessment purposes, we may fail to serve teachers' primary measurement needs. Measurement training that relies on traditional objective tests does not meet the day-to-day assessment needs of teachers. It disregards the full range of measurement options available to teachers and, more important, it fails to help teachers obtain the types of data needed to address the day-to-day decisions they face.

One promising path out of this dilemma is found in the growing interest in "classroom research," a subject we shall discuss later in this resource section.

Given the state of the art in assessment of psychomotor skills, then, the key issue is whether and to what extent an institution or program desires to address this domain. If the answer is a definite yes, then the first step is to develop a structure for the psychomotor domain.

Lenning (1977) offers a review of nine previously developed classifications. The Harrow taxonomy (p. 74), for one example, includes the following: reflex movements; basic/fundamental movements (locomotor, nonlocomotor, manipulative); perceptual abilities (kinesthetic discrimination, visual discrimination, auditory discrimination, tactile discrimination, and coordinated abilities); physical abilities (endurance, strength, flexibility, agility); skilled movements (simple adaptive, compound adaptive, and complex adaptive ones); and nondiscursive communication (expressive movement and interpretive movement). Berk (1986) offers both a discussion of the methodological issues and practical applications in the area of performance assessment, which is directly related to psychomotor skills (see chapters by Cascio and by Stiggins and Bridgeford). Key guidelines include explicit performance standards and direct observation as the basis of evaluation. The chief pitfall to avoid is allowing personal characteristics of students and other unrelated factors to influence the assessment.

Experimental Design

The classic research model for studying human behavior has been the experimental design. When applied to education, the intent is usually to test for effects of subject content, teaching technique or some other instructional or programmatic intervention (Byrnes & Kiger, 1988; Cottrell & St. Pierre, 1983; Serdahely, 1980; Yarber & Anno, 1981). This approach can best be used at classroom- and program-specific levels of assessment, where educationally and ethically students can be randomly assigned to different "treatments" or treatment levels (or educational experiences) designed to promote particular valued behavioral or performance outcomes. The usefulness of the resulting information can be increased by the accumulation of longitudinal data from "experiments" used with specific classroom or program treatments. Areas of emerging concern to colleges and universities hold promise for the use of experimental design: drug education, sexual behavior, health/wellness, sensitivity to racial differences, and knowledge about and use of the campus resources and environment (often a focus of new-student orientation programs).

Student Follow-up and Employer Satisfaction

Many outcomes require data after students leave the institution and are related to further educational performance, job performance, and behavioral manifestations of general education outcomes judged as important (e.g., leadership, moral development, citizenship). Student self-reporting as part of alumni surveys has been a primary means for documenting the outcomes of postsecondary education. Pace (1979) offers an extensive review of the history of efforts in this area. Bowen (1977) provides one of the most comprehensive reviews of the effects of higher education on students using data from government surveys of the general population (i.e., the census) and national surveys by polling agencies. The effects of the college experience on students are organized into the following categories (see chapters 5 and 6 of Bowen):

General traits of value in practical affairs

- Need for achievement
- Future orientation (planning ahead, saving, deferring gratification, prudently taking risks)
- Adaptability (being receptive to change)
- Leadership

Citizenship

- Attitudes
- Interest/involvement in political affairs
- Information on public affairs
- Party affiliation
- Voting
- Community participation
- Crime

Economic Productivity

- Quantity of product
- Quality of product
- Kinds of products (high/low value)
- Labor force participation
- Versatility-mobility
- Job satisfaction

The Family

- Sex roles
- Marriage

- Divorce
- Family planning
- Rearing of children

Consumer Behavior

- Allocation of consumer expenditures
- Savings and investment
- Ability to cope (dealing with red tape, asserting oneself)

Leisure

- How time is spent and amount of time for leisure

Health

- Use of health services
- Lifestyle related to health
- Health status

A major concern with the alumni or former-student survey approach in terms of assessment is the response rate, which determines to a great extent the perceived credibility of such studies by both internal and external constituencies. Since such studies deal with the total population, the concern is not with sampling or other methodological issues but with the response rate broken down by program or discipline and with the unknowns created by the nonrespondent population. The relevancy to faculty and policymakers will be determined primarily by their perception of an acceptable response rate, and thus, the only meaningful guideline for researchers is to strive for the highest response rate that can be obtained with the time and resources available.

One approach to the response-rate problem that is gaining favor across the nation and is specific to community colleges is cooperative interinstitutional projects involving data exchange. In Florida, Oregon, and other states, community colleges can match student records with employment security records maintained by the state (Walleri, 1990). This approach has produced match rates as high as 90% and provides information on the industry of employment and wages. A crosswalk between Classification of Instructional Programs (CIP) codes and the Standard Industrial Classification (SIC) system can be used to determine the rate at which students are employed within the field of their training. Cooperative efforts between community colleges and four-year institutions have focused on transfer rates and success in terms of community college students pursuing a bachelor's degree (Washington State Board for Community College Education, 1989).

Employer surveys offer yet another means of determining institutional effectiveness. Many institutions work regularly with business and industry with regard to training needs, cooperative work experiences, and placement. In terms of assessment, however, the issue is documentation. There are basically two approaches in surveying employers about their satisfaction with students' training or education and job performance. When the survey is tied to a specific student, as with employer surveys built from alumni survey results, care must be exercised to protect the student's confidentiality. In this case, student permission, gained through the alumni survey, for example, would be necessary. The drawback to this approach is that the employer population and response rate will be a function of the student response rate. The alternative is to survey the general population of employers known to employ graduates from the particular institution.

Change in behavior or performance using these approaches is noted across time, from one alumni or former-student group to the next. The change, however, may not be due to the college or program experience but rather to changes across time in characteristics of entering student populations. Thus, great caution must be taken in drawing causal inferences.

Other sources of information include the track record disclosure requirements under the Federal Student Loan Default Initiative and the vocational/technical program review requirements of the Carl Perkins Act. The track record disclosure requirements under the Federal Student Loan Default Initiative call on community colleges to inform prospective vocational students of the completion, certification, and placement rates of previous students by program of study. Although the track record disclosure requirements have been suspended by the Student Right To Know Act of 1990, this new legislation portends continued federal interest in having colleges and universities compile and publish student outcomes information. Similarly, the vocational/technical program review requirements of the Carl Perkins Act are specifically tied to assessing student performance through student self-report and employer satisfaction. The 1990 amendments (Section 115, Public Law 98-524-1984) to this act even go further by mandating "competency based instruction," with the states required to develop evaluation plans designed to measure occupation-specific competencies.

Data on the Use of the College Environment

To the extent that how the student uses the college environment influences or contributes to desired student outcomes, information about such use can complement the direct assessment of outcomes. In addition, use of the environment, such as the library, may be the desired student outcome that is used as an indicator of institutional effectiveness. An instrument designed to assess student use of the college environment is the College Student Experiences Questionnaire (CSQ), designed by C. Robert Pace (1984, 1986). The questionnaire asks students to report the frequency with which they have done different kinds of things while in attendance at the institution. Categories include use of classrooms, the library, facilities related to the arts, and the student union; experiences with faculty; experiences in writing; and topics of conversation. The 10 resulting scales include items that indicate "difficulty," from low to high, also called "quality of effort."

Institutional effectiveness, then, can be assessed across time by observing students' behavior as they use the college environment. To the extent that their quality of effort promotes desired student outcomes, direct assessment of their use of the social-psychological and physical environment can provide useful information about institutional effectiveness.

Product and Observable Performance Assessment

Direct assessment of products and performance typically involves one or more raters or judges describing the qualities of either a product (e.g., an essay, an architectural plan, a play, a movie) or a performance (e.g., a dance, a character portrayal in a play, a role play in a class, the process of replacing a transmission, the development of a participatory decision-making process in a small group). This approach to assessment can apply at the course, program, or institutional level. The special case of the Assessment Center is described in the following section.

Three important stages are involved in using the direct observation approach to assessing products and performances. First, the criteria to be used by the raters or judges must be identified and clearly specified. The development of the criteria might involve faculty as well as practitioners from the field who employ and supervise graduates of the program or institution. For instance, in rating a play, what qualities should be included? Specifically, what technical qualities should be reviewed? what artistic or creative qualities? Which are the qualities this particular program attempts to develop? For particular technical and professional fields, standards of performance may already exist and may be used as part of certification and licensing processes. For instance, international quality standards are beginning to have an impact on U.S. institutions as a consequence of requirements for conducting business with the European Community after 1992 (Johnson, 1990). The quality management standards of the International Standards Organization are similar to the student performance and employer satisfaction measures discussed here.

Examples will most likely be needed to clarify further what the specified criteria mean. For instance, in the case of an essay, if "persuasive" is a valued quality, what are some of the specific devices a student might use (that could be identified by a reviewer) to argue a particular position persuasively? In playing a character in a play, how might the rater or judge note the extent to which the performance was "convincing" or "well paced"?

Second, the raters or judges must be selected and provided the opportunity in advance to practice using the criteria to rate or judge a product or performance using rating scales, behavioral observation scales, checklists, the critical-incidence technique, and so on. Third, the level of interrater reliability should be determined and every effort made to increase such reliability. For further information, see Carroll and Schneier (1982), regarding performance appraisal techniques designed for on-the-job situations; chapters 7 and 8 in Worthen and Sanders (1987), for a discussion of performance standards and consumer- and expertise-oriented evaluation approaches; and Berk (1986), for a description of a wide variety of performance assessment methods and applications.

An alternative to the direct observation and rating of a product or performance is the use of paper-and-pencil instruments or interview schedules that ask the respondent questions designed to assess performance indirectly. For instance, in the field of educational administration many instruments of this kind are available (Arter, 1988). Critical issues here are the reliability and validity of the instrument or interview process. Evidence on each should be reviewed before adoption.

The Assessment Center

An assessment center is a support service that is separate from or external to the ongoing instructional process. The assessment center approach used by Alverno College (1979) is a special case of an institution's commitment to the use of multiple assessment techniques designed to document as well as promote the desired and valued learning (see also page 96). Many of the assessments are not paper-and-pencil tests and would fall in the category of behavioral, product-and-performance assessment strategies. The Alverno curriculum seeks to promote growth of the following eight general abilities: effective communication, analysis, problem solving, valuing in a decision-making context, effective social interaction, effectiveness in individual–environment relationships, responsible involvement in the contemporary world, and aesthetic responsiveness. Each student must demonstrate competence at six levels in each of these abilities.

The assessment center approach has earlier origins in business and industry (Thornton & Byham, 1982). Commonly used assessment techniques include the following (Moses, 1979, p. 4): "group exercises, business games, in-basket exercises, pencil-and-paper tests, and interviews. They may also include specially designed role-playing problems, phone calls, or simulated interviews." Another example of this approach is the Assessment Center program of the National Association of Secondary School Principals. The program involves a two-day assessment of performance, involving six to eight exercises (e.g., leadership group exercises, in-basket exercises involving simulations of decision-making situations, fact-finding exercises, structured interviews). Assessors are trained over a four-day period. Currently, 47 centers are operating in 35 states. Prospective principals are the primary audience for the center experience. According to Moses (1977, p. 9), successful centers, compared with less successful ones, involve assessors who are quite familiar with the job or duties they are assessing; use simulation exercises more than paper-and-pencil tests; and make predictions about "specific outcomes rather than . . . personality traits or individual characteristics."

For a concise, thoughtful discussion of assessment in professional education that describes and advocates the use of performance approaches (e.g., simulations, role plays, case study analyses, video-taped exercises, and auditing and feedback) of a master's level curriculum of the American Management Association, see Elman and Lynton (1985).

Naturalistic and Qualitative Approaches

Naturalistic (i.e., observing behavior in field or "natural" settings) and qualitative (i.e., nonnumerical treatment of data) approaches to assessing behavioral change and performance are especially appropriate if a goal is to understand or illuminate what is taking place or has taken place and the meaning those involved in the experience give to it. Included in these categories of approaches are ethnographic field studies; case studies; participant observation; the use of critical incidence logs; the keeping of journals or diaries; and the use of open-ended questions in interviews and surveys.

The use of full-blown ethnographic field studies and case studies as primary assessment strategies will most likely be limited due to time and personnel resource constraints. They can, however, provide rich information about student development and the role of the institution or program in such development. Classic studies such as the following provide illustrations of these approaches: Heath (1965), *The Reasonable Adventurer: The Development of Thirty-Six Undergraduates at Princeton*; Becker et al. (1961), *Boys in White: Student Culture in a Medical School*; and Clark (1960), "The Cooling-out Function in Higher Education," a study conducted at a community college.

The use of the other less elaborate approaches, however, is more likely. One important goal of these approaches is to prepare descriptive accounts or portrayals of the behaviors occurring in a natural setting or settings. The goal is to do more than simply document behavior; it is to increase our understanding about the how and why of such behaviors and what meaning they have to the individuals exhibiting them.

Fundamental to these methods is the assumption that as individuals we see the world differently and ascribe to experiences our own socially constructed reality. We make our own meanings. In simpler language, this means that what I do and what you do may look the same and be coded the same by an outside researcher or evaluator. Each of us, however, may ascribe to the behavior a very different meaning. Take the example of two individuals who have a consistent record of not voting in national elections. If we use voting record as one indicator of strength of citizenship, then both are measured low. Interviews might suggest a different conclusion. Imagine that one says she just doesn't have time to be involved in politics and really doesn't keep up on the issues. The other says she believes there really is no choice offered, that her decision not to vote is a political statement, and that she works instead with several special interest groups to bring about change in the society. Which individual demonstrates greater "citizenship"? The point being made here is that qualitative data, and data from ethnographic and case studies, can illuminate the meaning of behavior. The person behaving, the actor, helps the observer interpret the meaning of that behavior.

This section has been included to stimulate the development and use of these approaches in outcomes assessment, approaches we believe are being underutilized. Not all of them require an extensive commitment of time and resources (e.g., the use of diaries, critical incidence interviewing, collection and analysis of open-ended survey data). Good resources for learning more about these approaches are: Guba and Lincoln (1981), *Effective Evaluation*; Goetz and LeCompte (1984), *Ethnography and Qualitative Design in Educational Research*; Yin (1984), *Case Studies*; Webb et al. (1966), *Unobtrusive Measures*; Mc-Cracken (1988), *The Long Interview*; and Richardson (1965), *Interviewing: Its Form and Function*.

Classroom Assessment

K. Patricia Cross, in recent remarks at the first Classroom Research National Conference (held in Berkeley, California, on June 16, 1990, and attended by one of the authors), referred to the "three streams" in the assessment movement: statewide accountability (what the public has a right to know), institutional assessment (what the institution contributes) and classroom assessment (what students are learning and how an individual classroom makes a difference). She contended that institutional assessment must be more than classroom assessment, but that institutional assessment without classroom assessment will be too sterile and involve too few faculty. The assumption is that without significant faculty involvement, efforts to improve student learning in desired directions will likely be ineffective.

Much of the literature currently available about classroom assessment focuses on assessing specific cognitive skills and performance, and so is included in this resource section. Cross and Angelo (1988, p. 1) define classroom research as follows:

> We believe that classroom teachers can, through close observation, the collection of feedback on student learning, and the design of experiments, learn more about how students learn, and more specifically, how students respond to particular teaching approaches. We call this process of involving teachers in the formal study of teaching and learning Classroom Research.

We would add that, unlike some forms of assessment (for instance, that which is conducted to certify performance), classroom research is not punitive. The sole purpose is to help students to learn better and teachers to teach better.

In their search for and selection of classroom assessment techniques, 30 of which are described in their book, Cross and Angelo (1988, p. 4) used the following questions as a guide:

1. Will the assessment technique provide information about what students are learning in individual classrooms?
2. Does the technique focus on "alterable variables"—aspects of teacher or learner behavior that can be changed to promote better learning?
3. Will it give teachers and students information they can use to make mid-course changes and corrections?
4. Is the assessment technique relatively simple to prepare and use?
5. Are the results from the use of the technique relatively quick and easy to analyze?

The three sections of their handbook include techniques for assessing academic skills and knowledge, assessing students' self-awareness and self-assessment of learning skills, and assessing student reactions to teaching and courses. The techniques reflect current thinking about cognition, ways to obtain feedback on what is happening to students cognitively (e.g., critical thinking, skill in analysis, creative thinking, and skill with synthesis), and adults as learners.

We believe that during the next several years increasing attention will be given to practices in classroom assessment in pursuit of the goal of improving institutional effectiveness. For examples of classroom assessment activities taking place at a variety of colleges and universities, see Classroom Research Project, *Conference Proceedings* (1990).

A Perspective on the Future

Before closing this section, the authors are compelled to share their perspective on the future of outcomes assessment and institutional effectiveness. This perspective calls for equal attention by the assessment movement to behavioral and performance measures of outcomes *and* of institutional processes that limit or promote the desired outcomes. Dewey (1916/1944, p. 19) said:

We never educate directly, but indirectly by means of the environment. Whether we permit chance environments to do the work, or whether we design environments for the purpose makes a great difference. And any environment is a chance environment so far as its educative influence is concerned unless it has been deliberately regulated with reference to its educative effect.

As a result of this perspective, we offer three recommendations.

First, to promote student growth and development in our institutions, we must look beyond measures of behavior and performance of students to include measures of behavior and performance of aspects of the institutional environment that may promote or hinder student learning and development. We might assess directly aspects of the environment such as faculty roles and behaviors, the clarity of expectations for student performance, and the opportunity structure as it functions to promote student leadership or peer and student–faculty interaction.

Second, we should seek not only to document and report change in behavior and performance but to promote it. The assessment processes used should themselves promote or facilitate learning while at the same time providing documentation that learning has occurred and/or that the college experience has had an effect. Experiencing or participating in the assessment process should add something positive to a student's education. When this is not the case, most likely the student will not be motivated to perform at his or her best. And, we question the ethics of asking students to do something for which there may be little or no individual educational benefit.

Third, we are convinced that constructs such as "motivation" and "involvement" in the educational experience are important variables that help to account for the kinds and direction of learning that is taking place among our students. These constructs should be assessed directly as indicators of institutional effectiveness in their own right.

Summary

This resource section has described a variety of strategies for assessing student behavior and performance as indicators of institutional effectiveness. Many behavioral and performance outcomes are ones that are highly valued, are subject to influence by institutions, and offer the opportunity for documenting some of the more far reaching effects of college on students. In addition, a focus on these kinds of measures highlights the need for more attention to psycho-motor skills.

Those considering use of these strategies are advised to address a series of questions before diving in. Included are questions about the extent to which either behavioral data or direct appraisals of perfor-mance are relevant to assessing the valued outcomes; the specific behavioral manifestations of the valued cognitive, affective, or psy-chomotor outcomes sought; the unit of analysis; the time frame; cri-teria to be used in judging performance; and the time, resources, and expertise needed and available to adopt these approaches.

The specific assessment strategies reviewed included inventories and use of what is already available, student flow and tracking sys-tems, psychomotor skill assessment, experimental design, student follow-up and employer satisfaction, use of the college environment, assessment of products and observable performance, the assessment center, naturalistic and qualitative approaches, and classroom assess-ment. Three recommendations are offered: (1) Measure the behavior and performance of the institutional environment as well as the stu-dents, (2) promote change in behavior and performance through the students' experiences with assessment rather than conduct assess-ments solely to document behavior and performance, and (3) directly assess student motivation and involvement—key variables that are related to the kind and quality of student outcomes.

In conclusion, we challenge all those interested in improving our assessment practices, as they serve to improve institutional effective-ness, to develop instruments that help in assessing the extent to which higher education environments are designed and function to promote development. Also, we challenge our colleagues to develop and use simultaneously behavioral and performance measures of both environment and student.

References: Cited and Recommended

Arter, J. A. (1988). *Assessing leadership and managerial behavior*. Portland, OR: Northwest Regional Educational Laboratory.

Alverno College Faculty (1979). *Assessment at Alverno College*. Milwaukee: Alverno College.

Baird, L. (1988). Diverse and subtle arts: Assessing the generic outcomes of higher education. In C. Adelman (Ed.), *Performance and judgment: Essays on principles and practice in the assessment of college student learning* (pp. 39–62). Washington, DC: U.S. Department of Education.

Becker, H. S., Geer, B., Hughes, E. C., & Strauss, A. L. (1961). *Boys in white: Student culture in medical school*. Chicago: University of Chicago Press.

Berk, R. A. (Ed.). (1986). *Performance assessment: Methods and applications.* Baltimore, MD: Johns Hopkins University Press.

Bowen, H. R. (1977). *Investment in learning: The individual and social value of higher education.* San Francisco: Jossey-Bass.

Byham, W. (1988). Using the assessment center method to measure life competencies. In C. Adelman (Ed.), *Performance and judgement: Essays on principles and practice in the assessment of college student learning* (pp. 39–62). Washington, DC: U.S. Department of Education.

Byrnes, D., & Kiger, G. (1988, October 7). *Ethical and pedagogical issues in the use of simulation activities in the classroom: Evaluating the "blue eyes–brown eyes" prejudice simulation.* Paper presented at the annual meeting of the Northern Rocky Mountain Educational Research Association, Jackson, WY.

Carroll, S. J., & Schneier, C. E. (1982). *Performance appraisal and review systems: The identification, measurement, and development of performance in organizations.* Glenview, IL: Scott, Foresman.

Cascio, W. F. (1986). Technical and mechanical job performance appraisal. In R. A. Berk (Ed.), *Performance assessment: Methods and applications* (pp. 361–375). Baltimore, MD: Johns Hopkins University Press.

Clark, B. (1960). The cooling-out function in higher education. *American Journal of Sociology, 65,* 569–576.

Clarkson, Q., Neuburger, & Koroloff, N. (1977). A system for establishing evaluation standards. *CEDR Quarterly,* Spring, 17–19.

Classroom Research Project. (1990). Conference proceedings, University Extension, University of California, Berkeley, 2223 Fulton St., Berkeley, CA 94720.

Cottrell, R., & St. Pierre, R. (1983). Behavioral outcomes associated with HRA use in a college level health education course utilizing a lifestyle theme. *Health Education, 14*(7): 29–33.

Cross, K. P. (1990, June 16). Collaborative classroom assessment. In *Proceedings of the First National Conference on Classroom Research.* Berkeley, CA: University of California–Berkeley Classroom Research Project and University of California Extension.

Cross, K. P., & Angelo, T. A. (1988). *Classroom assessment techniques: A handbook for faculty.* Ann Arbor, MI: National Center for Research to Improve Postsecondary Teaching and Learning.

Dewey, J. (1944). *Democracy and education: An introduction to the philosophy of education.* New York: Free Press. (Original work published 1916)

Elman, S. E., & Lynton, E. A. (1985, October 13–15). *Assessment in professional education.* Washington, DC: American Association of Higher Education. Paper prepared for AAHE under contract to the National Institute of Education for the National Conference on Assessment in Higher Education, Columbia, SC.

Ewell, P. (1987). Principles of longitudinal enrollment analysis: Conducting retention and student flow studies. In J. Muffo & G. W. McLaughlin (Eds.), *A primer on institutional research* (pp. 1–19). Tallahassee, FL: Association for Institutional Research.

Gerber, L. (1990, April 22–25). *Planning for student success: Student outcomes and information sources—What counts with the faculty at Portland Community College?* Paper presented at the American Association of Community and Junior Colleges 1990 Conference, Seattle, WA.

Goetz, J. P., & LeCompte, M. D. (1984). *Ethnography and qualitative design in educational research.* Orlando, FL: Academic Press.

Grandy, J. (1988). Assessing changes in student values. In C. Adelman (Ed.), *Performance and judgment: Essays on principles and practice in the assessment of college student learning* (pp. 139–162). Washington, DC: U.S. Department of Education.

Guba, E. G., & Lincoln, Y. S. (1981). *Effective evaluation.* San Francisco: Jossey-Bass.

Harris, J. (1985). *Assessing outcomes in higher education: Practical suggestions for getting started.* Washington, DC: American Association of Higher Education. Paper prepared for AAHE under contract to the National Institute of Education for the National Conference on Assessment in Higher Education, October 13–15.

Heath, R. (1964). *The reasonable adventurer: A study of the development of thirty-six undergraduates at Princeton.* Pittsburgh, PA: University of Pittsburgh Press.

Johnson, F. (1990, May 13–16). *Quality measurements for postsecondary technical and vocational education.* Paper presented at the annual forum for the Association for Institutional Research, Louisville, KY.

Lenning, O. (1977). *Previous attempts to structure educational outcomes and outcome-related concepts: A compilation and review of the literature.* Boulder, CO: National Center for Higher Education Management Systems.

Lenning, O. (1988). Use of noncognitive measures in assessment. In T. Banta (Ed.), *Implementing outcomes assessment: Promise and perils* (pp. 41–52). New Directions for Institutional Research, no. 59, *XV*(3). San Francisco: Jossey-Bass.

McCracken, G. D. (1988). *The long interview.* Newberry Park, CA: Sage.

Moses, J. L. (1977). The assessment center method. In J. L. Moses & W. C. Byham (Eds.), *Applying the assessment center method.* New York: Pergamon.

National Center for Research in Vocational Education. (1990). *The 1990 agenda for the National Center for Research in Vocational Education.* Berkeley, CA: University of California–Berkeley.

Pace, C. R. (1979). *Measuring outcomes of college.* San Francisco: Jossey-Bass.

Pace, C. R.(1984). *College student experiences questionnaire.* Los Angeles: Higher Education Research Institute, Graduate School of Education, University of California-Los Angeles.

Pace, C. R. (1986). *Measuring the quality of college student experiences.* Los Angeles: Higher Education Research Institute, Graduate School of Education, University of California–Los Angeles.

Richardson, R., Jr. (1990). Strategies for serving underprepared students. *Leadership Abstracts, 3*(8).

Richardson, S. A., Dohrenwend, B. S., & Klein, D. (1965). *Interviewing: Its function and form.* New York: Basic Books.

Serdahely, W. (1980). A factual approach to drug education and its effects on drug consumption. *Journal of Alcohol and Drug Education, 26*(1), 63–68.

Stiggins, R. J., & Bridgeford, N. J. (1986). Student evaluation. In R. A. Berk (Ed.), *Performance assessment: Methods and applications.* Baltimore, MD: Johns Hopkins University Press.

Terenzini, P. T. (1987). Studying student attrition and retention. In J. Muffo & G. W. McLaughlin (Eds.), *A primer on institutional research* (pp. 20–35). Tallahassee, FL: Association for Institutional Research.

Thornton III, G. C., & Byham, W. C. (1982). *Assessment centers and managerial performance*. New York: Academic Press.

Walleri, R. D. (1990). Tracking and follow-up for communty college students: Institutional and statewide initiatives. *Community/Junior College Quarterly of Research and Practice*, 14(1): 21–34.

Washington State Board for Community College Education. (1989). *A study of the role of community colleges in the achievement of the bachelor's degree in Washington State*. Olympia, WA: Author.

Webb, E. J., Campbell, D. T., Schwartz, R. D., & Sechrest, L. (1966). *Unobtrusive measures: Nonreactive research in the social sciences*. Chicago: Rand McNally.

Worthen, B. R., & Sanders, J. R. (1987). *Educational evaluation*. New York: Longman.

Yarber, W., & Anno, T. (1981). Changes in sex guilt, premarital sexual intimacy attitudes and sexual behavior during a human sexuality course. *Health Education*, 12(5): 71–81.

Yin, R. (1984). *Case study research*. Beverly Hills, CA: Sage.

Assessment-Related Information from Institutional Data Systems

Bobby H. Sharp and Sheri Blessing

> Whenever possible, methods of assessment should be based on existing information. . . . Such attention to existing data will be both educationally and economically efficient (*Statement of principles*, 1988).

Institutions of higher learning routinely maintain and report vast amounts of data about themselves. Yet this source of assessment information may be overlooked as institutions focus attention on innovative ways to demonstrate their effectiveness. As ascertained during the "Initial Inventory and Evaluation of Assessment Procedures" phase (Figure 9), potentially useful indicators of institutional effectiveness may already exist and are available from institutions' own data systems and reports. Combined with additional data produced from tests and surveys, these existing institutional data can serve as critical evidence offered by institutions regarding their effectiveness.

This resource section is predicated on a basic assumption that is emphasized throughout this publication and depicted graphically in Figures 4 and 6 (pages 25 and 34): For existing institutional data to contribute meaningfully to outcomes assessment, those data must be fundamentally linked to appropriate statements of purpose by the institution and its various units. Taken alone, institutional data are of little, if any, value as evidence of institutional effectiveness. The meaningfulness of existing institutional data derives directly from their focus on specific statements of intentions that have been composed within the whole system of institutional effectiveness and assessment activities. The mere ability to generate impressive amounts of data is of secondary importance to its appropriateness to helping an institution tell whether it is accomplishing its stated goals. Institutional data generated to support institutional effectiveness must relate to intended educational, research, and service outcomes and administrative objectives established by the institution.

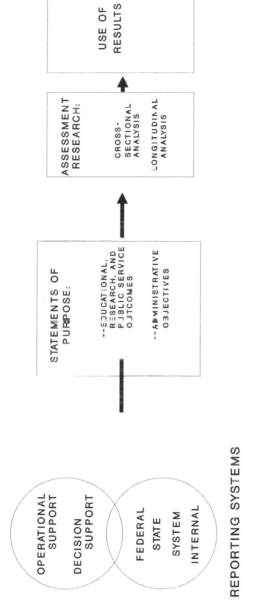

Figure 9

ASSESSMENT-RELATED INFORMATION FROM
INSTITUTIONAL DATA SYSTEMS

Purpose of the Resource Section

The purposes of this resource section are

1. To review currently maintained institutional data that may be used as indicators of institutional effectiveness;
2. To critique limitations of typical institutions' data and reporting systems when called on to support outcomes assessment;
3. To suggest ways for increasing the value of data and reporting systems to assessment activities.

The components of this resource section are represented graphically in Figure 9. Institutional data systems and reporting systems exist in some form at all institutions of higher learning. Statements of purpose serve as screens through which these data are filtered for use in assessment efforts. Thus, the considerable amount of institutional data will become focused and useful in assessing institutional effectiveness.

Throughout this resource section it is assumed that no two institutional data or reporting systems are alike, even when the same commercially available database and report-writing software are used. Unique institutional policies and procedures have resulted in quite diverse data-maintenance and -reporting systems.

Keeping this variety of institutional data systems in mind, an additional objective of this resource section is to stimulate individuals involved in assessing institutional effectiveness to (1) recognize the potential usefulness of existing data and reports, and (2) evaluate the capabilities of their own institutions' data systems to contribute to the assessment process. While recognizing the usefulness of existing data systems, the inadequacies of these systems also may be examined. In some cases, relatively minor modifications to the systems may be feasible to assist institutional assessment efforts more readily.

Institutional Data Systems

In reviewing current institutional data systems, most reflect the two primary types of activities or processes they were designed to support.

Operational Support

Routine but complicated institutional activities such as registering students, collecting and recording student fee payments, maintaining accurate student records, and meeting faculty and staff payrolls have been quite suited to automation with the use of computers. These data systems obviously provide valuable support to institutions in carrying out essential operations. However, the initial implementation of these data systems was largely to support the many transactions that routinely occur within institutions rather than to provide easily accessed, aggregated information to high-level policymakers.

For that reason, their usefulness to institutional effectiveness and outcomes assessment may be limited to those stated purposes or objectives that pertain to operating procedures and practices by selected offices or departments. Examples of how transactional data systems can be focused on administrative goal statements are as follows:

1. Financial and budgetary units may use revenue and expenditure data to focus on objectives related to effective budget control, accounting practices, and financial reporting;
2. A Registrar's Office may use course registration data to focus on objectives related to the mechanics of the registration process, the prompt production of class rolls, or the timely release of student grades;
3. An Office of Financial Aid may use financial aid data to focus on objectives related to the timeliness and fairness of financial aid awards.

Decision Support

Traditional data systems also offer information that is used in administrative decisions and policy setting. On many campuses, data elements are added to operational support systems in order to provide information used by top-level administrators. With the availability of sophisticated "executive information systems" (EIS), "executive support systems" (ESS), and "decision support systems" (DSS), attention is being drawn to the development of data systems to provide readily accessible information on multiple levels of aggregation.

Decision support data systems have most often been developed in such policy areas as

1. Admissions and institutional marketing dynamics,
2. Student graduation and attrition,
3. Faculty hiring practices,

4. Faculty workload and productivity measures,
5. Faculty salary summaries,
6. Space utilization rates,
7. Course and program offerings,
8. Academic and support services (e.g., library holdings),
9. Sponsored research values.

The importance of such data to administrators in setting policy cannot be overemphasized. This has been confirmed by El-Khawas's (1986, 1987, 1988, 1989) annual *Campus Trends*. The vast majority of those administrators responding to the American Council on Education surveys on practices in higher education included many of those data as appropriate measures of institutional effectiveness.

For decision support data to be of value as indicators of institutional effectiveness, however, they must be focused on articulated statements of objectives or expected outcomes. For example, graduation rates after 4 years, an indicator of institutional effectiveness frequently used by senior institutions, have meaning only when assessing intended educational outcomes that pertain to students completing degree requirements within a specific period of time. When appropriately applied, decision support data may provide key information about the extent to which various policies implemented throughout the campus are successful.

Institutional Reporting Systems

Federal Reports

Data to support the assessment of many institutional objectives may be available in the various reports routinely submitted to federal agencies. Once part of the Higher Education General Information Surveys (HEGIS) system of reports, one set of reports is now collected under the aegis of the Integrated Postsecondary Education Data System (IPEDS). The purpose of HEGIS/IPEDS has been to obtain information about institutions—who attends them and who completes degree programs at them, what degree programs are offered, and what human and financial resources are used in providing higher education services. In addition to HEGIS/IPEDS reports, other reports have been routinely submitted to various federal agencies such as the Office of Civil Rights (OCR), the Office of Vocational and Adult Education (OVAE), the Office of Postsecondary Education (OPE), and the Equal Employment Opportunity Commission (EEOC).

On many campuses several offices have shared responsibilities for submitting the HEGIS/IPEDS and other federal reports. Thus, one of the first tasks may be to assemble copies of these reports into a complete set for use in the assessment effort. These reports contain a considerable amount of information on students, faculty, and finances, and taken together, represent a rich historical data source for use in an institutional effectiveness program. In addition, these reports represent a concerted effort to adhere, over time, to consistent and standard data definitions. This effort adds credibility to the information contained in these reports.

The specificity of these reports necessitates carefully applying the data contained within them. In reporting degrees awarded, for instance, the levels of disaggregation reach to the six-digit Classification of Instructional Programs (CIP) level by gender of the degree recipient. Enrollment is typically disaggregated by CIP, by level of the program, by racial/ethnic status, and by gender. Faculty salaries are usually reported by rank, by gender, and by tenure status. Library loan transactions are reported by type of collection. Clearly, such detail has meaning only to the extent that it is focused on intended educational, research, or service outcomes. When particular institutional objectives are articulated in ways that allow for direct linkages between the objectives and the information reported to the federal agencies, these reports are ready-made sources of evidence of institutional effectiveness.

State and System Reports

To supplement the reports submitted to federal agencies, state and system agencies often require their own data reports. These reports should also be assembled and reviewed for their usefulness to the assessment program. These reports, like those submitted to HEGIS/IPEDS, typically have been developed through thought and deliberation, lending credibility to their contents.

An increasing number of states are mandating state-level assessment reporting. Ewell, Finney, and Lenth (1990) indicated that 27 of the 48 states that responded to a survey "report having in place an identifiable 'assessment initiative' consisting of legislation or board policy" (p. 4), and another 6 states provide incentives for assessment efforts.

Indicators included in state-mandated assessment reports vary widely and include such standard reporting elements as academic preparation of enrolling students, enrollment in academic programs, demographic diversity, retention rates, graduation rates, and other similar measures. In addition, other measures of student achievement include reporting licensing and certification exam performance, job placement data, alumni follow-up studies, and external program evaluation results. Institutions located in states that require various assessment-related data obviously may incorporate the state-mandated reports into the overall institutional assessment program. The design and implementation of the institutional assessment effort can allow for both meeting the state mandate and utilizing the data within the institution's own planning process.

Internal Reports

Another source for decision support information that may be useful to a program of institutional assessment includes the myriad of both routine and ad hoc studies and reports produced within every institution. These studies range widely and include such subjects as admissions practices (e.g., rates of applications, acceptances, and matriculation), graduation rates, affirmative action practices (e.g., hiring, promoting, and terminating practices), faculty flows, and faculty salaries. As expected of internal studies, the level of sophistication and the usefulness of these reports vary. Nevertheless, part of the inventory of assessment procedures phase (Figure 5, p. 32) should involve compiling an inventory of the federal, state, and any additional reports and internal studies available. A detailed look at the different definitions or procedures of these reports and studies is necessary to apply these data to the assessment process. In some instances, reconciling incongruous figures may be required.

Orientation of Data Systems

Cross-Sectional Orientation

Despite the vast amount of data maintained and reported by institutions, many data systems have an inherent weakness when called on to support outcomes assessment. That weakness is the cross-sectional orientation of data elements and report formats within those data systems.

Institutional "census files," from which many of the reports mentioned thus far are generated, typically represent snapshots of operational and decision support files. Because operational and decision support files constantly change as fields of data are overwritten with "updates," the snapshots show the contents of the files at an instant in time. For most institutions, these snapshots become the historical record for each reporting period and represent the institutional condition at a given point in time.

Since outcomes assessment examines change over time, cross-sectional studies alone will be inadequate. The practice of inferring change from cross-sectional studies is, of course, common among researchers. For example, if in a given semester the proportion of all seniors reported in a certain department is significantly less than the proportion of all freshmen reported in that department, and there is no known recent upsurge in the popularity of that department's programs, it may be inferred that the department is not retaining its majors through graduation. This analysis is limited in scope due to other possible explanations for observed differences between or among subgroups.

Longitudinal Orientation

One way to overcome the limitations of cross-sectional analysis is to use census files to study changes over time by comparing measures across multiple snapshots. The composition of the subpopulations usually changes from point to point, but trend studies or time-series studies can be very informative. A common example is the comparison made in admissions acceptance and yield rates over consecutive years. Another example is a multiyear comparison of average salaries for various subpopulations of faculty. In both examples, relative differences and trends are identifiable through comparing cross-sectional snapshots across time. Quite useful indicators of institutional effectiveness may be readily available through this method.

Such analyses, however, are based on comparisons of different populations or subpopulations at different points in time. They do not track individuals' experiences over time. Outcomes assessment requires at least some analyses that allow for that type of study. These analyses, commonly referred to as panel studies, follow a group of individuals (i.e., the panel) across multiple reporting periods.

Panel analysis is particularly suited to student data. Progress of individuals through their educational programs can best be shown when various measures of their performance are collected and maintained across successive time periods. Built-in referents for measuring progress then exist. Traditional data systems thus may require modification or supplementation in order to provide the longitudinal orientation crucial to outcomes assessment.

Along with developing the capability of data systems to support longitudinal orientations, analysts must develop proficiency in handling these data and in applying appropriate research methods to them. For example, thoroughly understanding experimental design may be necessary. Or, interpreting panel attrition's effect on the generalizability of the findings, a typical problem for researchers using panel data, may require new research skills. Procedures used to analyze panel data, such as repeated-measures analysis, are not as well known to researchers as are other research techniques. This will mean that the development of unfamiliar, specialized research skills may be necessary at many institutions.

Data Elements Supportive of Outcomes Assessment

The particular data elements used to support outcomes assessment necessarily will depend on an institution's assessment program. However, for most institutions there are at a minimum two types of data elements that can be maintained and will be required for either cross-sectional or longitudinal studies:

1. *Demographic data elements*—These typically will come from admissions data files and may not change throughout the tracking period. Included here are such variables as the following:
    a. Student identifier
    b. Birth date
    c. Race
    d. Sex
    e. Entrance test scores
    f. High school grades
    g. High school rank
    h. Prior institution(s) attended
    i. Prior degree(s) earned
    j. Proposed major and degree
    k. Predicted college success measures (e.g., predicted grade point average)

These data elements both broaden the scope of outcomes analysis and offer referents against which progress may be measured.

2. *Academic progress data elements*—"Term" files usually provide most of these data elements. That is, these data elements are term specific, varying from one term to the next. Examples of these data elements include the following:
   a. Declared major each semester
   b. Financial aid and tuition status each semester
   c. Current semester course-taking data (e.g., number, name, section, credit hours, grade)
   d. Semester and cumulative grade point average (GPA) or quality points
   e. Graduation data (e.g., date, major, degree), when available.

These data elements allow the tracking of academic performance by term or by year, if preferred. Among questions answered by this collection of data elements are those related to the history of majors declared as well as the calculation of retention/attrition and graduation rates. Data are then available to assess the progress of an entire cohort, a subgroup, or even an individual student.

Most institutional data systems are fairly well equipped to provide the demographic and academic process data elements just identified. The primary task would be to extract them and assemble them into a longitudinally designed file. Various hardware and software tools are now available to facilitate that process.

A file developed with typically available institutional data, however, still will require additional academic progress data elements important to an outcomes assessment program. Increasingly, institutions are collecting a considerable amount of data from attitudinal surveys and cognitive tests. Other sections of this chapter address the development and use of these instruments within outcomes assessment. The results of these surveys and tests measure academic progress and should be incorporated and used along with those progress-type data elements previously listed. For example, responses to items in an entering freshmen survey can be compared to responses to items in other surveys administered both during students' enrollment and after they graduate from or otherwise leave an institution. These survey responses also can be related to current major, current GPA, or other measures captured in the file. Test performances at various times during students' enrollment also can be compared as measures of academic progress. To make such analyses possible, however, institutional data systems must contain these types of measures.

Using Institutional Data Systems in Assessment

How institutional data systems are used in outcomes assessment depends on several factors.

1. The extent to which data systems are automated will either limit or expand the opportunities for their use. During systematic outcomes assessment over time, a considerable amount of data will be collected for analysis. Sufficient and accessible automated storage will be essential. The capability of extracting data from institutional data systems is assumed. Powerful, easily used data analysis tools (e.g., statistical packages) will be necessities. Already limited computing facilities simply may be overburdened by extensive longitudinal data files, thereby constraining users of longitudinal data. As has been demonstrated by Ewell (1983; 1987a) and others, however, modest but quite effective longitudinal tracking files can be built using microcomputers with sufficient hard disk storage. In general, mainframe computing support will be required.
2. As indicated in Chapter 1, the way assessment data will be used depends on the commitment of institutional leaders to the entire institutional effectiveness and outcomes assessment program. The best possible outcomes data will be of little use to an institution when the initial question why has not been addressed. To get the most use out of assessment data, institutions must have thoughtfully articulated why they are collecting it in the first place.
3. Potential users of assessment data must be taught how those data can be used. Thinking in terms of longitudinal data collection and analysis is a relatively novel approach and is unfamiliar to many researchers. As a new way of measuring the effectiveness of all aspects of institutions, outcomes assessment data require the development of users. However, once involved in applying sound assessment practices, users will see benefits of this approach and explore new uses for the collected data.

Possible uses of institutional data systems in assessment are numerous. Many have been suggested and alluded to already in this resource section. Thus, those offered in the following section are but a few among many.

Calculating Retention and Graduation Rates

In El-Khawas's (1986) report, 88% of those higher education administrators surveyed indicated that retention and graduation rates were appropriate measures of institutional effectiveness. Their appropriateness, as emphasized throughout this publication, depends on statements of institutional and departmental intentions that have been formulated. For most institutions, however, facilitating the successful progress of students through academic programs to graduation represents a fundamental purpose for their existence. Measuring the extent to which students persist to graduation thus may offer indications of how effectively institutions have accomplished one of their fundamental purposes.

Thorough analysis of retention and graduation rates can best be conducted by using a longitudinal-oriented data system. Then cohorts of students entering the enrollment "pipeline" can be followed as long as information on them is deemed important to the assessment program.

Questions about retention and graduation rates usually require disaggregation into subgroups. That is, it is one thing to know that a certain percentage of entering full-time freshmen will persist to graduation, but it is quite another to know retention and graduation rates of student subgroups and to be able to identify those that are relatively high risk and in need of special intervention programs. These disaggregated retention and graduation rates provide institutions with considerably more useful information in answering pertinent questions, such as

1. For an entering freshmen cohort, how do retention and graduation rates differ among ethnic groups? among entry-level skill groupings?
2. How do retention and graduation rates differ among majors?
3. How do retention and graduation rates differ among ethnic groups within majors?
4. If there are differences that cause concern, how will the outcomes of strategies adopted to deal with the issue be measured?

The answers given to questions such as these may determine the success or failure of institutional effectiveness and assessment programs.

The questions posed in the preceding paragraph reemphasize the importance of having a carefully designed longitudinal data system.

Systems that permit answering only the first or second question (i.e., regarding rates for ethnic groups, for certain entry-level skill groupings, or for majors), but not the third (i.e., rates for ethnic groups within majors), may be limited in their usefulness in identifying those individuals most in need of remediation and developmental programs. The extent of the disaggregation should be considered in conjunction with the levels of cross-analysis anticipated.

Comparison of Successive Test Scores and Inventory Results

Some institutions have begun employing batteries of cognitive tests as part of their outcomes assessment. Institutions promoting a "value-added" concept of higher education, for example, must develop means to demonstrate that students perform better academically as a result of their educational experiences. One way to do this has been to require standardized test scores for students at different points in their educational experience. Thus, entering freshmen, rising juniors, and graduating seniors may be required to take standardized tests and have their scores maintained in longitudinal data systems.

Taken individually, the test scores offer little evidence of "value" having been "added." Compared over time, however, the results of the exams may indeed serve as measures of educational progress and may stimulate changes in such areas as curricula and course offerings. Studies comparing successive test scores may employ such statistical procedures as repeated-measures analysis to examine the data.

Along with cognitive tests, opinion and attitudinal surveys may be administered over successive time periods and may serve as useful indicators of educational progress. Differences in responses between the point of entry as freshmen and the point of exit as graduates can tell institutions how students perceive their own progress as related to the academic and support programs offered to them. The capacity to compare successive inventory results, though, presupposes some kind of longitudinal data system.

In comparing both cognitive test scores and inventory results over time, institutions should remember that the focus is on *institutional effectiveness*, not individual student performance. The purpose of various tests and inventories administered to students is to assess the effectiveness of institutions and their subunits. Students do not pass or fail these instruments. Rather, their performances on these tests and inventories should be used by institutions as but one means among many for evaluating policies intended to enhance institutional effectiveness.

Determining Course-Taking Patterns

A longitudinal data system that retains students' course enrollment histories also can provide useful information about educational progress. When considered along with other assessment indicators such as retention and graduation rates as well as cognitive test scores, the results obtained can be especially useful in several ways. For instance, information learned from relating graduating students' cognitive test scores to their course-taking patterns may help improve

1. Curricular requirements/offerings,
2. Student advising programs,
3. Course offerings,
4. Faculty teaching assignments,
5. Space allocation.

Results of such an analysis thus range from happier, more successful students to improved use of institutional resources.

Providing Follow-up Information on Students

Among the data elements within longitudinal data systems that support outcomes assessment are those pertaining to activities of students following graduation. Over 80% of the administrators responding to El-Khawas's (1986) survey indicated that "honors and other achievements of recent graduates," "job placement rates of graduates, by field," and "graduates' performance on the job" each were appropriate measures of institutional effectiveness. Paulson (1990) found alumni follow-up studies to be a common assessment initiative within the states responding to the Education Commission of the States' survey. Mechanics of conducting alumni surveys can be found in various publications as well as in workshops offered by professional organizations. The subject is also treated in another resource section in this volume.

Along with follow-up studies of graduates, surveys of students who elect not to return to school can also reveal useful information. Institutions may find these students' evaluations of educational and associated programs to be one helpful means of assessing the effectiveness of those programs.

Equally important indicators of institutional effectiveness are an institution's graduates who successfully continue their education at other institutions; for example:

1. Two-year institutions whose missions include preparing students to complete their baccalaureate degrees at four-year institutions need to know how their graduates perform at the senior institutions.
2. Four-year institutions need to know how their baccalaureate graduates perform when they enroll in graduate programs.
3. Master's degree programs need to know how their graduates perform in doctoral degree programs.

To support outcomes assessment, then, institutions at all levels should prepare for providing "feeder" institutions and programs with follow-up information on their former students. Longitudinal data systems containing data elements for prior institutions attended and prior degrees obtained, along with current status and performance measures, will facilitate the interinstitutional cooperation required. Regular reports provided to feeder institutions can then become part of the longitudinal data systems supportive of those institutions' assessment programs.

The provision of such data to feeder institutions is authorized under USCS 1232g, Family Educational and Privacy Act. In that legislation, information other than "directory information," as defined in the act, may be released to

(F) Organizations conducting studies for, or on behalf of, educational agencies or institutions for the purpose of developing, validating, or administering predictive tests, administering student aid programs, and improving instruction, if such studies are conducted in such a manner as will not permit the personal identification of students and their parents by persons other than representatives of such organizations and such information will be destroyed when no longer needed for the purpose for which it is conducted;

(G) Accrediting organizations in order to carry out their accrediting functions.

The release of student data to feeder institutions assumes the data will be used for "improving instruction," a component within the overall institutional effectiveness initiative. Further, the stipulations regarding use of the data and protecting the individual student's anonymity must be strictly enforced.

Summary

Successful efforts to assess institutional effectiveness must be supported by appropriate data systems. For most institutions, a considerable amount of useful data already exists and only (!) requires cataloging and formating into useful information. Examples of these data are the many federal, state, system, and internal reports regularly produced over many years. These existing reports may be a quite efficient and relatively inexpensive means of demonstrating institutional progress toward stated goals.

Many institutions, however, will find that their data systems lack a sufficiently longitudinal orientation to fully support their outcomes assessment. Inherent in measuring institutional effectiveness is the capability for following the progress of individual students over time. Data systems must be configured to support longitudinal analyses relating demographics to academic performance and personal development. Research such as calculating retention and graduation rates, comparing cognitive test scores over time, analyzing course-taking patterns, and providing interinstitutional follow-up data on students will then be facilitated.

The commitment of resources to adapt, supplement, or otherwise modify institutional data systems to support institutional effectiveness should be considered early in the institutional effectiveness initiative. It is most important that institutional data systems link directly to the institution's and departments' statements of intentions. This tie-in with the statements of outcomes gives institutional data systems their utility. When these systems are focused correctly on intended educational, research, and service outcomes and administrative objectives, expenditures to more fully utilize existing data may be among the most cost-effective actions that institutions can take.

References: Cited and Recommended

Banta, T. W. (Ed.). (1988). *Implementing outcomes assessment: Promise and perils.* New Directions for Institutional Research, no. 59, *XV*(3). San Francisco: Jossey-Bass.

Berk, R. A. (Ed.). (1986). *Performance assessment: Methods and applications.* Baltimore: Johns Hopkins University Press.

Criteria for accreditation: Commission on colleges. (1989–1990). Atlanta, GA: Southern Association of Colleges and Schools.

El-Khawas, E. (1986). *Campus trends, 1986* (Higher Education Panel Report No. 73). Washington, DC: American Council on Education.

El-Khawas, E. (1987). *Campus trends, 1987* (Higher Education Panel Report No. 75). Washington, DC: American Council on Education.

El-Khawas, E. (1988). *Campus trends, 1988* (Higher Education Panel Report No. 77). Washington, DC: American Council on Education.

El-Khawas, E. (1989). *Campus trends, 1989* (Higher Education Panel Report No. 78). Washington, DC: American Council on Education.

Ewell, P. T. (1983). *Information on student outcomes: How to get it and how to use it.* Boulder: National Center for Education Management Systems.

Ewell, P. T. (Ed.). (1985). *Assessing educational outcomes.* New Directions for Institutional Research, no. 47, *XII*(3). San Francisco: Jossey-Bass.

Ewell, P. T. (1987a). Establishing a campus-based assessment program. In D. F. Halpern (Ed.), Student outcomes assessment: What institutions stand to gain (pp. 9–24). New Directions in Higher Education, no. 59, *XV*(3). San Francisco: Jossey-Bass.

Ewell, P. T. (1987b). Principles of longitudinal enrollment analysis: Conducting retention and student flow studies. In J. Muffo & G. W. McLaughlin (Eds.), *A primer on institutional research* (pp. 1–19). Tallahassee, FL: Association for Institutional Research.

Ewell, P. T. & Lisensky, R. P. (1988). *Assessing institutional effectiveness.* Washington: Consortium for the Advancement of Private Higher Education.

Ewell, P. T., Parker, R., & Jones, D. P. (1988). *Establishing a longitudinal student tracking system: An implementation handbook.* Boulder: National Center for Education Management Systems.

Ewell, P. T., Finney, J., & Lenth, C. (1990). Filling in the mosaic: The emerging pattern of state-based assessment. *AAHE Bulletin, XLII*(8), 3–5.

Gray, P. J. (Ed.). (1989). *Achieving assessment goals using evaluation techniques.* New Directions in Higher Education, no. 67, *XVII*(3). San Francisco: Jossey-Bass.

Halpern, D. F. (Ed.). (1987). *Student outcomes assessment: What institutions stand to gain.* New Directions in Higher Education, no. 59, *XV*(3). San Francisco: Jossey-Bass.

Handbook of accreditation, 1990–92. (1990). Chicago: North Central Association of Colleges and Schools; Commission on Institutions of Higher Education.

Harris, J. (1985). *Assessing outcomes in higher education: Practical suggestions for getting started.* Unpublished manuscript, David Lipscomb College, Nashville, TN.

Howard, R. D., Nichols, J. O., & Gracie, L. W. (1987). Institutional research support of the self-study. In J. Muffo & G. W. McLaughlin (Eds.), *A primer on institutional research* (pp. 79–88). Tallahassee, FL: Association for Institutional Research.

Kauffman, J. F. (1984). Assessing the quality of student services. In R. A. Scott (Ed.), *Determining the effectiveness of campus services* (pp. 23–36). New Directions in Institutional Research, no. 41, *XI*(1). San Francisco: Jossey-Bass.

Keller, G. (1983). *Academic strategy* (see especially pp. 131–133). Baltimore: Johns Hopkins University Press.

Klepper, W. M., Nelson, J. E., & Miller, T. E. (1987). The role of institutional research in retention. In M. M. Stodt & W. M. Klepper (Eds.), *Increasing retention: Academic and student affairs administration in partnership* (pp. 27–

37). New Directions in Higher Education, no. 60, *XV*(4). San Francisco: Jossey-Bass.

Melchiori, G. S. (Ed.). (1988). *Alumni research: Methods and applications*. New Directions for Institutional Research, no. 60, *XV*(4). San Francisco: Jossey-Bass.

Miller, R. I. (1981). Appraising institutional performance. In P. Jedamus, M. W. Peterson, & Associates (Eds.), *Improving academic management* (pp. 406–431). San Francisco: Jossey-Bass.

Mingle, J. R. (1985). *Measuring the educational achievement of undergraduates: State and national developments*. Unpublished manuscript, State Higher Educational Executive Officers, Denver.

Paulson, C. P. (1990). *State initiatives in assessment and outcome measurement: Tools for teaching and learning in the 1990s*. Denver: Education Commission of the States.

Resource manual on institutional effectiveness. (1989). Atlanta, GA: Southern Association of Colleges and Schools.

Seldin, P. (1988). *Evaluating and developing administrative performance*. San Francisco: Jossey-Bass.

Statement of principles on student outcomes assessment. (1988). Washington, DC: National Association of State Universities and Land Grant Colleges.

Terenzini, P. T. (1987). Studying student attrition and retention. In J. Muffo & G. W. McLaughlin (Eds.), *A primer on institutional research* (pp. 79–88). Tallahassee, FL: Association for Institutional Research.

CHAPTER FOUR

Detailed Design at the Departmental Level

The activities accomplished at the institutional level during the first year of the process are preparatory to the majority of the campus's efforts toward implementation of institutional effectiveness or outcomes assessment that will take place within the academic and administrative departments beginning in the second year of implementation (see Figure 10). The *Departmental Guide to Student Outcomes Assessment and Institutional Effectiveness* has been provided as a complementary work to assist departmental administration in this effort. (J. Nichols, 1991 New York: Agathon Press.)

Among the more difficult tasks that must be accomplished in implementation during this second year is gaining the confidence and active support of academic and administrative department chairpersons and/or heads. What are the obstacles to be overcome in gaining this confidence and support?

Probably the first obstacle is the "inertia" of academic and administrative practices, which have for years focused almost exclusively on the processes that take place in a department rather than the end "results" or outcomes to which those departmental processes contribute. In the academic sector, these processes relate to class scheduling, grade reporting, and so forth. Within administrative departments, process-oriented activities such as conducting registration, acquiring books, cutting the grass, and preparing the payroll all seem more familiar and urgent than outcomes assessment.

Second, implementation of institutional effectiveness will be an additional task rather than a replacement for any of the process-oriented tasks required in continuation of day-to-day operations. This will be a particularly difficult obstacle to overcome at relatively

Figure 10

The Second Year of a Four-Year Plan for
Implementation of Institutional Effectiveness
and Assessment Activities on a Campus

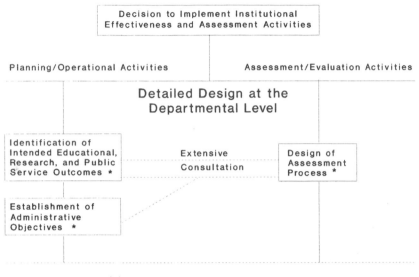

* Resource section(s) included in the chapter to support

smaller institutions or in smaller departments within larger institutions, where the departmental-level administrative personnel may already be overburdened with process-oriented requirements for which little release time or support is provided.

A third major obstacle to departmental leadership support will, in all likelihood, be a large measure of skepticism regarding implementation of institutional effectiveness as just another fad or redirection of effort and doubt about the institution's commitment to following through with implementation. Many departmental administrators have witnessed the great fanfare surrounding announcements of significant institutional initiatives in the past, which proved to be only lip service.

Given these obstacles, winning the confidence and active support of departmental administrators for implementation will take a concerted effort. However, this confidence can be stimulated by the following:

1. Visible commitment in word and deed by the institution's CEO and chief academic officer (CAO)
2. Complete and professionally executed staff work at the institutional level during the first year of implementation
3. Implementation plans that identify each department as one component of an ongoing project involving other departments and extending into the future
4. Presence of an external stimulus, such as an accrediting or state governmental agency, requiring implementation

Gaining the active support of departmental administrators will require their choice of institutional effectiveness implementation over, or at least along with, their process-oriented responsibilities. Such a choice will doubtlessly require the extension of various incentives for implementation, such as those referenced earlier in Chapter 2. However, it is also important that the institution avoid apparent punishment of those units in which implementation is not being aggressively pursued.

Although activities on the planning/operational and assessment/evaluation tracks remained relatively separate during the first year of implementation, extensive coordination between such activities is required in the second year. As the various academic and administrative departments go about establishment of their intended outcomes and administrative objectives, it is important that the departments identify (in general) the means through which assessment of their actual results will take place. At the same time, those parties designing the institution's assessment/evaluation process need to be well informed regarding the objectives on which that process will focus. Neither the interests of the planning/operational track nor those of the assessment/evaluation track should be paramount in this relationship. Rather, a give-and-take process should occur between the two, yielding the most appropriate intended departmental/program outcomes or objectives that can be supported by a feasible assessment plan.

Planning/Operational Activities

During this second year of implementation, planning/operational activities are extended to the departmental/program level through establishment of "Intended Educational (Instructional), Research, and Service Outcomes/Objectives" in administrative departments.

All of these results-oriented statements should be carefully linked to support of the institution's expanded statement of purpose (see

All of these results-oriented statements should be carefully linked to support of the institution's expanded statement of purpose (see Figure 11). On some campuses, the Expanded Statement of Institutional Purpose will be utilized as the starting point, and results-oriented statements will flow "down" from this statement to the individual departments. At other institutions, departmental/program statements of intentions will be directed "up" to support the Expanded Statement of Institutional Purpose. Whether these results-oriented statements are voluntarily originated by the institution's departments or are directed from a central level, it is imperative that a clear and identifiable linkage be established between the expanded statement of purpose and such departmental results-oriented statements of intentions.

In the instructional area, results-oriented statements of intentions will primarily take the form of "Intended Educational Outcomes" by degree program offered. It may also be desirable to establish separate statements of intended outcomes regarding educational programs (such as general education, premedicine, or certificate programs) not resulting in a specific degree.

Additionally, intended outcomes should be identified for the other two traditional areas included in statements of purpose (research and public service). These statements of "Intended Research and Public Service Outcomes" should be linked to the Expanded Statement of Institutional Purpose.

Finally, the institution's administrative and educational support units should play a major role in accomplishment of institutional effectiveness through establishment of "Administrative Objectives" supporting the Expanded Statement of Institutional Purpose. Direct linkage with portions of the expanded institutional statement of purpose by some units (payroll, auditing, physical plant, etc.) may be difficult to achieve. In this case, the objectives established by these units should focus on creation of an academic and administrative environment conducive to more direct support of the Expanded Statement of Institutional Purpose by other departments/programs. Nonetheless, such statements of objectives or intentions should be established in all institutional units.

In the resource sections entitled "Setting and Evaluating Intended Educational (Instructional) Outcomes" and "Setting and Evaluating Objectives and Outcomes in Nonacademic Units," these concepts are discussed further (see pages 168–187 and 188–208). Appendix C contains a series of examples of results-oriented statements linked to the sample Expanded Statements of Institutional Purpose contained in Appendixes A and B.

Figure II

Undergraduate English Program

Example of Linkage between
Expanded Statement of Institutional Purpose,
Departmental/Program Intended Outcomes/Objectives, and
Assessment Criteria and Procedures at Our University

Expanded Statement of Institutional Purpose

Mission Statement:

The principal focus of Our University's curricular program is undergraduate education in the liberal arts and sciences combined with a number of directly career related and preprofessional fields.

Goal Statements:

Each graduate of Our University will be treated as an individual, and all graduates of baccalaureate-level programs at the University will have developed a depth of understanding in their major field and been afforded the opportunity to prepare for a career or profession following graduation.

Departmental/Program Intended Outcomes/Objectives

1. Students completing the baccalaureate program in English will compare very favorably in their knowledge of literature with those students completing a similar program nationally.

2. Graduates will be able to critique a brief draft essay, pointing out the grammatical, spelling, and punctuation errors and offering appropriate suggestions for correction of the deficiencies.

3. Students completing the baccalaureate program will be capable of writing a brief journal article and submitting it for publication.

Assessment Criteria & Procedures

1a. The average score of the graduates of the baccalaureate program in English on the "Literature in English" MFAT subject test (which they will be required to take shortly before graduation) will be at or near the 50th percentile compared to national results.

1b. Ninety percent of the graduates of the English baccalaureate program will "agree" or "strongly agree" with the statement "In the field of literature I feel as well prepared as the majority of individuals nation-wide who have completed a similar degree during the past year."

2a. As part of a departmental comprehensive examination administered during the students' final semester prior to graduation, they will critique a short draft essay; identify grammatical, spelling, and punctuation errors; and offer suggestions for correction of the deficiencies. Eighty percent of the program's graduates will identify and offer suggestions for remediation of 90% of the errors in the draft essay.

3a. All graduates of the baccalaureate level program in English will prepare a journal article for submission and forward it to the English department.

3b. Eighty percent of those journal articles submitted will be judged acceptable for publication by a jury of English department faculty from an institution comparable to Our University.

3c. Twenty percent of those articles submitted will be published in student or other publications.

Assessment/Evaluation Activities

Based on the institutional-level activity in the previous year (initial design and implementation of attitudinal surveys, inventory of existing assessment procedures, adjustments of institutional data systems, identification of cognitive tests, etc.), assessment/evaluation activities in this second year of implementation also shift to the departmental/program level.

By the beginning of the second year of implementation, those charged with implementing assessment procedures on the campus should be prepared to work closely with each department/program in identifying appropriate ways to assess accomplishment of the statements of intention being developed within the unit. These means of assessment will include the following:

1. Attitudinal measures
2. Measures of cognitive learning
3. Behavioral change
4. Performance measures
5. Information drawn from the institution's automated files
6. Other means

Data from these sources will be derived from both locally developed and standardized instruments, tests, and procedures.

In the educational (instructional) sector of the institution, a wide variety of assessment means probably will be brought to bear on departmental/program statements of "Intended Educational Outcomes," although it should be understood that not all accomplishments identified in such statements can be measured or ascertained. Attitudinal surveys and more direct measures (counts of patrons, external funding received, library circulation, etc.) will predominate in the institution's administrative departments.

The resource section entitled "Statements of Outcomes/Objectives and Assessment at the Departmental Level" contains not only a much more detailed review of the concepts just described but also a discussion of the importance of multiple assessment procedures for each intended outcome or objective, the design of feedback mechanisms, and logistical support of the assessment process.

Together with the second-year implementation activities illustrated in Figure 10, these three resource sections can be used to guide the final preparations for implementing institutional effectiveness operations the following year.

Statements of Outcomes/Objectives and Assessment at the Departmental Level

Linda Pratt

In designing a campus-wide assessment process, it is important to assure that each unit's objectives and statements of outcomes are clearly linked to the institution's expanded statement of purpose and that the specific assessment procedures are appropriate for evaluating the extent to which the institution as a whole is moving toward achievement of its goals. The focus in implementing institutional effectiveness is, by definition, at the institutional level. The linkage of academic and administrative outcomes and objectives to an Expanded Statement of Institutional Purpose is necessary to assure that subunits support the institution-wide mission.

Linkage of Assessment Results through Outcomes and Objectives to Statement of Purpose

There are a variety of formats for writing objectives and defining desired outcomes. The *Resource Manual on Institutional Effectiveness* (1989), published by the Commission on Colleges of the Southern Association of Colleges and Schools (SACS), suggests one format for development of outcomes/objectives at the unit level that ensures linkage between the institution's statement of purpose and the unit objectives by including an excerpt from the mission as a part of the objective. Assessment criteria and procedures, as well as ways assessment results will be used, are then described. This format and any other which ensures that the assessment results are consistent with the intended outcomes/objectives and that the linkage with the institution's statement of purpose is assured provide solid evidence concerning accomplishment of institutional-level intentions.

In order to ensure linkage of institutional and department/program statements of intention, SACS suggests the development of a series of matrices that relate planning and evaluation components to each of the traditional areas of institutional mission (e.g., teaching, research, public service) as well as to an institution's major operational areas such as admissions, curriculum, instruction, faculty, library, physical resources, and so forth. Essential planning and evaluation components identified by SACS include

1. The statement of institutional purpose
2. The definition of expected results (outcomes or objectives)
3. The description of appropriate means of evaluation
4. The assignment of responsibility for implementation
5. The description of the use of evaluation results (SACS, 1989, pp. 11–13)

Sometimes difficulties arise in attempting to link the Expanded Statement of Institutional Purpose (mission statement and goals statements) and their related outcomes/objectives. As Fincher (1978) notes, "Goals may not be present at the beginning of an activity or function, but they are believed to be a future state, destination, or end product that will help guide and direct the progression of that activity or function" (p. 4). Not all outcomes are intended, encouraged, planned, or anticipated, and side effects may be as important as intended outcomes. In this case, Institutional Effectiveness may on occasion be as concerned with movement in "the right direction" as with the measurable achievement of narrowly defined outcomes/objectives. Thus, although institutions must attempt to state clearly their missions, goals, and outcomes/objectives, they must maintain sufficient flexibility to permit revisions as the process unfolds.

Linkage of the Expanded Statement of Institutional Purpose from the "top down" is probably preferable to linkage from the "bottom up" on many campuses. Certainly this type of linkage more nearly matches many familiar planning models. Such top-down linkage is more appropriate for institutions with a clearly articulated Expanded Statement of Institutional Purpose, for smaller institutions, and for selected colleges or universities where the existence of a unique ethos is all-pervasive. Charismatic presidential leadership or strong traditions of centralized leadership may also increase the likelihood of common acceptance of a well-defined mission statement that guides the development of institutional goals as well as departmental/ program statements of intentions.

On the other hand, the bottom-up linkage of intended outcomes/ objectives to an Expanded Statement of Institutional Purpose may be more effective for some institutions. In larger research institutions with diverse units, the tradition of decentralized funding patterns and governance structures may mean that institutional goals emerge from the broad statements of a loose confederation of largely autonomous schools and departments. In these instances, the Expanded Statement of Institutional Purpose springs from the activities of the institution's subunits.

Finally, in many institutions, a combination of bottom-up and top-down development may be preferable. For example, in large universities, each school or college may develop goals for top-down use by departments while, at the same time, the amalgamation of the goals of the schools or colleges may drive the institution's Expanded Statement of Institutional Purpose in an essentially bottom-up process.

General Factors to Be Considered

In identifying and defining intended outcomes/objectives and the assessment procedures for measuring those outcomes/objectives within the various administrative units on campus, key factors to consider are the time and effort needed to develop the outcomes/ objectives and to implement the assessment process. If the number of outcomes/objectives is too large or the assessment procedure is too cumbersome, the process is likely to be abandoned in midstream. As Miller (1980) indicated, "The process of collecting data should be established in such a way that it can continue beyond the first self-assessment as a routine function of the master planning and decision-making process" (p. 425). For this to occur, the number of such departmental statements of intentions should be reduced to those that can be effectively addressed in any single time period, and the outcomes/objectives and related assessment procedures should be simple and directly related to the most important goals of the institution and of the individual unit.

It is not necessary or even desirable for any unit of the institution to develop a comprehensive set of outcomes/objectives that describe every detail of the operations of that unit. Rather, each unit must identify the most important or key outcomes or objectives and concentrate on assessment of those outcomes. In practice, this may mean choosing outcomes/objectives related to an area identified as being troublesome, addressing only those related to new or revised initiatives, or selecting only those outcomes deemed absolutely essential to unit operations. As an example, a department with a faculty that has an excellent reputation in the teaching area might want to increase its emphasis on faculty research and publication. The department could identify the accomplishment and publication of significant research findings as an intended outcome but would not, at the same time, identify improvement in teaching as an area for increased emphasis. An Alumni Office that has had an efficient system for identifying and tracking graduates of the institution since 1960 might set as an objective the improvement of the database of pre-1960 alumni. Critical to the success of any such effort is the identification of outcomes/objectives judged important to the operation of the unit and linked as directly as possible to the Expanded Statement of Institutional Purpose.

Once a set of departmental/program outcomes/objectives has been identified, the next step is to further refine and complete these statements for use within institutional effectiveness assessment. The format for describing intended outcomes/objectives may vary according to the reference, but the questions to be answered remain consistent:

1. Is the outcome/objective consistent with the institution's Expanded Statement of Institutional Purpose?
2. Does the outcome/objective describe a reasonable or achievable outcome?
3. Is the outcome/objective clear and measurable?
4. Is the outcome/objective written at a reasonable level of specificity?
5. Does the outcome/objective specify the time frame in which it will be accomplished?

Within the context of these general questions, there are many formats for presenting objectives. The National Laboratory for Higher Education (1974) recommended that an objective (or intended outcome) take the form of a single statement with the following elements:

1. Responsibility—what person or unit is responsible for carrying out the objective
2. Outcome (or result)—what is expected to occur
3. Time—when the goal will be completed
4. Measurement (or assessment)—what will be used to measure accomplishment of the objective

5. Performance standards—what level of attainment is required
6. Conditions—what conditions must be met before the objective can be accomplished

An example of an objective written in this format is the following:

By fall of the 1992–93 academic year [*time*], the Admissions Office [*responsibility*]—assuming that there are tuition increases of no more than 7% [*condition*]—will enroll an entering class [*outcome or result*] of 1,200 [*performance standard*]; the number of full-time registrations will be used to verify achievement [*measurement*].

Translated into the format suggested by one regional accrediting association, the Commission on Colleges of the Southern Association of Colleges and Schools (SACS) (*Resource Manual*, 1989), this objective would read as follows:

Statement of Purpose—Our University will recruit students of high academic credentials.

Expected Results (outcome/objective)—By fall of the 1992–93 academic year, Our University will admit 2,000 students from a pool of 3,200 applicants, yielding a fall semester entering class of 1,200 students.

Assessment Procedures—The number of full-time registrations for first-time freshmen in the fall semester, as indicated by the records in the Registrar's Office, plus the number of applicants and number of students accepted for admission during those periods, as indicated by the records in the Office of Admissions, will constitute the basic data for assessment of the extent of accomplishment.

Administration of Assessment Procedures—The Office of Institutional Research will report the number of applicants, the number of those accepted, and the number of entering freshmen as a part of the regular fall enrollment report. The Office of Admissions will verify the applicant and admission data, and the University Registrar will verify the number of first-time freshmen.

Use of Assessment Findings—The Office of Admissions will review the results on a yearly basis and, if the results are below expectation, either initiate procedures to increase the number and the quality of applicants, or raise the matter for consideration at the institutional level.

Note that the SACS format includes a description of the way the assessment results will be used. Addition of this, or a similar, section to each objective improves the probability that the assessment process will become more than an exercise. The format just described might be slightly altered so that the "Expected Results" and "Assessment Procedures" sections are completed early in the fiscal or academic year with additional sections describing the results of the assessment and the use of the assessment results completed at the end of the period as part of an annual update or an annual report.

These are only two examples of formats for writing objectives. Each institution must identify a format that is compatible with its own planning and evaluation system. The format itself is not as important as the elements included, and many perfectly acceptable statements of departmental/program intentions will not explicitly contain all of the elements suggested. The sample outcome/objective just described, for example, could also have been presented in the form of a table or with separate paragraphs for each element, and the second could have been written as a single statement with all of the elements included.

Selection of Assessment Procedures

One of the most challenging aspects of writing objectives and of identifying outcomes for higher education, particularly for administrative units, is the problem of selecting the assessment procedures to determine whether expected outcomes have been achieved. While in the process of developing new outcomes/objectives, the department or administrative unit can easily identify assessment procedures that will be so time- and resource-consuming that they will become an end in themselves and not a means of determining whether a specific outcome/objective has been achieved. If this occurs, the long-term result is likely to be abandonment of the process.

Pratt and Reichard (1983) recommend developing, wherever possible, assessment procedures using existing institutional records such as registration records, logs of student or public contact, monthly or weekly records of books checked out of the library, or any other records, particularly those that can be reduced to monthly, quarterly, or yearly reports. If such records are not available or if the existing records are not appropriate for assessing a particular outcome/objective, special reports must be developed. Even in this case, the more completely the assessment procedures can be incorporated into existing operations of a unit, the more likely the assessment is to be continued over the long term. In a few instances, the particular academic or administrative unit may wish to collect data through a special procedure such as a survey of students, faculty, alumni, or local business operators. If this form of assessment is undertaken, it should generally be regarded as a long-term, repetitive effort, with the initial survey data used to form a baseline for future studies as well as to answer immediate assessment needs. Institutions should seriously consider centralization of the logistical aspects of such surveys to avoid duplication of effort and excessive cost.

As the individual assessment plans are developed for each outcome/objective, the use of subjective measures should not be neglected. Although objective measures are generally easier to collect and less open to question, they are not appropriate in every case. As Miller (1980, pp. 425–426) indicated:

> Institutional evaluation should use objective data where available and purposeful but make no apologies for using subjective data. Or, it is better to be generally right than precisely wrong. Objective data is important, yet considerable variation exists in the availability and quality of such evidence. . . . The lack of "hard" data should not deter careful and systematic decision making about important institutional matters. Solid bases for decision making can be developed by using whatever hard data are available along with experience, judgment, and common sense. Important institutional process-type decisions often are made on much less.

Whatever the source of data, whatever the type of evidence available, the careful selection of educational, research, and service outcomes and administrative objectives is one of the most important activities in the process of assessment. If outcomes and objectives are important and meaningful to the department/program, if the assessment procedures are easily incorporated into ongoing operations, and if those procedures provide useful information that can be used to improve those operations, then the process is likely to be sustained over time.

Importance of Multiple Assessment Procedures for Each Outcome/Objective

In any area of research, the reliability of the results depends in part on the various procedures used to develop the situation and collect the data and in part on the appropriateness of the particular measure chosen. As in other research endeavors, reliability can be improved by the use of "multiple measures." Although the term *multiple measures* is generally interpreted to mean two or more different measures of the same effect, it can also mean repeating the same measure at different intervals or, more rarely, having more than one observer measure the same effect at a single point in time.

Some outcomes are stated in such a way that a single measure will provide appropriate information for assessment of that objective. For example, Our University has a goal to "increase the level of organized or sponsored research expenditures by 5% per year for the next 5 years." An audit report indicating the increase in expenditures each year would be a single measure adequate to assess that goal. On the other hand, the goal to "study Our University's general education program to determine whether revisions are desirable" would probably require more than one outcome/objective measure for adequate assessment. Some type of test or examination measuring student achievement might be paired with measures of student success in subsequent upper-level courses, evaluation of course syllabi to determine whether course content is consistent with the goals of the program, and possibly a review of the program by an outside group or individual. A third goal, to "give increased emphasis to recruitment of minority students (Hispanic, black, Asian, and Native American) and increase their representation in the overall student population" might best be assessed by establishing a base of the number and percentage of students in each racial category and monitoring changes in both number and percentage over a period of several years. In this case, repeated measures of the same data element provide the most appropriate method of assessment.

In summary, as in selecting the specific method of assessment, the determination of the number of different methods of assessment or the number of times each needs to be repeated to establish trend data is a decision that must be made based on the content of the goal or objective.

Progressive Revision of Standards

As the Expanded Statement of Institutional Purpose objectives and outcomes are reviewed on a continuous basis, the standards by which their achievement is measured also need to be reconsidered periodically. If, for example, the percentage of students successfully passing board exams in nursing increased at the rate of 2% per year over a 3 years, it might be logical to consider adopting statements of intentions that would require progressively higher percentages of students to pass such exams. Judgment will play a crucial role in determining realistic performance standards.

Design of Feedback Mechanisms

Based on the assessment of outcomes and objectives, reports for presentation to academic and administrative departments should be prepared. Mechanisms for providing feedback from the evaluation should include written documents, probably in the form of a report addressing each of the stated outcomes/objectives as well as tabular data. Although narrative descriptions of the findings are suggested, graphic presentations are usually more effective. An objective of the assessment process might be to summarize the data for each outcome/objective on one page through either a table or graph, with a short explanatory paragraph highlighting the major findings. Faculty and staff committees may be involved in analyzing and reporting the information that is disseminated to the entire department for review. Time for faculty and staff to discuss the report and to offer their interpretation of the results is essential. Rather than discussing the results at a regular departmental meeting, the chairperson or director may identify a special meeting at the beginning of the academic year for the interpretation of the assessment findings. A retreat or workshop may be the best mechanism for communicating how well the department met its objectives. Combining oral presentations with supporting visual materials can effectively draw attention to the data.

Interpretation of the data requires comparison of the results to norms or expectations, depending on how the standards are established. When outcomes are presented as desired states, then comparisons of obtained results with desired outcomes may be effective in focusing on strengths and weaknesses. If standardized instruments are used, comparison of the department's performance with an appropriate normative sample aids in interpretation of the results. If an institution-wide survey is conducted, the department can be compared to the institution as a whole or some subgroup, such as a division, college, or school. At the very least, the same data should be collected over a period of time to show progress toward goals. Graphical presentations can clearly illustrate trends over time and progress toward goals.

After the results have been interpreted, faculty and staff should focus on the implications for changes in courses, curriculum, instructional methods, faculty development, advising, andother areas. The assessment findings must be communicated to an institution's chief executive officer (CEO) or an institutionwide committee that has responsibility for the evaluation of institutional effectiveness. This will be facilitated by processing assessment results through a centralized clearinghouse for assessment results.

Peter Ewell (1984) cited three examples of "self-regarding institutions" that engage in a continuous assessment process and use assessment results for curriculum and institutional improvement. Alverno College, Northeast Missouri State University (NMSU), and the University of Tennessee at Knoxville (UTK) differ in their approaches to assessment as well as in their motivation for carrying out assessments. However, both NMSU and UTK link the results of assessment to budgeting processes, and NMSU uses the results in its budget requests to the state. UTK is responding to the Tennessee Higher Education Commission's "performance funding" program, which distributes additional state money based on measures of student outcomes and program evaluations.

Given Ewell's analysis of effective assessment programs of post-secondary institutions, I conclude that, to be effective in promoting institutional change, the review of departmental outcomes must be incorporated into the regular resource-allocation and budget-planning processes. The linkage of departmental evaluations to institutional-level assessment is most effectively accomplished through the planning and budgeting processes. Departmental requests for budgets could be presented to an institution-wide committee for review of progress toward last year's goals and objectives and determination of resource needs to support the proposed objectives.

If the departmental evaluations result in increases or decreases in budgets to support change and improvement, then faculty and staff will view the process as more than a mere exercise. The tangible ramifications of the evaluation process will lead to serious efforts to demonstrate departmental outcomes, although a tendency to set aspirations or intentions that are easily attained and/or to lower standards over time may be observed in some departments. Therefore, senior administrators or an institutional committee should carefully review the revised outcomes and objectives to ensure that criteria and standards are appropriate.

The institutional review will result in revisions of outcomes and objectives in light of institutional goals and resource availability. The senior administrator or the institutional committee and department heads can negotiate the outcomes and objectives for the next cycle to ensure compatibility with the Expanded Statement of Institutional Purpose and feasibility within given resources.

At the departmental level, the reports of assessment findings are reviewed, discussed, and revised by members of the department. After discussions with senior administrators or the institutional committee, the director or department chairperson/head can agree to certain revisions in objectives. Finally, the director or department chairperson should communicate these changes to the faculty and staff. Resource allocations would be directly linked to the proposed objectives and to the departmental strengths and weaknesses identified in the evaluation reports.

The Logistical Support of Assessment

Assessment can be a costly process, in terms of both money and human resources. Throughout these resource sections the authors have encouraged the use of simple assessment procedures. Both academic and administrative units have repeatedly been encouraged to use existing data wherever possible, to minimize the use of special reports, and to use special instruments and surveys sparingly. However, even the most carefully designed process will require extra expenditures and added effort on the part of faculty, administrators, and staff.

Student outcomes assessment is one area where additional expense is almost unavoidable. Although attitude assessment instruments are relatively inexpensive, the total cost of administering a survey can be high. The costs of an initial mailing, return postage, and the mailing of one or more follow-up postcards must be considered as well. A simple alumni survey of a graduating class of 1,000 could cost well over $1,000, depending on the particular survey and the method of scoring and analysis. Academic assessment instruments are even more costly. Freshman placement testing can be less expensive, provided instruments are scored on campus, but even this is a major expenditure. A decision to purchase commercially available surveys or services rather than invest one's own staff resources ends up as a trade-off requiring judgment as to which resource is most limited.

Each campus should review the assessments planned—particularly those that require student testing or surveying of campus or outside groups—to determine whether the needs of several units can be met by a coordinated effort. In many cases, a single survey can meet the needs of not only several administrative units but also several academic departments or schools. Where this is possible, the time and effort to prepare, administer, and score the instrument as well as the actual costs of mailing and follow-up can be greatly reduced. As an added benefit, the return rate is likely to be higher if the same individuals do not receive multiple instruments from different units within the college or university.

As the assessment procedures are being developed and identified, campus planning groups should be identifying sources of funds to be used for assessment. The success of a student outcomes assessment process will depend, in large part, on whether assessment can become a regular budget item. If new sources of funds must be identified each year, the process will eventually die as other priorities intervene. It is also important for some person or group to be given responsibility for carrying out those parts of the assessment that are coordinated and for that individual (or group) to be given the time and resources to complete the tasks on an ongoing basis.

As the assessment process progresses, a large body of data concerning the students and the operations of the university will accumulate. At this point, two questions arise: (1) How will the information be stored or maintained? and (2) Who will have access to what data? Each campus will need to determine, for each type of information, who is to have access and who is to maintain that data. The campuses will then need to identify an office that will be responsible for maintaining a consolidated list of information sources, a library of reports, and documented computer files of survey and student academic assessment data. Following the campus determination of access, that office would serve as a clearinghouse for assessment data. Most information would be available in either raw data or report form. Some information, such as that included in detailed annual reports, might be available only in the offices generating the reports and the files of supervisors receiving the reports. However, even in those cases, the clearinghouse would maintain copies of unit outcomes and objectives reports indicating which assessments are appropriate and the current assessment results relating to each.

As indicated by this discussion, a major assessment program—even one carefully planned to decentralize and simplify the procedure—requires a major commitment by the institution. This commitment must take the form of providing resources as a part of the regular budget and of assigning responsibility for overall coordination to a single office or individual.

Summary

It would be a mistake to picture the design of the assessment process solely in terms of the blueprint analogy utilized by Yost in a preceding resource section concerning the development of the Expanded Statement of Institutional Purpose, because the assessment process must by its design be reactive in nature. Rather, those charged with responsibility for coordination of assessment activities must gather the best materials available, apply these assessment materials to the blueprint provided by intended outcomes/objectives, assist in development of new materials to fill the gaps in assessment coverage, seek to make the application of various assessment methodologies across the campus as efficient as possible, and feed back the information to the various levels of the institutions as effectively as possible.

Institutions can expect a considerable degree of variance in the technical merit of statements of departmental/program intended outcomes/objectives. Particularly at the inception of institutional effectiveness operations, such differences are not only acceptable but desirable to the extent that they reflect active involvement by the institution's departments. However, this resource section and the examples contained in Appendix C suggest that outcomes/objectives should be linked to the Expanded Statement of Institutional Purpose, exhibit (explicitly or implicitly) many of the attributes described earlier, and in most cases be subject to ascertainment of accomplishment.

References: Cited and Recommended

Ewell, P. T. (1984). *The self-regulating institution: Information for excellence*. Boulder, CO: National Center for Higher Education Management Systems.

Fincher, C. (1978). Importance of criteria for institutional goals. In R. H. Fenske (Ed.), *Using goals in research and planning* (pp. 1–15). New Directions for Institutional Research, no. 19, *V*(8). San Francisco: Jossey-Bass.

Miller, R. I. (1980). Appraising institutional performance. In P. Jedamus, M. W. Peterson, & Associates (Eds.), *Improving academic management*. San Francisco: Jossey-Bass.

National Laboratory for Higher Education. (1974). *Developing measurable objectives*. Durham, NC: Author.

Pratt, L. K., & Reichard, D. J. (1983). Assessing institutional goals. In N. P. Uhl (Ed.), *Using research for institutional planning* (pp. 53–66). New Directions for Institutional Research, no. 37. San Francisco: Jossey-Bass.

Resource manual on institutional effectiveness. (1989). Atlanta, GA: Commission on Colleges of the Southern Association of Colleges and Schools.

Setting and Evaluating Intended Educational (Instructional) Outcomes

Brenda Rogers

At the level of the academic department, successful implementation depends on the involvement and commitment of faculty, who are the direct link to students and the educational process. Educational outcomes, defined as changes that result from instruction, must be focused on student learning and the improvement of teaching and learning. Specifically, academic departments must state in relatively behavioral terms their expectations for student achievement. Because faculty have responsibility for developing the curriculum and courses, as well as for teaching and testing students, they should also be responsible for defining reasonable expectations of students.

Setting Intended Educational (Instructional) Outcomes

In the normal cycle for curriculum planning and course development, educational outcomes originate from the faculty. The plan for implementing institutional effectiveness integrates course and curriculum planning with institutional planning processes. The degree to which institutional effectiveness is implemented at the academic department level depends largely on faculty perceiving that the activities are appropriate departmental planning and evaluation processes. Convincing the faculty that the process will enhance normal departmental planning and will link departmental planning with the institutional budgeting cycles is imperative.

That faculty must be intimately involved in setting the educational outcomes for the academic departments is a fact accepted by virtually all members of the higher education community. For any other group to do so would be usurping the power of the faculty over curriculum and course development. In fact, a major source of faculty resistance to the assessment movement in higher education is this perceived threat to their academic freedom in the selection of course content and instructional methods, the development of testing procedures, and the establishment of grading standards.

In general, faculty support is enhanced when the actions as well as the rhetoric of the administration demonstrate a commitment to assessment "as a tool for the improvement of teaching and learning" (Chandler, 1986, p. 5). Peter Ewell (1985), in a description of successful assessment programs, notes that model programs often have "an explicit focus on the assessment and improvement of an individual curricula" and that "many programs fail because assessment and improvement is only undertaken for the institution as a whole" (p. 22). Incentives for planning and evaluation activities, such as seed money to support a faculty planning retreat or to develop a set of assessment measures, are visible signs of that commitment. Departments that set challenging objectives and have creative ways of measuring their accomplishments should be recognized and rewarded, if the means are available.

The Study Group on the Conditions of Excellence in American Higher Education (1984) emphasized assessment as a form of feedback to improve teaching and learning. This group specifically recommended faculty involvement in the design and implementation of assessment programs for the following reason:

> The best way to connect assessment to improvement of teaching and learning is to insure that faculty have a proprietary interest in the assessment process . . . such involvement will help faculty to specify—far more precisely than they do at present—the outcomes they expect from individual courses and academic programs. And the more precisely they can specify the outcomes, the more likely they are to match teaching approaches to those ends. (p. 45)

The success of assessment efforts depends on more than focusing those efforts on academic departments, the curricula, and courses; it also depends on faculty agreement as to the appropriate means for assessing their own departmental outcomes. Faculty will be skeptical if they are not convinced that the assessment information is relevant for the improvement of teaching and learning processes. A standardized test measuring computational and writing skills, adopted by the institution to measure "general education," will probably not be meaningful to the art, drama, and music departments, although their courses may satisfy some of the general education requirements. The faculty may, however, accept measures of critical thinking applied specifically to their disciplines as appropriate outcomes.

Faculty must also agree on the proper use of the assessment results. Although faculty may agree that normative data will assist in evaluating their program, they may be rightfully concerned about the misuse of the data. Faculty need answers to the following questions: Who will have access to the departmental information, and how will this information be used? Will programs be eliminated based on student outcomes? Will results be used to promote and terminate faculty? To minimize these legitimate concerns about the misuse of the assessment results, faculty must engage in discussions at the planning stage, during which the ground rules for the dissemination and use of the information are established. Unless faculty are assured that they will maintain control over the information at the academic department level, they may not provide the essential support in setting meaningful educational outcomes for their programs.

Thus, from the very beginning of the implementation process, the administration must consult faculty and use their advice in making decisions about assessment of institutional effectiveness. Faculty representing a wide range of academic disciplines should serve on every committee and should have input about the way assessment will be carried out.

However careful the facilitators of the planning and evaluation processes are, faculty participation in the planning and implementation processes will not ensure that all faculty fully support institutional efforts. Rarely do faculty reach total consensus on any issue. However, for the implementation of institutional effectiveness to have the desired impact on the overall quality of the institution, the majority of the faculty, particularly those who function as strong leaders, should support the planning and evaluation efforts, if not every activity.

Clearly, the faculty, as the specialists in their academic disciplines and as the direct link to students in the classroom, must be responsible for defining and revising intended instructional outcomes. At the departmental level, outcomes must form a bridge between institutional goals for student learning/development and specific course and curriculum content. The educational outcomes must be broad enough to encompass the total curriculum yet concrete enough to have implications for changes in instructional methods and curriculum design. Therefore, faculty should limit the number of outcomes to be assessed to those that are meaningful at the departmental level and are related to institutional goals. Concentration on assessment of a few crucial outcomes is more productive than incomplete coverage of all departmental expectations.

As desired states of behavior, outcomes should focus on problem areas where improvements are needed and changes are expected. A continuation of the current conditions, although important, is not appropriate in an outcome statement. Thus, outcomes should be stated in terms of expected behaviors within a set time frame. Educational outcomes focus primarily on student behavior; however, faculty development can also be included, since changes in faculty may have indirect effects on student learning.

How do departmental faculty begin the process of developing meaningful outcomes statements? A good resource is the manual *Developing Measurable Objectives* (National Laboratory for Higher Education, 1974), which contains a dscussion of procedures for developing program goals and objectives. A beginning step is to complete a content analysis of current courses and curricula. A review of course syllabi and the study of the overall curriculum should be conducted, perhaps as a part of a regular program review. This curriculum review should not be limited to current local course offerings alone but should extend to other institutions that offer strong academic programs in the same field which may serve as models for the institution to emulate. In addition, faculty should consult other sources of information, including reports from national commissions and professional associations. Desirable outcomes of academic programs are often described in such reports. Then faculty can select those outcomes that are appropriate for their students as well as consistent with both the purpose of the institution and the overall orientation of the department.

To ensure that outcomes are aimed at appropriate levels of performance, faculty must know the achievement levels of the typical entering student in order to set the expected performance level of the typical exiting student. Outcomes frequently are statements of gains or changes that occur as a result of the college experience. Knowledge of high school preparation will assist in setting reasonable outcomes for first- and second-year college students. In some disciplines it is highly desirable to have placement test data not only to establish valid procedures for assigning students to remedial or advanced courses but also to describe skills and knowledge of the typical entering student. For upper-level undergraduate programs, faculty need to be familiar with prerequisite courses taught not only at their institution but at institutions from which students transfer.

A more difficult question is the expected level of performance for the exiting student, which should be stated in the educational outcomes. (Within departments that primarily provide required courses at the freshman and sophomore levels contributing to the institution's general education requirements, outcomes may include the knowledge, skills, and attitudes judged necessary for success at upper-division levels. Some questions for departments to consider are the following:)Do the expectations differ for those students who major in the discipline versus those who take only the introductory courses? Do the courses teach general skills that should continue to develop in other courses outside of the department? When is the appropriate time during the student's academic career to measure the attainment of these outcomes?

For departments offering degrees, diplomas, or certificates, what outcomes are necessary for graduates to succeed in jobs or advanced academic programs? If the undergraduate degree provides the foundation for graduate or professional programs, faculty must be aware of the performance levels that institutions offering these programs expect of entering students. If the degree, diploma, or certificate is primarily aimed at preparing graduates for entry into jobs, then the outcomes must relate to job preparation and performance. If a requirement for job entry is passing a licensing, certifying, or qualifying examination, then the knowledge and skills have already been defined, probably by a professional organization. In the absence of such examinations, faculty must work with other professionals to conduct job analyses of entry level positions. A job analysis specifies the skills, knowledge, and behaviors necessary for the recent graduate to perform the job adequately.

Institutional goals in the educational area are not limited to development of "a depth of understanding in the major field and pre-professional programs preparing the graduate for employment" (Appendix A, p. 251). In the Expanded Statement of Institutional Purpose of the hypothetical institution, Our University, academic programs are to lay an "academic foundation in liberal studies in order to enhance students' communication and analytic skills, to provide an understanding of their intellectual and cultural heritage, and to assist them in the development of self-awareness, responsible leadership, and the capacity to make reasoned moral judgments" (Appendix A, p. 249). Thus, departments must address areas of social and personal development as well as cognitive development, which is usually the primary focus of curriculum objectives. Faculty must consider how their academic disciplines contribute to social and personal development. For example, the study of foreign languages may contribute to students developing an interest in and tolerance of people from different cultures. The sociology, political science, and business management programs may focus on defining "responsible leadership" and having students judge the value of such leadership to our society.

Thus, outcomes should not be limited to the cognitive domain but should adequately cover the affective and skill areas. The classification of outcomes into these three areas—cognitive (knowledge), affective (attitudes), and skills (performance)—is helpful to ensure broad coverage of student changes. The cognitive domain, as described in Bloom's taxonomy of educational objectives (Bloom et al., 1956), includes knowledge, comprehension, application, analysis, synthesis, and evaluation. Faculty should specify the level of cognitive complexity required for students to demonstrate that learning has occurred. Is it sufficient for the student to pass an objective test that measures knowledge, or is the application of knowledge in simulation exercises a more appropriate measure?

The affective domain, described by Krathwohl, Bloom, and Masia (1964), includes attitudes, beliefs, values, goals, and expectations which predispose a person to behave in certain ways. Affect or attitude must be directed toward a person, object, place, or idea. For example, to say that a student has a positive attitude is meaningless, but to add "toward writing" allows us to make some predictions about the student's behavior. We might expect the student to write more often, to write with observable pleasure, or to ask for help in writing.

Although such outcomes are generally not stated in course objectives, faculty frequently want to increase student interest in the subject matter—an affective outcome. Departments may be less inclined to state affective outcomes because of the problems associated with the measurement of attitudes. Henerson, Morris, and Fitz-Gibbon (1978, p. 13) describe those problems. First, it is impossible to measure attitudes directly; we must infer attitudes from behavior. Second, there may be inconsistency between attitudes and behavior; thus, more than one observation of behavior is essential in order to infer the attitude. Third, it is difficult to develop instruments that meet the accepted standards for reliability; attitudes change, and stability in measuring them over time is often unattainable. Finally, since attitudes are constructs that cannot be directly observed, people disagree on the conceptual and operational definitions of specific attitudes.

Skills include, but are not limited to, psychomotor tasks that develop through imitation and practice. Physical education departments; the performing arts; professional programs like nursing, teaching, and dentistry; and technical, vocational, and trade programs all focus on skill development. Although knowledge of information may be a necessary condition to perform certain tasks, knowledge alone is not sufficient; practice is often the key to psychomotor performance. For example, the music department cannot adequately assess the aspiring musician through an objective test that measures recognition of musical notes, time, and rhythmic patterns. Actual performance of several pieces in which a student demonstrates the ability to read music and play musical instruments, using correct time and rhythms, is necessary to determine the student's level of proficiency.

In addition to psychomotor skills, general skills expected of all students are usually identified. The Expanded Statement of Institutional Purpose for Our University explicitly states five general skills that all students should master before exiting the institution. Our University's students are expected to

1. Express themselves clearly, correctly, and succinctly in a written manner;
2. Make an effective verbal presentation of their ideas concerning a topic;
3. Read and offer an analysis of periodical literature concerning a topic of interest;
4. Complete accurately basic mathematical calculations;
5. Demonstrate a sufficient level of computer literacy.

These skills are usually addressed in the general education component of the curriculum, which crosses academic departments. Reading, writing, speaking, mathematical computation, and computer literacy may be directly related to specific courses; however, the skills should continue to develop across the entire curriculum. For example, students may be required to take a speech course that will provide them with fundamental skills in developing an idea and presenting it orally. However, students should use these skills in many other courses, through class discussions if not formal oral presentations. Although the speech department should accept more responsibility for this skill, all academic departments should provide students with both practice in and evaluation of oral presentations.

Who should be responsible for setting the educational outcomes for general education? This is a question that each institution must address, for it also implies responsibility for assessing these skills.

Perhaps, as with our hypothetical institution, these should be institutionwide outcomes, set by a faculty committee that broadly represents the academic community. This approach supports the notion of shared responsibility for the development of general education skills. The task confronting each department is to determine how its courses and programs foster development of the skills and to define the outcomes for its own courses and programs in ways that can be assessed.

The academic department then has responsibility for reviewing its courses and programs, examining the professional literature, and collaborating with colleagues from other institutions—including high schools, two-year colleges, four-year colleges, institutions with professional and graduate programs, and employers—to determine desirable outcomes for its students. In addition to student outcomes, however, expectations for faculty development may also be described. Such outcomes may address improved teaching through involvement in professional meetings where the latest findings in their disciplines are discussed, presentation and publication of original research, and participation in workshops designed to enhance teaching effectiveness.

Each academic department must develop for its students and faculty meaningful educational outcomes that capture the overall objectives of the courses and curricula within the context of the institution's purpose. Although defining procedures for assessing outcomes is the next step, the process of setting educational outcomes should not be restricted by measurement considerations. Often the most meaningful objectives may be less amenable to direct observation or testing. If faculty are committed to the educational outcomes, they may find very creative and innovative ways to infer the accomplishment of these objectives. Creativity and innovation should be encouraged, not stifled by measurement considerations.

Evaluating Intended Educational (Instructional) Outcomes

As emphasized previously, it is important to allow educational outcomes to emerge without overemphasis on assessment procedures. Probably some separation in time between the development of the outcomes and the selection of assessment procedures is healthy. However, once meaningful objectives are established, the next step is to define in operational terms how the educational outcomes will be evaluated.

For faculty to agree on which outcomes are important for their students to attain is difficult enough, but then to agree on the operational definitions of those outcomes—how they will be observed and measured—may be a major stumbling block in the process. Multiple measures that use different techniques (for example, interest inventories, interviews, and direct observation of behavior) may be essential for faculty to reach agreement regarding the assessment of educational outcomes.

In evaluating student outcomes, faculty first should inventory existing data collection efforts and assessment procedures. Chapter Three, beginning on page 31, contains a detailed discussion of this process. It may be that departments or the institution is currently conducting a follow-up survey of graduates that may be useful in the assessment of educational outcomes.

Most institutions maintain computerized files with historical data on students, faculty, and staff. A wealth of information about retention, enrollment and graduation trends, grades, and course-taking patterns is available from student information systems. Computerized files and report programs may have to be designed to answer important questions—for example, on the average, how long it takes an undergraduate to complete a baccalaureate degree in a particular discipline. However, the data are available without new collection efforts. Peter Ewell (1987) has described the basic principles in building cohort files and conducting retention studies from data maintained on college campuses, and this subject was explored in some detail in the resource section beginning on page 130.

To assist in the evaluation of departmental outcomes, computerized reports must present separate analyses for each department. Assuming that a fourth-generation language, like SAS (1985), is used to build the files and generate the reports, a programmer can slightly modify the standard program to produce departmental reports. Coordination with the institutional research office or administrative data processing is essential to ensure that reports, like retention studies, answer questions at the departmental level.

Routine reports required by the governing board, state agencies, the federal government, and professional accrediting agencies offer additional sources of information. The IPEDS (formerly HEGIS) reports required by the federal government are useful if the data are analyzed over several years to identify trends in enrollment and graduation. The Institutional Research Office should be able to identify the standard reports that may help departments with assessment.

If, however, existing data do not provide information appropriate for assessing departmental outcomes, then other approaches will have to be considered. Faculty must reach agreement as to the approaches that will generate the most meaningful information about their students. Not only tests and surveys but also direct observations, interviews, student performances, journals and other written materials, portfolios of student work, oral presentations, and self-evaluations should be considered as sources of information about educational outcomes and student learning. The major consideration is whether the method provides useful, credible information about the accomplishment of the educational objectives.

Faculty may choose qualitative methods in order to explore student change and development. Qualitative approaches may utilize unobtrusive observations of students, unstructured interviews, content analysis of historical documents, analysis of autobiographies or journals, and holistic judgments of student performances or products, such as oral presentations or writing samples. Qualitative approaches do not yield scores; rather, faculty use the information to make overall judgments about the attainment of the stated outcomes. A good introduction to qualitative research methods is *Qualitative Data Analysis: A Sourcebook of New Methods* (Miles & Huberman, 1984).

It will be helpful for faculty to categorize the educational objectives as pertaining to cognitive, affective, and psychomotor outcomes. Educational testing will be most appropriate for cognitive outcomes. Surveys, interviews, and qualitative approaches may be more appropriate for affective, rather than cognitive, outcomes. Performance measures and direct observations are good techniques for measuring psychomotor skill attainment. A variety of approaches will be reviewed, with emphasis on resource materials helpful to academic departments.

Assessment of Cognitive Outcomes

In the past few years the dominant approach toward the assessment of cognitive outcomes in general education and the academic major has been standardized tests. However, institutions have reported limited success in using the results effectively for improving teaching and learning. Often the standardized cognitive instruments do not provide adequate coverage of the content nor do they tap the more complex cognitive processes that college requires of students. We would do well to heed the remarks of Shulman, Smith, and Stewart (1987, p. 8): "There's some magical thinking going on in the assessment community. And that magical thinking is that if we can somehow lay a comprehensive 90-minute exam on top of an otherwise absolutely disintegrated curriculum, we're doing general education."

Testing that is not preceded by sound curriculum planning and development is a useless activity. Furthermore, testing cognitive processes and content unrelated to the course and curriculum objectives is a waste of time if the aim is the improvement of teaching and learning at the departmental level. In fact, finding an existing standardized test that matches the aims of the academic program is somewhat unlikely. Baird (1988) argues strongly that existing measures of "generic academic outcomes," such as those developed by testing companies, are not linked to the specific goals of the institution and the academic programs, and therefore scores from such measures are not effective measures of student learning and teaching strategies at the program and course levels. Rather than limiting assessment to the search for the "right test," faculty should select from a broad array of methods, using multiple measures to increase the reliability of the results.

While cognizant of the limitations of standardized measures of cognitive outcomes for departmental use, departmental faculty should conduct a critical review of existing instruments. New instruments are being marketed every day, and the research literature and technical manuals accompanying the instruments can attest to the validity of the instruments for specific purposes. Assessment instruments are available not only from testing companies but also from individuals who have developed instruments for research purposes. A thorough review of existing instruments includes an evaluation of the following:

1. Content validity—The match between the test content and the departmental objectives
2. Reliability—The consistency of scores over time and across alternate forms
3. The appropriateness of the instrument for the target population
4. The normative data to assist in interpreting the measures or scores

Several resources will assist in the search for published tests. In *Tests in Print III: An Index to Tests, Test Reviews, and the Literature of Specific Tests*, Mitchell (1983) attempts to list all commercial tests printed in English. The *Mental Measurements Yearbook* series contains reviews of tests as well as factual information about the author, publisher, publication date, cost, administrative time, and grade levels for which appropriate. Instruments published after 1972 are reviewed in the ninth edition (Mitchell, 1983). However, tests published prior to 1972 may also be contained in the recent edition of the *Yearbook* if new versions of the test have been released or new information is available.

Research instruments developed by individual researchers may be obtained simply by requesting copies and permission to use them from the authors. One resource cited by Anastasi (1988) for identifying these unpublished instruments is *Tests in Microfiche*, available from Test Collection, ETS. Often these questionnaires and scales are available free of charge simply by contacting the researcher. In their *Directory of Unpublished Experimental Mental Measures: Volume V*, Goldman and Osborne (1990) list a number of experimental test instruments (i.e., tests that are not currently marketed commercially). This volume serves as a reference enabling the reader to identify potentially useful measures. The validity of all such instruments for program evaluation may not be established, so an initial step may be validation of the instruments for their intended use.

With a grant from the Fund for the Improvement of Postsecondary Education, the University of Tennessee at Knoxville has developed the *Bibliography of Assessment Instruments* for colleges and universities referred to in the resource section entitled "Cognitive Assessment Instruments: Availability and Utilization." This bibliography includes tests used to assess cognitive and affective changes in students and provides descriptive information about the purpose, publisher and address, target audience, cost, scoring procedures, and administrative time. Copies of this publication are available from

Dr. Trudy Banta, Director
Center for Assessment Research and Development
1819 Andy Holt Avenue
Knoxville, TN 37996-4350
Telephone: (615) 974-2350

Banta and Schneider (1988), at the University of Tennessee at Knoxville, have reported on the use of faculty-developed exit examinations. The process undertaken by academic departments in the development of the examinations is briefly described in the article.

An excellent discussion of "Assessment Through the Major" is provided by Mark I. Appelbaum (1988). A variety of approaches for evaluating the quality of education obtained by the student majoring in a discipline is presented. Issues surrounding the assessment of the major are explored in some depth.

The development of tests to measure cognitive gains is a time-consuming task requiring much expertise in the field of tests and measurement. Departments that choose to develop their own achievement tests will likely need assistance from testing experts. Testing companies will work with institutions in the development of instruments. As indicated in the resource section on cognitive instruments, some institutions committed to outcomes assessment have established their own assessment centers, staffed with experts to assist departments in the process of setting outcomes and selecting or developing appropriate measures. However, most institutions will be hard pressed to justify such an expenditure without specific external funding.

Although speaking primarily about elementary and secondary education, Morris and Fitz-Gibbon (1978) have described the general process for measuring achievement as one part of a program evaluation. To construct a departmental achievement test, faculty must carefully state the outcomes/objectives to be covered in the test. The objectives should include specification of both the content and the cognitive processes. Test items are then constructed to measure the outcomes/objectives, with the item format carefully chosen to require the cognitive processes described by the objectives. Items and the reliability of the instrument should be analyzed. Finally, validity of the scores for the intended use should be examined. Although many excellent references describe the process of developing achievement tests, this is not a simple task. However, when no existing achievement test adequately covers the program outcomes/objectives, the only alternative is the development of departmental examinations.

Another approach is the use of an external examiner, as proposed by Bobby Fong (1987) at the American Association for Higher Education Assessment Forum. He suggests that an outside expert in the academic field can be an "effective way to assess both student learning and curricular coherence in a major," which can lead to "valuable information and recommendations as to where curricular requirements need to be more specific and how course offerings need to be strengthened" (p. 17). The outside consultant could be asked to address the outcomes specified by the departments and to critique the curriculum.

Separate resource sections at the end of Chapter 3 have expanded on specific instruments used to assess cognitive outcomes.

Assessment of Affective Outcomes

The resource section on attitudinal surveys to assess institutional effectiveness provides a thorough review of survey instruments (see page 55). The ETS instruments most appropriate for use at the academic department level are the Program Self-Assessment Service and the Graduate Program Self-Assessment Service. The perceptions of three constituencies—currently enrolled students, alumni, and faculty—concerning the strengths and weaknesses of the program can be compared. The ability to add up to 20 items to the standard questionnaire offers the opportunity to obtain information directly relevant to the affective objectives of the program.

Another attitudinal instrument is the College Student Experiences Questionnaire (CSEQ), developed by UCLA's Robert Pace (1979). This is a self-report instrument measuring student involvement in 16 college activities, 21 areas in which students estimate gains as a result of attending college, and 7 dimensions of the college environment. Comparative data are available for participating institutions. The CSEQ assesses student behaviors, such as the percentage of students using the library or various student services. Thus, it may be particularly helpful in establishing baseline measurements for a range of activities, which may be helpful in setting institutional or subunit goals. Although the research is promising, the primary application of research findings thus far has been at the institutional, rather than the departmental, level.

The research literature on college student development is a good resource for identifying measures of affective outcomes. The *Journal of College Student Personnel* should be reviewed regularly for new instruments and innovative approaches to assessment. *Scales for the Measurement of Attitudes* (Shaw & Wright, 1967) provides a listing of research instruments. If changes in values or level of motivation are the focus of departmental objectives, then Grandy (1988) and Graham (1988) provide good reviews of existing instruments as well as of the issues relating to the measurement of these affective outcomes.

In the absence of existing surveys that match the educational objectives, the department must develop its own surveys, if surveys of students, alumni, and/or faculty are judged as the best sources of information. Attitudinal surveys are generally easier to construct than achievement tests. The key is to develop items that elicit truthful responses and relate to the intended outcomes. ACT has an item bank of attitudinal items from which institutions can select those relevant to their needs. Existing surveys should be examined for examples of the types of questions and response formats. After the questionnaire is constructed, it should be reviewed by experts for their suggestions and then pretested with students.

Faculty should explore methods other than surveys to assess affective outcomes. Attitudinal surveys may lack specificity or may be so reactive in nature that faculty will question the validity of the results. In such cases, faculty must select alternate assessment methods and possibly develop new approaches.

Unobtrusive measures offer alternatives to paper-and-pencil measures (Grandy, 1988; Terenzini, 1986; Webb, Campbell, Schwartz, & Sechrest, 1981). Examples of unobtrusive measures are records of student use of facilities and services. For example, professors often place supplemental reading material on reserve in the library. Frequency of use is an indicator of students' interest in the subject. Physical education departments may be able to monitor student use of recreational and exercise facilities outside the classroom. Such "counts" of student behavior may be good indicators of attitudes.

Interviewing students is another way to collect evaluation data on affective outcomes. Questions may be highly structured and standardized, or they may emerge as a skilled interviewer probes the responses for underlying meaning. In either case, interviewers should be trained and have a very clear understanding about the goal of the interviews. Either individual or group interviews may be used. Focus groups are one method used to explore attitudes and perceptions.

The interview method, if conducted properly, may yield a wealth of both quantitative and qualitative data regarding students' perceptions, expectations, and values. If faculty or advisors conduct the interviews, an unintended outcome may be an increase in meaningful dialogue between students and faculty/advisors. A study of changes in students over their 4 years at Stanford University, *Careerism and Intellectualism Among College Students* (Katchadourian & Boli, 1985), illustrates the use of the interview method to analyze change in undergraduates over the college years.

From observations of student behavior we may draw inferences about attitudes. Observations can be highly controlled with checklists for recording and quantifying discrete behaviors. On the other hand, faculty may observe during classroom settings, later recording and interpreting events. Students' responsiveness, from which interest in the subject matter is inferred, may be observed in the classroom. Faculty advisors may observe and record in advising notes the way students make educational and career decisions during their college years. From such notes, inferences may be made about students' career maturity, attitudes toward college and work, and academic motivation. The less obtrusive and the more naturalistic the observations, the more likely the behavior is reflective of student attitudes rather than a desire to please or exhibit socially desirable behavior.

Self-reports from students and faculty offer another alternative. The degree of structure in self-reports can vary from inventories and checklists to life histories, journals, and self-evaluations. As a part of course assignments or faculty advising, students may be asked to report their attitudes toward the course content, instructional methods, their own progress in attaining the goals of the course, or their growth and development as a result of taking a course or majoring in a subject. Faculty may report their own attitudes toward teaching, research, and departmental and institutional service. As with all measures of attitudes, self-reports can be faked; therefore, it is important that self-reports be used only in areas where there is clearly no "right" or desirable attitude. Also, student grades and faculty evaluations for promotion, tenure, or merit moneys should be clearly divorced from these self-reports.

Because attitudes are not directly observable but must be inferred from observations of behavior, it is even more important to use multiple methods for measuring affective outcomes. Conclusions based on the convergence of results from multiple methods will stand up under close scrutiny, whereas a single measurement, based on one observation, is probably a very unreliable indicator of attitudes.

The Assessment of Skills and the Psychomotor Domain

Having experts observe performance is the most appropriate way of ascertaining the attainment of psychomotor skills as well as other skills, such as writing, speaking, problem solving, managing, and leading. Physical education instructors observe students in sports and physical activities and rate the level of skill attainment. Similarly, faculty in the performing arts rate their students based on actual performances of music, dance, and drama. Products created in studio art and design classes are judged by faculty. Technical and vocational instructors observe their students performing tasks related to job skills and judge how adequately prepared they are for job entry.

Performance assessments are also appropriate for judging highly complex cognitive processes that require demonstration, such as writing and speaking (Dunbar, 1988). Performance measures, such as writing a paper, delivering a speech, or using a computer to solve a problem, are appropriate for many general education outcomes. In fact, performance measures may be more relevant to the instructional methods and intended outcomes than multiple-choice questions.

The degree to which the performance task is structured and planned, related to theory, systematically observed, and reduced to numerical ratings determines whether the method is quantitative or qualitative. Rating separate components of writing, such as grammar, paragraph structure, complexity of sentence structure, and diction, will yield a quantitative measure of writing. A holistic approach—in which someone examines the entire piece of writing and makes an overall judgment as to how well the purpose is accomplished—is a qualitative assessment.

Some other examples of performance assessments appropriately adopted by academic departments are field experiments; interviews with students in a foreign language to determine their fluency and comprehension; diagnoses by medical students; clinical interviews by students in counseling, psychology, and social work; and practice teaching and simulations of classroom teaching by education students. A more complete review of performance and behavioral assessment is contained in the resource section beginning on page 104.

Portfolio assessment, a method for determining student change and growth over time, is discussed beginning on page 96. A portfolio is a collection of student performance information over time, which may be judged in terms of growth or change in knowledge, skill, and values. The portfolio may contain written works, such as essays, journals, and autobiographies; self-evaluations; audiotapes and videos of speeches delivered or other performances; a collection of artwork, drawings, designs, and so forth; or computer programs written or printouts demonstrating mastery of programming. The performances selected for the portfolio may be left up to the students' imaginations, or they may be assigned by the faculty. Typically, the portfolio follows the student throughout his or her college career and is assessed at different points in time. At Evergreen State College in Washington, the student's portfolio replaces the college transcript, and the portfolio contains written assessments of the student by faculty members.

Some outcomes of higher education may be shared by many departments but transcend the specific content of any single discipline. *Life competencies* is a term used to describe behaviors that are best observed, such as leadership, decision making, communication, plan-

ning and organizational skills, problem analysis, innovation, and social interaction (Byham, 1988). One approach to assessing life competencies, originally adopted by business and industry but feasible
for institutions of higher education, is the assessment center. The
assessment center is defined as "a comprehensive, standardized process in which techniques such as situational exercises and job simulations (e.g., discussion groups and presentations) are used to evaluate individuals" (p. 256). The assessment center requires a full-time
director and many part-time assessors who are trained observers.
Faculty might participate as observers, particularly for the evaluation
of objectives directly related to their departmental student outcomes.
In fact, the credibility of the results from assessment centers would
probably depend in large part on the involvement of faculty in defining the simulation exercises and in judging the performances.

Summary

Educational outcomes can describe changes in students in the cognitive, affective, and psychomotor dimensions. Departments should
limit the outcomes to those that are most important for their students
and most significantly related to the institutional purpose. The process of identifying educational outcomes should be a natural, ongoing
part of course and curriculum planning; however, the new dimension
in the process is developing the linkages between institutional purpose and departmental activities.

A variety of approaches should be explored for the assessment of
educational outcomes. Methods closely related to the teaching and
learning processes are likely to be successful, whereas the administration of instruments—tests, surveys, and so on—with little connection to regular course activities may yield useless data. Methods appropriate for the type of educational outcome should be selected.
Achievement tests, as well as written work and other products, are
appropriate measures of cognitive outcomes. Surveys, interviews,
observations, and portfolio analysis may be appropriate measures of
affective outcomes. Skills, including psychomotor, interpersonal, life
competencies, and complex cognitive skills, may best be evaluated
through performance measures. The assessment procedures must
match the objective and yield information that will be useful to faculty
in changing teaching strategies, improving course content, and revising curricula.

References: Cited and Recommended

Anastasi, A. (1988). *Psychological testing* (6th ed.). New York: Macmillan.

Appelbaum, M. I. (1988). Assessment through the major. In C. Adelman (Ed.), *Performance and judgment: Essays on princples and practices in the assessment of college student learning* (pp. 117–137). Washington, DC: U.S. Department of Education, Office of Educational Research and Improvement.

Baird, L. L. (1988). Diverse and subtle arts: Assessing the generic outcomes of higher education. In C. Adelman (Ed.), *Performance and judgment: Essays on principles and practices in the assessment of college student learning* (pp. 39–62). Washington, DC: U.S. Department of Education, Office of Educational Research and Improvement.

Banta, T. W. (1988). *Selected bibliography on outcomes assessment.* Knoxville, TN: Assessment Resource Center, University of Tennessee.

Banta, T. W., & Schneider, J. A. (1988). Using faculty-developed exit examinations to evaluate academic programs. *Journal of Higher Education, 59,* 69–83.

Bloom, B. S., Englhard, M., Funst, E., Hill, W., & Krathwohl, D. (Eds.). (1956). *Taxonomy of educational objectives: The classification of educational goals: Handbook I: Cognitive domain.* New York: David McKay.

Byham, W. C. (1988). Using the assessment center method to measure life competencies. In C. Adelman (Ed.), *Performance and judgment: Essays on principles and practices in the assessment of college student learning* (pp. 255–278). Washington, DC: U.S. Department of Education, Office of Educational Research and Improvement.

Chandler, J. W. (1986). *The college perspective on assessment.* Paper presented at the ETS Invitational Conference on Assessing the Outcomes of Higher Education, New York, NY.

Dunbar, S. (1988). States of art in the science of writing and other performance assessments. In C. Adelman (Ed.), *Performance and judgment: Essays on principles and practices in the assessment of college student learning* (pp. 235–254). Washington, DC: U.S. Department of Education, Office of Educational Research and Improvement.

Ewell, P. T. (1985). *Levers for change: The role of state government in improving the quality of postsecondary education.* ECS working paper. Denver, CO: Education Commission of the States.

Ewell, P. T. (1987). Principles of longitudinal enrollment analysis: Conducting retention and student flow studies. In J. A. Muffo & G. W. McLaughlin (Eds.), *A primer on institutional research* (pp. 1–19). Tallahassee, FL: Association for Institutional Research.

Fong, B. (1987). *The external examiner approach to assessment.* Paper commissioned by the American Association for Higher Education Assessment Forum for the Second National Conference on Assessment in Higher Education, Denver, CO.

Goldman, B. A., & Mitchell, D. F. (1990). *Directory of unpublished experimental mental measures: Volume V.* Dubuque, IA: W. C. Brown.

Graham, S. (1988). Indicators of motivation in college students. In C. Adelman (Ed.), *Performance and judgment: Essays on principles and practices in the assessment of college student learning* (pp. 163–186). Washington, DC: U.S.

Department of Education, Office of Educational Research and Improvement.

Grandy, J. (1988). Assessing changes in student values. In C. Adelman (Ed.), *Performance and judgment: Essays on principles and practices in the assessment of college student learning* (pp. 139–161). Washington, DC: U.S. Department of Education, Office of Educational Research and Improvement.

Henerson, M. E., Morris, L. L., & Fitz-Gibbon, C. T. (1978). *How to measure attitudes*. Beverly Hills, CA: Sage.

Katchadourian, H. A., & Boli, J. (1985). *Careerism and intellectualism among college students*. San Francisco: Jossey-Bass.

Krathwohl, D. R., Bloom, B. S., & Masia, B. B. (Eds.). (1964). *Taxonomy of educational objectives: The classification of educational goals: Handbook I: Affective domain*. New York: David McKay.

Miles, M. B., & Huberman, A. M. (1984). *Qualitative data analysis: A sourcebook of new methods*. Beverly Hills, CA: Sage.

Mitchell, J. V. (Ed.). (1983). *Tests in print III: An index to tests, test reviews, and the literature on specific tests*. Lincoln, NE: Buros Institute of Mental Measurements.

Mitchell, J. V. (Ed.). (1985). *The ninth mental measurements yearbook*. Lincoln, NE: Buros Institute of Mental Measurements.

Morris, L. L., & Fitz-Gibbon, C. T. (1978). *How to measure achievement*. Beverly Hills, CA: Sage.

National Laboratory for Higher Education. (1974). *Developing measurable objectives*. Durham, NC: National Laboratory for Higher Education.

Pace, C. R. (1979). *College student experiences*. Los Angeles: Higher Educational Research Institute, University of California.

SAS Institute, Inc. *SAS® • Language and Procedures: Usage, Version 6, First Edition*. (1989). Cary, NC: SAS Institute, Inc.

Shaw, M. E., & Wright, J. M. (1967). *Scales for the measurement of attitudes*. New York: McGraw-Hill.

Shulman, L. S., Smith, V. B., & Stewart, D. M. (1987). *Three presentations: From the Second National Conference on Assessment in Higher Education*. Washington, DC: American Association for Higher Education.

Study Group on the Conditions of Excellence in American Higher Education. (1984, October 24). Text of new report on excellence in undergraduate education. *Chronicle of Higher Education*, pp. 35–49.

Terenzini, P. T. (1987). The case for unobtrusive measures. In *Assessing the outcomes of higher education* (pp. 47–61). Proceedings of the 1986 ETS Invitational Conference. Princeton, NJ: Educational Testing Service.

Webb, E. J., Campbell, D. T., Schwartz, R. D., & Sechrest, L. (1981). *Unobtrusive measures* (2nd ed.). Chicago: Rand McNally.

Setting and Evaluating Objectives and Outcomes in Nonacademic Units

Marilyn K. Brown and
Donald J. Reichard

The emphasis of the institutional effectiveness movement to date has been primarily on instructional programs. If an institution of higher education is to be effective in achieving its total mission through its principal activities of instruction, research, and public service, the effectiveness of all its operations must be evaluated. Effective instructional, research, and public service programs may be jeopardized by poor administrative support. Therefore, evaluating the organizational performance of support units becomes important to assure that they are operating effectively in consonance with institutional goals.

Interest in the evaluation of administrative support units has grown for a variety of reasons. Although many administrative units may be small, the cumulative resources required for their continued support may be substantial. The existence of ongoing procedures for academic program review may lead to increased interest in administrative unit reviews as administrative structures increase in size. Such factors may result, as in Illinois, in requirements by state coordinating boards that administrative units be evaluated regularly (Wilson, 1987).

Regardless of the motivation for undertaking reviews of nonacademic units, the reviews should ultimately be cost-free in the sense that the return should equal the investment (Wergin & Braskamp, 1987, p. 97). Because the goal of evaluation is overall institutional improvement, such evaluations, when devised in accordance with the institutional mission, may lead to new ways of looking at a unit's role within the institution as well as a redefinition of important priorities for the unit.

One way of promoting effectiveness in operating units is to subject them to formal reviews based on established criteria. In this chapter we define a model for a formal academic support unit review process that is theoretically sound and workable. Also, we cite a growing body of literature and note mechanisms that are available for setting and evaluating research and public service outcomes in a variety of nonacademic units.

Review of Assessment Methods Available for Research and Service Outcomes and Administrative Objectives

Most four-year institutions incorporate references to research and public service in their mission statements and may employ a wide range of resources in setting Research and Public Service outcomes and administrative objectives. One of the most helpful general references is the *Outcomes Measures and Procedures Manual* (Micek, Service, & Lee, 1975); this document specifies measures that administrators might wish to employ as well as definitions, data sources, and procedures for collecting such measures. Other means of assessing outcomes and setting administrative objectives include direct measures, attitudinal measures, measures derived from standard administrative practice, and data system indicators. Examples from the research and public service areas are used to illustrate how desired outcomes and objectives may be derived from a variety of sources.

Direct Measures

In the area of research services, the identification of outcomes employed in measuring institutional effectiveness may have several sources. First, and most common, is the specification of direct measures of research program activity. Here, the number and dollar amounts of proposals developed, submitted, and funded often serve as the primary reference point. Such data are usually collected routinely as requirements by state and federal agencies for reporting purposes. Such readily available baseline external funding statistics may serve as ideal benchmarks for formulating intended research outcomes. Goals identified in the Expanded Statement of Institutional Purpose may also be stated and analyzed in terms of the sources of restricted revenue (federal, state, or local governments, private gifts and contracts) from which sponsored research moneys were sought and obtained.

Public service/community impact measures that institutions may wish to consider include (a) enrollment levels/community participation in program offerings; (b) the extent to which an institution participates in community affairs or makes its social, cultural, and recreational programs and facilities available to the community; (c) the economic impact of an institution on its local community; and (d) the extent to which an institution, through its industrial and educational enterprises, assists the community in the development and application of new technologies.

Attitudinal Measures

Beyond the usual quantitative outcome indicators, attitudinal indicators gathered primarily through satisfaction surveys of the users are helpful in formulating outcome indicators. The most common focus of such surveys would be feedback regarding the scope of desired services coupled with measures of satisfaction with existing services.

Several types of surveys may be helpful in the assessment of progress in reaching program outcomes and objectives in the sponsored research and community service areas. The first type of attitudinal measure may be a needs survey seeking input from faculty, students, or community clientele about the most-needed services or educational programs.

Once services and programs have been implemented in response to defined needs, user surveys may be quite helpful in assessing the degree of satisfaction and eliciting suggestions for the improvement of existing or expanded programs and services. Longitudinal follow-up studies of program participants may be helpful in assessing the long-term effects of an institution's program and service offerings. All too often, institutions survey only the clientele whom they are currently serving. Efforts must also be made to obtain reactions from persons who express interest in program offerings but do not actually participate in an institution's activities. Such surveys may help identify obstacles to program participation that may be remedied in the future.

Data System Indicators

In the research and public service areas, as in most areas of institutional activity, the institution's normal operations may provide a range of data system indicators useful in assessing outcomes and progress toward stated administrative objectives. Normal federal data-reporting procedures will yield financial data on research and public service activities via the IPEDS Financial Statistics Report. Often, additional reports required at the state level will also yield standard indicators of the extent of sponsored program or public service activities. The National Science Foundation (NSF) surveys, as well as survey responses to a number of collegiate guides at the graduate and undergraduate levels, may also provide a variety of outcomes indicators.

Administrative Practice

Standard administrative practices such as the conduct of a management audit or submission of a unit's annual report may also provide suitable objectives for assessment. Information obtained from a management audit may be helpful in formulating outcomes related to an assessment of research services. The primary focus in this regard is on the efficiency of procedures employed in administering contracts and grants. Such procedures are generally designed to assure the orderly commitment of external and internal funds in administering contracts for special projects and programs. Audits may be performed by a team of internal or state auditors or by independent accounting firms.

Virtually every administrative unit will file an annual report with the office to which it reports. Information in these reports may provide a starting point in assessing progress toward goals and objectives. In short, if an office maintains any type of database on a central administrative computer or a microcomputer, it has the capability of transforming its operational data into analytical information suitable for evaluating program and administrative objectives.

Professional Standards

The statement of Research and Public Service outcomes and objectives may flow logically from the Expanded Statement of Institutional Purpose. If it does not, efforts to develop standards or statements of recommended professional practice for research and public service may also serve as a source for establishing administrative objectives. Often the administration of grants and contracts is carried out by an institution's Business Office, whereas assistance in obtaining research funds and services is provided to faculty from an office reporting to the Academic Affairs Office or the Graduate School Office. In the former instance, familiarity with contract and grant procedures developed by the National Association of College and University Business Officers (NACUBO, 1987) may be helpful. In the latter instance, information concerning desired research services and information sources useful in obtaining grants and contracts is available through the activities and information networks of such professional organizations as the National Council of University Research Administrators (NCURA) or the Society of Research Administrators (SRA).

In the area of public service, continuing educators have focused considerable attention on the definition of standards and the formulation of principles of good practice. The Principles of Good Practice for Continuing Education (Council on the Continuing Education Unit, 1984) are designed to serve sponsors, providers, and users of continuing education in collegiate and noncollegiate settings. Development of more current standards for continuing education was preceded by a study of attitudes toward previously existing standards of good practice in a variety of organizational settings (House, 1983). The 18 general principles and 70 statements of good practice in relation to learning needs, learning outcomes, learning experiences, assessment, and administration of continuing education programs may serve as a model for research, public service, or other units of various types.

Educational Support Services

Educational support services are equivalent to "Academic Support Services" in the illustrative Expanded Statement of Institutional Purpose contained in Appendix A of this *Handbook*. Collier (1978) defines academic support services as "those activities carried out in direct support of one or more of the three primary programs (Instruction, Research, Public Service)" (p. 37). Subprograms or areas of academic support include library services, museums and galleries, educational media services, academic computing support, academic administration and personnel development, and course and curriculum development.

There may not be universal agreement when one attempts to define the administrative areas included under a given functional area. The broader Program Classification Structure (PCS), described by Myers and Topping (1974), helps to define administrative units falling under the primary PCS areas of instruction, research, public service, academic support, student service, and institutional support.

The emergence of new areas such as enrollment management, for which Dolence (1989) has developed a series of evaluation criteria, complicates attempts to define administrative areas and, at the same time, illustrates the fluid nature of college and university organization.

Areas such as library services and computing services are frequently structured as independent units. These units, in particular, must coordinate their objectives with those of the academic units, which, in turn, should coordinate their plans with the support service units to be sure that intended outcomes requiring substantial increases in resources or services are feasible. For example, the library may have an objective of automating its catalog and providing on-line catalog search service to all departments. If the departments are not aware of this intention and have not requested funds for appropriate equipment in their budgets, this objective will not be achieved fully. Automating the catalog can be achieved by the library without support from other units, but the use of an on-line service by academic units depends on the purchase of equipment out of departmental budgets. Unless academic units allocate funds for equipment, the service will very likely be unused.

The assessment procedures developed by academic support units may differ from those developed by academic units, in that examination of records, logs of activities, and supporting documents for annual reports may play a much larger role. A library can document that its catalog is automated by reporting details of the development procedure and having the catalog available for review. An art museum can document that it has increased its collection in a particular area by listing new acquisitions in a simple report, assuming that dated sales agreements or letters describing donations are on file and assuming that the new acquisitions are available for examination. In summary, academic support units will most often be documenting activities using routine record keeping and reports and will rarely have to use special data collection methods or surveys.

Evaluation of Nonacademic Units

The trend toward self-regulation on the part of individual- and institution-based professional associations, combined with increased interest in the evaluation of such services and programs on the part of single institutions, has led to the emergence of a growing, but somewhat fugitive, literature base on the evaluation of noninstructional areas.

Professional Associations

With regard to self-regulation, the work of the Council for the Advancement of Standards for Student Services/Development Programs (CAS, 1989) and the Student Services Program Review Project (SSPRP, 1986) have been especially notable.

CAS developed a set of evaluation standards and guidelines for evaluating 16 functional administrative areas. The work of CAS was carried out over 6 years through the efforts of 22 CAS professional associations with support and encouragement from the American Council on Education's Advisory Committee on Self-Regulation Initiatives and the Council on Postsecondary Accreditation (COPA).

In the development of the CAS standards and guidelines, no particular organizational or administrative structure was presupposed or mandated. Therefore, the standards that emerged apply to all types of postsecondary institutions. General standards were developed for each of the following functional areas: mission, program, leadership and management, organization and administration, human resources, funding, facilities, legal responsibilities, equal opportunity, access and affirmative action, campus and community relations, multicultural programs and services, ethics, and evaluation.

Academic support services for which CAS standards were developed include academic advising, learning assistance programs, faculty development programs, and computing services. Student service areas addressed in the CAS standards and guidelines include career planning and placement, college unions, commuter student services, disabled student services, fraternities and sororities, housing and residence life, judicial programs, minority student services, recreational sports, religious programs, student activities, and orientation programs. In the area of institutional support services, CAS standards and guidelines were proposed for the evaluation of research and evaluation services.

The SSPRP, developed in California, is of particular interest to the community college sector but has general applicability to all postsecondary institutions. The goal of the project was to develop and pilot test evaluation designs in order to assist colleges in implementing program evaluations for selected campus-based student service programs. Over a 3-year period, more than a thousand persons were involved in the development and testing of evaluation designs—including goals, criteria, measures, and methods—that were field based and field produced. The following were the specific objectives (SSPRP, 1986, p. 3):

1. Develop evaluation models.
2. Develop data collection, data analysis, and information-reporting procedures.
3. Pilot test evaluation models and procedures.
4. Widely disseminate models and procedures.
5. Develop support materials and services to assist colleges in implementing program evaluations appropriate to their institutions.

The SSPRP project developed evaluation designs and procedures for admissions and records, assessment services, career/life planning, counseling, financial aid, job placement, student affairs, and tutorial services.

Rather than focusing on existing generalized program evaluation models and their applicability to administrative settings, Wergin and Braskamp (1987) have discussed issues and strategies for evaluating specific programs. They presented specific criteria and evaluative schema are presented for institutional planning, business affairs, intercollegiate athletic programs, student support services, counseling centers, faculty development programs, and campus computing services. Key questions addressed are as follows: (1) How can institutional researchers and academic administrators authorize and produce information on program effectiveness that is useful for decision making? and (2) How are administrators to know how well these administrative and support services are working and what might be done to improve them?

Campus-Based Evaluation Plans for Nonacademic Units

A number of campus-based plans for the evaluation of nonacademic units have emerged in recent years (Brown, 1989; Haberaecker, 1990; Northwestern University, 1989). The Northwestern University review process has been applied to some 93 academic department centers and administrative units from the 1985-86 through 1988-89 academic years. Appendix E contains an "Executive Summary and Table of Contents" for these processes. In this section, however, we shall pay particular attention to the development of the process for the review of nonacademic units that is operating at the University of Maryland at College Park as described by Brown (1989).

The assessment process must not be so labor intensive and time-consuming that it becomes an end in itself. All of the institutionally based processes noted here are involved and lengthy processes. However, the Northwestern and College Park evaluation processes operate on a 7-year cycle—each unit is reviewed only once in 7 years. Elements of the process, such as surveys of users, can be performed on a more routine basis. Both processes also include follow-up procedures that assure continued, but less stringent, assessment procedures. The College Park process is conducted in each nonacademic unit using a modified self-study approach.

Self-study is a process familiar to members of the campus community. It is used in the accreditation review process and in the academic unit review process. Utilization of a modified self-study concept requires the formation of a self-study committee to oversee the evaluation. This committee should comprise representatives of the several constituencies with an interest in the unit. Constituencies to be represented would include senior administrators, unit managers, unit staff, campus users of the unit's services, external suppliers or users, and the unit head (usually a director). This committee, appointed by the senior administrator in charge of the unit, in consultation with the unit director, would oversee the self-study and prepare a report using the UMCP framework as a guide.

A study by Brown (1990) reinforced the need to select the members of the oversight committee very carefully. The chair must be viewed as objective and have some stature on campus. He or she must also be interested in the review process. Committee members must be willing to devote considerable time and effort to the process. Selecting users who were critical of the unit to serve on the self-study committee was shown to have a positive effect on the attitude of these constituents.

Upon completion of the self-study, two or more external consultants would be brought to campus to perform an independent evaluation of the unit. Their report would be incorporated into the report of the self-study committee. The UMCP framework for the review of nonacademic units is based on the seven issues critical for a successful evaluation (Cameron & Whetten, 1983; Goodman & Pennings, 1980; Steers, 1975).

Purpose of Evaluation. Since significant resources in the form of both staff time and money will be invested in this evaluation process, the evaluations should produce results that are useful to everyone involved, especially the senior administrator responsible for the unit and the director of the unit, but also the unit staff and other constituents as well. Therefore, the evaluation will be "utilization focused" (Patton, 1978). By its nature, utilization-focused evaluation is formative, rather than summative, evaluation. The primary purpose of the assessment of academic support units is to collect information that can be used to improve and further develop the unit.

It is also important to recognize that evaluation "is partly a political process" (Patton, 1978, p. 49). Through the generation of information for prediction and control, decision makers use evaluation results to reduce uncertainty. Unit heads could utilize the evaluation process to influence constituencies and use the results of the evaluation to garner additional resources. The stated purpose of this evaluation process is to assess the effectiveness of the units. More to the point, however, is the purpose of the evaluation as viewed by the senior administrator as well as the unit head. The first step in a utilization-focused evaluation is to have the self-study committee discuss the evaluation with these administrators and determine particular issues and/or problems they would like to have explored during review of the unit (Patton, 1978). The evaluation cannot be useful if it does not provide the specific information these administrators need to make decisions and improve the operation of the unit. The primary purpose of the evaluation, then, is to meet the requirements of administrators for information concerning the effectiveness of their unit.

Another purpose of evaluation in any organization is to improve the quality of the organization. This is particularly important in an institution of higher education that is striving to achieve excellence. If a college is to achieve academic excellence, its leaders must also be concerned with the performance and quality of the institution's nonacademic units (Keller, 1983). It is equally important for senior administrators, as well as the college's constituencies, to know whether the resources being expended on nonacademic support are being utilized as effectively and efficiently as possible.

Level of Analysis. The nature of the evaluation process has determined that in the nonacademic area the unit is the level at which the evaluation will be conducted. Goodman and Pennings (1977) support assessment at this level: "It seems strategically advantageous to focus on subunits' characteristics, including their technological and human resources and the social structure and processes that they have developed" (p. 150).

Constituents to Be Included. The perspectives of all identifiable constituents of the unit should be considered in the evaluation. There are two ways of assuring that the perspectives of all constituents are considered in a review: (1) A representative of the constituency can serve as a member of the self-study committee, and (2) constituents can be surveyed.

The UMCP framework strongly recommends that senior administrators (an assistant vice president, perhaps), subunit supervisors, and staff of the unit be represented on the committee. The director of the unit should be included as well. Without these constituents the evaluation is not a self-study. Additionally, it is in the interest of the unit and the campus that the evaluation be perceived as a positive event and not a "witch hunt." It is normal for staff and supervisors of a unit to be apprehensive if their performance is being examined— perhaps someone is "out to get them." These fears can be allayed somewhat by appointing one or more representatives of the supervisory and support staffs to the self-study committee. This is also a mechanism for providing the staff with insight into the perspectives of other constituents. When interviewing staff who participated in the process, Brown (1990) learned that they were deeply interested in working on the self-study committee. They wanted to do whatever they could to improve the operation of their unit.

Users of the unit's services should also be represented. Some units have several distinct categories of users or "customers." For instance, the purchasing department in a university serves several kinds of departments. Some rarely buy anything more than office supplies and an occasional piece of office equipment. There are departments with large research components whose purchases comprise very sophisticated equipment required for conducting specific research projects and/or for instruction. Finally, there are users such as the physical plant who buy large quantities of building materials and supplies, heavy equipment, and motor vehicles. Each of these types of customers has different requirements that translate into different goals for the purchasing department. Somehow all of these users' perspectives must be considered in the review. It would be advisable to include at least one of the large-volume purchasers on the self-study committee while utilizing the second method of recognizing constituent perspectives (i.e., surveys) to consider the views of the less-frequent customers. In fact, a more complete picture of all customers' views would be obtained if all types of customers were surveyed (in addition to having large-volume users serve on the self-study committee).

Other constituencies whose perspectives are important in an evaluation are groups in the external environment who interact on a regular basis with the nonacademic unit. These external constituents frequently are the source of constraints on the focal unit. Their rules and regulations, whether formal or implicit, can hamper the effectiveness of an operation. It is important to include representatives of these constituencies for two reasons: (1) to obtain their perspectives on the operative goals and processes of the unit, and (2) to make them aware of the extent to which their rules act as constraints and inhibit the effectiveness of the unit.

As noted earlier, including constituents who are known to have a negative view of the unit can, in the long run, be quite positive. As described by Brown (1990), one director at the University of Maryland at College Park invited a few of his strongest critics to serve on the self-study committee. Once these people came to realize the constraints placed on the unit by oversight agencies, they became the unit's strongest supporters and lobbied to have regulations that hampered the effectiveness of the unit changed.

External environment in this context has two meanings: First, it includes departments outside of the focal unit but inside the college. As an example, if the Registrar's Office were being evaluated, it would be important to consider the perspective of the Administrative Computer Center, which provides the data-processing support for the Registrar's Office. Second, individuals and/or organizations outside of the university are also part of the external environment. For some departments, such as purchasing, this includes suppliers and contractors with whom the university does business. While campus users of the Purchasing Department expect the department to provide prompt service and quality products at the lowest possible price, suppliers and contractors want to make the best "deal" and be paid promptly. Resolving these two possibly conflicting goals could be problematic, although enlightening, for the self-study committee.

It should be reiterated here that it is practical for representatives of only a few constituencies to sit on the self-study committee. The political decision concerning who the "most important" constituents are must be made by the senior administrator and the director. The self-study committee itself might later decide to add one or more constituents. Nonrepresented constituencies and/or all of the members of the constituencies that are represented can be surveyed using paper surveys, phone surveys, focus groups, personal interviews, or group forums to assure that all perspectives are considered.

Domains of Activity to Be Considered. The inclusion of the perspectives of all constituencies leads to the evaluation of activity in all of the domains in which the unit operates. Domains arise from the activities or primary tasks that are emphasized in the organization, from the competencies of the organization, and from the demands placed on the organization by external forces (Cameron, 1981; Miles, 1980). The Office of Institutional Research at many universities can serve to illustrate this point. The traditional responsibility of this office has been the collection and reporting of institutional data to federal and state agencies, as well as to senior administrators. The conduct of analytical studies in support of decision making has also been the responsibility of this office. These activities represent two domains. When institutional assessment became required, the Office of Institutional Research was usually assigned the responsibility. The "competencies of the organization" as well as "external demands" thus created another domain of activity for the office.

Cameron and Whetten (1983) point out that "no organization is maximally effective in all its domains" (p. 271). Nevertheless, the self-study committee must examine the effectiveness of the unit in all of the areas in which the unit operates. Senior administrators, however, must not expect an equal level of performance in all domains. The evaluation might be useful in helping the unit director and senior administrator set priorities concerning domains of activity so the highest levels of performance can be achieved in those areas deemed most important to the campus at any given point in time. In some instances, the senior administrator might elect to exclude one or more domains of a unit's activities from the review process. In order to do this successfully, the domain must be a clearly separate activity. An example might be the records function in the Registrar's Office. If a particular function has recently undergone major change and/or reorganization, it might be too early to review the results of the changes. In this case, the senior administrator, in consultation with the unit head, might decide not to review that particular domain of activity.

As the self-study committee considers the domains in which the unit operates, it should consider the structure or organization of the unit. Are routine functions centralized and automated to the fullest extent possible? Are functions requiring creativity decentralized to allow staff the freedom they need to perform effectively? Are job responsibilities distributed in the most efficient manner. Is the unit, within each domain, employing the appropriate technology, that is, knowledge and machines? Is there evidence of creativity and innovation? Are new ideas and methods tested and adopted if they work? Is there evidence of a willingness on the part of staff as well as supervisors to adapt and change as the requirements of the environment change? Such attributes of unit performance must be considered in judging effectiveness (Hage, 1980).

One domain should exist in every unit, and it deserves close scrutiny by the committee. This activity is the acquisition and utilization of resources for the purpose of obtaining additional resources. Does the unit attract and utilize bright, competent, dedicated employees? The reputation of a unit for having a high degree of competency brings respect and helps attract additional able employees. The unit should also use the skills and competencies of its employees to get the most from its human energy. The acquisition and effective use of information can lead to innovation.

Another resource that is not often recognized is the goodwill of the units' users. Garnering goodwill can lead to improved effectiveness through cooperation and even to additional funding.

Time Frame. The concept of self-study requires that the time frame considered in the evaluation be current. What is going on now, and what results are being achieved? The committee might consider plans for change that are in the process of being implemented and comment on the expected results. The committee's report might also recommend changes that should be considered for the future.

Type of Data Utilized. Two kinds of data can be used in an evaluation—objective and subjective. Objective data are obtained from organizational records. Some examples appropriate to unit review are budget data, staff turnover rates, number of units processed (i.e., circulation data, items processed from purchasing, audiovisual services performed), personnel evaluations, and absentee rate, to name some of the obvious. Subjective data are perceptual and are obtained from surveys or personal interviews. Cameron (1980) cautions that objective and subjective data are sometimes contradictory. Nevertheless, both kinds of data can contribute to the study of effectiveness.

Budget levels over time suggest whether a unit is being properly funded as its domains of activity expand or shrink and the number of units processed changes. Turnover rates can indicate the level of staff morale. Changes in units processed per employee can indicate the appropriateness of staffing levels. These are a few examples of ways in which organizational (objective) data can be used in the evaluation process.

Perceptual (subjective) data also play a role in evaluation. The importance of examining the perspectives of all the identifiable constituents of the unit—the perceptual data—has already been discussed. When considering subjective data, the committee must recognize that by their nature such data are biased. It is possible that lack of information or even dishonesty on the part of respondents can hinder the reliability ofthe data. It should also be noted that the nature and time frame of the self-study do not permit the testing of survey instruments for reliability and validity. The instruments used will be designed by the committee or its designee and are likely to be used only once during the review process.

Referents. Referents are the standards against which the effectiveness of the academic support unit will be judged. The UMCP framework includes the use of several referents. Since this evaluation process examines the perspectives or goals of the unit's several constituencies, use of the goal-centered approach is suitable. How well is the unit achieving the goals of the various constituents? As was the case in the discussion of domains, differential levels of goal achievement among constituents are to be expected. Again, the unit director and senior administrator must set priorities.

It is appropriate to compare the unit with similar units. Two sources of referents are applicable. First, if industry or government standards of performance are available for the type of activity conducted by the unit, they can be used to measure effectiveness. Such might be the case for personnel (e.g., number of job applicants processed per employee), purchasing (e.g., number of purchase orders filled per employee), or accounts payable (e.g., number of invoices processed per employee). Many units have no counterpart outside of higher education. Comparable data for these units (registrations, admissions, bursar, and student affairs units, to name a few) must be obtained from peer institutions. In selecting peers for comparison, care must be taken that only comparable institutions are selected. The admissions process at Harvard is probably quite different from the process at Penn State. Using Harvard's data as a measure of effectiveness at Penn State would be inappropriate. The instrument for collecting peer data must be very carefully designed to assure the clarity of the request. The director of the unit can offer the best advice on the development of such an instrument, whether the data are collected with a paper survey, by phone, or even in person.

A method for collecting peer data in order to compare the efficiency rates of nonacademic units is described by Haberaecker (1990) and is used at Northeastern Illinois University. The process results in a ratio of headcount or FTE students per budgeted staff in nonacademic units. It is another example of the use of referents in the review process.

Another form of comparative evaluation will occur when outside experts visit the campus and evaluate the unit. These experts will each have his or her own set of referents against which the unit will be judged.

Steps to Follow in Conducting a Nonacademic Unit Review

When a nonacademic unit is being reviewed, the following activities should occur:

1. The senior administrator and the unit director form a self-study committee and consider appropriate external reviewers.
2. The committee, the senior administrator, and the unit director discuss particular issues to be addressed in the review.
3. The committee prepares a self-study plan and budget and submits them to the senior administrator.
4. The senior administrator approves the plan and budget or makes suggestions for changes.
5. The committee conducts the self-study, addressing the following general issues and using the UMCP framework as a guide:
   a. Expectations of the various constituencies
   b. Domains in which the unit is operating
   c. Structure, task differentiation, and technology of the unit relevant to the expressed goals of the constituencies
   d. Conformance with performance standards
   e. Constraints imposed by the external environment (includes funding and staffing levels)
   f. Satisfaction of users with the unit's services
   g. Qualifications/competencies and morale of the staff
   h. General environment of the workplace
   i. Recommendations
6. The committee prepares a self-study report.
7. The committee submits the self-study to the senior administrator and external reviewers.
8. The external reviewers conduct an on-site evaluation.
9. The external reviewers submit an evaluation report.
10. The external review results are incorporated into the self-study report.
11. The director prepares a response and a plan to implement the recommendations.
12. The senior administrator and unit director discuss the report, the

director's response, and the plans to implement the report's recommendations.
13. The report and action plans are submitted to the chief executive officer.

Shortcomings of the Framework

Even though it draws from a variety of models of organizational effectiveness, the UMCP framework has several shortcomings.

1. There is no explicit evaluation of efficiency in the framework. Hannan and Freeman (1977) include efficiency in their definition of effectiveness, since resource constraints exist within most organizations. Evaluators could calculate a cost-per-output ratio and compare it with similar ratios from other peer institutions. The problem that frequently confounds such a comparison is the likelihood that no units in higher education institutions are exactly alike. Whereas different structures and/or technology should not prevent comparison of efficiency ratios, differing domains of activity should. If one Admissions Office evaluates transfer students' transcripts for transferable credits and another does not, their efficiency ratios are not comparable. Usually the self-study committee would not be aware of such subtleties. Because such efficiency comparisons are problematic they have not been included in the framework. (Haberaecker [1990]) describes a process for developing comparable efficiency ratios.)
2. Evaluations will not be identical in all units. The framework sets general guidelines, but a self-study is subjective. Different committees will emphasize different areas for scrutiny. The senior administrator and the unit director will suggest different issues for concentrated study. Some committees will have a stronger commitment to the process than others; there is probably no way to avoid such differences completely. The senior administrator has some control, since he or she will approve the committee's plan. However, as long as the senior administrator and the unit director receive the information they require from the evaluation, one need not be overly concerned with consistency as long as the basic framework is applied.
3. Unit evaluations over time are not likely to be consistent for the same reasons evaluations among units might not be consistent. Ideally, in subsequent evaluations, the report from the prior eval-

uation would be considered and the committee would note whether the recommendations had been implemented. It is possible that from one review to another constituencies and domains would change. Of necessity, the review would be somewhat different. Lack of consistency over time is not a serious problem.

4. Negativism concerning the evaluation can be a problem, especially for the first units to be reviewed. Unit directors, as well as staff, might be threatened by such close scrutiny of their unit. It is incumbent on senior administrators to allay such fears by describing the process beforehand and pointing out the positive aspects of the self-study. As was previously mentioned, involving the director and subunit managers and staff in the evaluation process will also place the process in a more positive light.

5. The UMCP framework describes a multistage process that is expensive to implement. Each self-study takes close to a year from planning to final report. A significant portion of the time of the unit director and the staff who serve on the committee is required for the self-study. Additional people are not hired to assist with the normal workload. In addition, other university employees are asked to serve on self-study committees as representatives of various constituencies. Employees provide their services to the self-study committee by either slacking off on other responsibilities or, more likely, by spending more time on the job. Either way, the service exacts a price. Other costs are also involved in the conduct of surveys and the preparation of committee working materials. The most significant financial outlay is required to bring to campus experts for every evaluation. As many as six to eight reviews can occur in any given year on campus. The collective cost of conducting so many evaluations has not been estimated, but it is generally high.

Benefits of Review

Such an expensive process should provide some tangible benefits. What will the university gain? Probably the most obvious and desired benefit of unit evaluation is the diagnosis of problem areas and the resulting improvement in operations and decisions. Of equal importance, however, is the opportunity to discover and acknowledge excellence in an operation. In fact, evaluation is likely to be viewed more positively by those being assessed if this possible outcome of review is emphasized.

Brewer (1983) pointed out that another benefit of unit evaluation is complacency reduction. In the course of working with the self-study committee, unit personnel, and particularly the unit director, must clarify their own goals. Such introspection leads to clarity about what has to be done and the best way to do it. The unit review process provides an opportunity for unit personnel to step back from the pressure of routine demands and think about what they are doing and how they are doing it.

The UMCP framework draws representatives of identifiable constituencies into the evaluation process. As the goals of the several constituencies are discussed, there is an opportunity for each constituent to recognize the goals of the others. Constituents will also be in a position of seeing the constraints they, and the others, place on the focal unit. A better understanding of all of the demands placed on a department, coupled with the knowledge of budget and staff limitations, should serve to make constituents less critical when their own expectations are not met.

Finally, the evaluation activity itself could enhance the image of the institution. This outcome of assessment is also mentioned by Brewer (1983). Such activity is commonplace in industry, and introducing the practice should send a signal to those who provide funding, both public and private, that the university is committed to achieving the highest level of effectiveness and quality in its operations. By developing an evaluation system on its own initiative, the university might forestall any effort on the part of state agencies to mandate such practices. Although the process of assessing the effectiveness of non-academic units may be difficult, time-consuming, and expensive, many benefits can be gained from such a practice.

Summary

Institutions can expect a considerable degree of variance in the technical merit of statements of program intent, outcomes, and objectives. Particularly at the inception of institutional effectiveness operations, such differences are not only acceptable but desirable to the extent that they reflect active involvement by the institution's administrative units. However, this resource section and the examples contained in Appendix B suggest that outcomes/objectives should be linked to the Expanded Statement of Institutional Purpose; should exhibit (explicitly or implicitly) many of the attributes described earlier; and, in most cases, should be measurable.

Note: Substantial portions of this resource section are adapted from "Developing and Implementing a Process for the Review of Nonacademic Units" by M. K. Brown, 1989, *Research in Higher Education, 30*(1), pp. 89–112. Adapted with the written permission of the publisher.

References: Cited and Recommended

Brewer, G. D. (1983). Assessing outcomes and effects. In K. S. Cameron & D. S. Whetton (Eds.), *Organizational effectiveness: A comparison of multiple models*. New York: Academic Press.

Brown, M. K. (1989). Developing and implementing a process for the review of nonacademic units. *Research in Higher Education, 30*(1), 89–112.

Brown, M. K. (1990). An analysis of the academic support unit review process in operation at the University of Maryland at College Park. Unpublished dissertation, College Park, MD.

Cameron, K. S. (1981). Domains of organizational effectiveness in colleges and universities. *Academy of Management Journal, 24*, 25–47.

Cameron, K. S., & Whetton, D. S. (1983). *Organizational effectiveness: A comparison of multiple models*. New York: Academic Press.

Collier, D. V. (1978). *Program classification structure*. (Technical Report No. 106). Boulder, CO: National Center for Higher Education Management Systems (NCHEMS) at Western Interstate Commission for Higher Education.

Council for the Advancement of Standards for Student Services/Development Programs. (1989). *CAS standards and guidelines for student service/development programs*. College Park, MD: Office of Student Affairs, University of Maryland.

Council of the Continuing Education Unit. (1984). *Principles of good practice in continuing education*. Silver Spring, MD: Council of the Continuing Education Unit.

Dolence, M. G. (1989). Evaluation criteria for an enrollment management program. *Planning for Higher Education. 18*(1), 1–13.

Fincher, C. (1978). Importance of criteria for institutional goals. In R. H. Fenske (Ed.), *Using goals in research and planning* (pp. 1–15). New Directions for Institutional Research, no. 19. San Francisco: Jossey-Bass.

Goodman, P. S., & Pennings, J. M. (1977). *New perspectives on organizational effectiveness*. San Francisco: Jossey-Bass.

Goodman, P. S., & Pennings, J. M. (1980). Critical issues in assessing organizatonal effectiveness. In N. E. Lawler, D. A. Nadler, & C. Cammann (Eds.), *Organizational assessment: Perspectives on the measurement of organizational behavior and the quality of life*. New York: Wiley.

Haberaecker, H. J. (1990). *Developing interinstitutional comparisons of nonacademic units for use in the review process*. Paper presented at the 1990 Association for Institutional Research Forum, Louisville, KY.

Hage, J. (1980). *Theories of organization*. New York: Wiley.

Hannan, M. T., & Freeman, J. (1977). Obstacles to comparative studies. In P. S. Goodman, J. M. Pennings, & Associates (Eds.), *New perspectives on organizational effectiveness*. San Francisco: Jossey-Bass.

Harris, J. (1985). Assessing outcomes in higher education. In C. Adelman

(Ed.), *Assessment in American higher education: Issues and contexts*. Washington, DC: U.S. Department of Education.

House, R. M. (1983). *Standards of practice in continuing education: A status study*. Silver Springs, MD: Council on the Continuing Education Unit.

Keller, G. (1983). *Academic strategy*. Baltimore, MD: Johns Hopkins University Press.

Micek, S. S., Service, A. L., & Lee, Y. S. (1975). *Outcome measures and procedures manual: Field edition*. (Technical Report No. 70). Boulder, CO: NCHEMS at Western Interstate Commission for Higher Education.

Miles, R. H. (1980). *Macro organizational behavior*. Santa Monica, CA: Goodyear.

Miller, R. I. (1980). Appraising institutional performance. In P. Jedamus, M. W. Peterson, & Associates (Eds.), *Improving academic management* (pp. 406–431). San Francisco: Jossey-Bass.

Moore, K. M. (1986). Assessment of institutional effectiveness. In J. Losak (Ed.), *Applying institutional research in decision making* (pp. 49–60). New Directions for Community Colleges, no. 56. San Francisco: Jossey-Bass.

Myers, E. M., & Topping, J. R. (1974). *Information exchange procedures activity structure*. (Technical Report No. 63). Boulder, CO: NCHEMS.

National Laboratory for Higher Education. (1974). *Developing measurable objectives*. Durham, NC: Author.

Northwestern University. (1989). *Academic and administrative review procedures*. Evanston, IL: Office of the Vice President for Administration and Planning.

Pace, C. R. (1983). *College student experiences*. Los Angeles: Higher Education Research Institute, UCLA.

Patton, M. Q. (1978). *Utilization-focused evaluation*. Beverly Hills, CA: Sage.

Perrow, C. (1961). The analysis of goals in complex organizations. *American Sociological Review, 26*(December), 854–866.

Pratt, L. K., & Reichard, D. J. (1983). Assessing institutional goals. In N. P. Uhl (Ed.), *Using research for institutional planning* (pp. 53–66). New Directions for Institutional Research, no. 37. San Francisco: Jossey-Bass.

Resource manual on institutional effectiveness. (1989). Atlanta, GA: Commission on Colleges of the Southern Association of Colleges and Schools.

Scott, R. A. (1984). *Determining the effectiveness of campus services*. New Directions for Institutional Research, no. 41. San Francisco: Jossey-Bass.

Steers, R. M. (1975). Problems in the measurement of organizational effectiveness. *Administrative Science Quarterly, 20*, 546–556.

Student Services Program Review Project (SSPRP). (1986). *They said it couldn't be done*. Santa Ana, CA: Author. (ERIC ED 280 518)

Wergin, J. F., & Braskamp, L. A. (Eds.). (1987). *Evaluating administrative services and programs*. New Directions for Institutional Research, no. 56. San Francisco: Jossey-Bass.

Wilson, R. F. (1987). A perspective on evaluating administrative units in higher education. In J. F. Wergin & L. A. Braskamp (Eds.), *Evaluating administrative services and programs* (pp. 3–13). New Directions for Institutional Research, no 56. San Francisco: Jossey-Bass.

CHAPTER FIVE
Initial Implementation

Following 2 years of preparation at the institutional and, subsequently, departmental levels, the institution should be ready for initial operational implementation of institutional effectiveness at the beginning of the third year (shown on Figure 12). By that time the institution should have in place the following key elements developed during the first 2 years of preparation:

1. Expanded Statement of Institutional Purpose—developed during the first year of implementation preparation
2. Statements of Intended Educational, Research, and Service Outcomes as well as Statements of Administrative Objectives—prepared during the second year by each department/program and closely linked to the expanded statement of purpose
3. Assessment Plan—designed in close coordination with departmental/program statements of intentions during the second year

With these three important components serving as the foundation, the institution is ready to begin operational institutional effectiveness implementation; however, a modest amount of institutional remotivation may be necessary to refocus the institution's attention on the task immediately at hand.

At the beginning of the third year, the institution should reflect on what has been accomplished regarding institutional effectiveness, then current operational implementation activities, and the ultimate value of complete implementation. This process could be accomplished by distribution of a well-prepared document covering these points; however, it probably would best be accomplished through either a single campuswide convocation or through multiple smaller meetings highlighting these points as the document is distributed.

Figure 12

The Third Year of a Four-Year Plan for Implementation of Institutional Effectiveness and Assessment Activities on a Campus

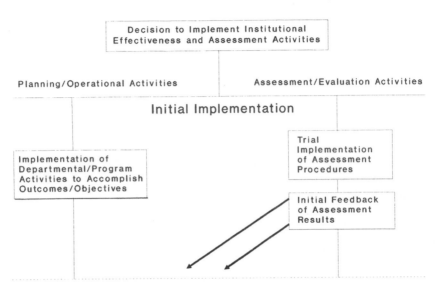

The purpose of this activity, whether written or covered in meetings or, preferably, both, is to rekindle the enthusiasm and energy with which implementation activities commenced several years earlier and to demonstrate the CEO's continued high level of interest in the subject. Regardless of the success that the first 2 years of preparatory activities have enjoyed, the best and most successful implementation effort will begin to "wilt" after several years of steady work. It is essential that an implementation "pep rally," in one form or another, be held as actual operational implementation begins in order to revitalize those taking part in the implementation process.

As shown on Figure 12, implementation during this third year continues on both the planning/operational and assessment/evaluation tracks. However, the bulk of developmental or new work is focused in "Trial Implementation of Assessment Procedures," while the institution's academic and administrative departments conduct relatively normal operations designed to accomplish their intended outcomes/objectives.

Planning/Operational Activities

Following the considerable amount of departmental/program effort required to establish statements of intended outcomes or objectives during the second year, the degree of involvement by academic and administrative department/program personnel early in the third year of implementation may seem to some like a respite from previous preparatory activities directed toward implementation. In fact, the only activity scheduled on the planning/operational activities track during the third year is "Implementation of Departmental/Program Activities to Accomplish Outcomes/Objectives." Stated differently, academic and administrative departments are not required to do anything except their functional tasks (teaching, research, public service, student registration, maintenance of fiscal records, etc.) and, possibly, assist in the "Trial Implementation of Assessment Procedures" later during the third year of implementation.

Superficially, this appears to be a relatively easy year for the academic and administrative departments/programs within the institution; however, in reality, many departments/programs will be implementing new or substantially revised curricular patterns or services growing from development of their statements of intended outcomes or objectives.

The very act of specifying their intended outcomes or objectives during the second year will lead many departments to consider and then implement improved educational or service activities during the third year. An academic department may have determined that, in order for its degree program graduates to accomplish a particular cognitive outcome, a new course will be required. A research-oriented department may have concluded that to reach its level of intended grant commitment by external agencies, a shift or change in grant application procedures is necessary. In order to accomplish specified objectives regarding student residential life, administrators and staff in student affairs may have determined it necessary to modify greatly the social and educational programs taking place at the institution. In all of these examples the central point is similar: Even as operational implementation of institutional effectiveness is begun and before the implementation of any formal assessment, many of the institution's departments/programs will begin to benefit from their natural response to the challenge of setting intended outcomes or objectives and then seeking to conduct departmental/program operations so as to accomplish those ends.

Within these departmental efforts toward accomplishment of their intended outcomes or objectives, some units may wish to conduct informal or departmental midyear mini-assessments of their progress. However, in those units in which substantial changes have taken place in operations, it may well take several years for the full impact of their revised operations to become evident through assessment.

Assessment/Evaluation Activities

Clearly, the bulk of the activity during this initial year of operational implementation of institutional effectiveness will be involved with initiation of assessment procedures and feedback mechanisms.

Both the second year of implementation and the first half of this third year will undoubtedly be filled with the design of and planning for assessment, but it is in the later half of the third year of implementation that "Trial Implementation of Assessment Procedures" will take place. Assuming that implementation years roughly parallel academic years, trial implementation and feedback would take place between March and August of the third year. This period of time should be evenly divided between assessment activities conducted primarily during the months of March, April, and May and results processing and feedback during June, July, and August.

The assessment-and-feedback cycle should be initiated by the end of the academic year and be completed before the next academic year begins. These timing restraints mean that the majority of the work in this area will take place as faculty and students, who might otherwise be engaged in supporting these activities, are preparing to leave the campus or have actually departed for the summer. Hence, institutions should seriously consider employment of several faculty members (perhaps one from each college or school) and a number of students during the trial implementation summer to assist in processing the data received and preparing the necessary feedback for presentation to the faculty and staff at the beginning of the next academic year. What activities can be expected in the "Trial Implementation of Assessment Procedures"?

The "Trial Implementation of Assessment Procedures" will result in a considerable amount of effort in at least four major areas of endeavor: (a) standardized cognitive testing, (b) administration of attitudinal surveys, (c) information drawn from institutional databases and other institutional data sources, and (d) departmental reports of assessment means implemented within the department.

Standardized Cognitive Testing

Undoubtedly, the fulfillment of many statements of intended educational outcomes will be assessed through students' performance on standardized cognitive tests. Hence, a substantial increase in the number of students taking such examinations can be anticipated. The procedures implemented regarding such testing should ensure that students have ample opportunity to take such tests and that students applying for graduation in a particular program register to take the appropriate test. Three basic questions will emerge concerning increased student participation in cognitive testing:

1. Who pays for such standardized examinations?
2. Should achievement of a specific score be required for graduation?
3. How can the institution motivate students to take such examinations seriously if a "passing" score is not required for graduation?

The answer to the first two of these logical inquiries relates to the primary purpose for the administration of the standardized examinations—assessment of institutional effectiveness. Although performance on such examinations will reflect on individual students, the primary intent is to assess the effectiveness of the institution's educational programs, not its students. Hence, either asking students to pay directly for taking standardized tests or setting a passing score for students to attain before graduation appears to be inconsistent with the primary purpose of administration. However, this statement should not be construed as opposition to increasing the general student activity fee or tuition sufficiently to cover assessment-related costs.

Assuming that students are not required to pay directly for taking such standardized tests, how are institutions going to get students to take such examinations seriously? The answer is that each institution must seek and encourage voluntary compliance by specifically explaining to students why their taking the examination is important to continued institutional improvement. Institutions may further seek voluntary compliance by describing to students the potential benefit of having such standardized examination results on file when they graduate. Some institutions, having failed to gain student commitment intrinsically, suggest extrinsic motivational means, such as altering the sequence of preregistration or distribution of student parking permits to reward students who achieve certain scores on standardized cognitive measures routinely administered at the end of their second year in attendance. However, the undeniable fact remains that, short of requiring a passing score, institutions cannot force students to take standardized examinations. Given this realization, institutions should limit the pressure placed on students to take such standardized examinations and be prepared to disregard test scores that appear to reflect half-hearted participation.

Attitudinal Surveys

Also taking place during this period of time will be distribution to and return of attitudinal surveys by those students completing educational programs at the institution. These instruments, designed and pilot tested earlier in the implementation process, are best distributed and collected during the student's administrative processing for graduation. Some institutions may find it useful to distribute the survey when students obtain their application for graduation and to collect the completed questionnaire when a diploma fee is paid.

Other attitudinal surveys such as those of alumni, students leaving the institution prior to graduation, or employers are less constrained within the March-to-August time frame. In order to spread the workload of the trial assessment procedures implementation over the entire year, institutions should consider distribution of attitudinal surveys to such recipients during the period prior to March to avoid scheduling this activity concurrently with other assessment procedures more directly tied to the last half of the year.

Information Drawn from Institutional Data Systems

As the academic year draws to a close, data concerning student achievements, retention, and other subjects should be drawn from the institution's data system (as well as the data systems of other institutions) to support the assessment process. Data drawn from other institutions' data systems will be necessary to ascertain the success of students transferring from two-year colleges to four-year institutions and later to gauge the success in graduate school of baccalaureate program graduates.

Departmental Reports

During May and June, the institution's academic departments can be expected to be administering various cognitive and performance measures that they have designed both for assessment of the extent to which their intended programmatic outcomes have been achieved and, potentially, as requirements for student graduation. Although such means of assessment must be administered at the departmental level, there must also be institutional responsibility and effort to ensure that such activities are actually undertaken by the responsible departments and that the results are forwarded to a central point for compilation with other assessment results relating to the program.

Assembly and Processing of Assessment Results

During the early to mid-summer of the third year of implementation, the institution should be literally awash in assessment-related data. Student scores for standardized cognitive tests taken earlier should be arriving. The results of attitudinal surveys (particularly the graduates' survey) will become available. Data drawn from institutional sources and other databases should have been processed. Departmental assessment results should be available. How should this flood of data be organized and refined into useful assessment information for the departments/programs and the institution?

The key to organizing this variety of assessment data is the establishment of a centralized agency (office, department, etc.) to which all such data are forwarded for compilation. Within that agency (staffed by both its own permanent employees and temporary faculty and students), separate folders or files for each department/program es tablishing intended departmental outcomes or objectives should be established. The folder should contain a copy of the departmental statements of intention (including their proposed means for assessment) and all of the trial assessment implementation results relating to that department/program. During the early part of the summer, it will be necessary that an outcome-by-outcome (or objective-by-objective) comparison of the proposed means of assessment with the results in the folder be conducted. The comparison and subsequent follow-up will determine which data are missing from the folder but available within the institution and which means of assessment were, for one reason or another, not accomplished. By the end of June all assessment data available should have been collected and filed in the appropriate folder by department/program prior to analysis and preparation of feedback to the departments.

Initial Feedback of Results

Once the results of the trial assessment procedure implementation are received and filed, analysis of the results and preparation of feedback should commence. Analysis of such results will always remain a matter of subjective judgment at the departmental/program level, and only limited centralized analysis of results need, or indeed should, be provided to the department. On the other hand, centralized organization of the information to focus on departmental statements of intentions, summarization of individual student results into departmental/program averages, or interpretation of departmental/program results in light of institutional or national normative data may greatly enhance a department's willingness and ability to analyze and apply the results of the trial assessment procedures.

Although little direct analysis of results needs to be provided to the departmental/program level, a general need exists at the institutional level for insight into the extent to which the institution is accomplishing its Expanded Statement of Institutional Purpose. If the statement of purpose portrays the institution as a selective entity whose graduates should excel academically, but the trial assessment results indicate that its students are consistently exhibiting cognitive learning levels that might be expected of graduates at a substantially less selective institution, the institution should seriously consider adjusting its Expanded Statement of Institutional Purpose. Those individuals responsible at the institutional level for analysis and departmental/ program information preparation will undoubtedly form general opinions concerning the extent to which departmental/program statements of intentions are being realized. Through these generalizations (subject to confirmation by individual departmental personnel) a basic understanding of the extent to which intentions expressed in the Expanded Statement of Institutional Purpose are being accomplished can be established.

The means for and timing of the feedback of assessment results to the departmental/program level are crucial to their use for improvement of the institution. During design of the assessment process, considerable thought should have been given to the data processing needed to obtain the desired data layouts and tables regarding each means of assessment. Following assembly of the various assessment results relating to each department/program by intended outcome/ objective, a relatively standardized set of data presentation formats— designed earlier—for the results of each assessment means (cognitive test, attitudinal survey, etc.) should be completed.

There is no intention to homogenize departmental/program data analysis or presentation by use of standardized information formats. Rather, the intention is to devote considerable time and expertise to design of a professionally developed set of data formats that can be quickly and efficiently adapted to each outcome/objective and assessment means. The use of such formats also precludes the expenditure of an inordinate amount of time summarizing the data for each outcome/objective by an individual (faculty or student) very possibly not trained in data analysis or presentation techniques.

To the maximum extent feasible, feedback of the assessment results should be part of a face-to-face report presented by a representative of the assessment team to the department/program. Such a presentation not only explains the results more clearly and provides an opportunity for the answering of questions but also enhances the professional and collegial image of the assessment team and stimulates greater use of the results within the department/program. The use of faculty employed during the summer to support the assessment effort in feedback seminars in their college/school should be given serious consideration.

Without much doubt, the most appropriate time to present assessment feedback results is as the institution begins its next academic year. At that time all of the faculty will be present, and the tradition of starting anew will facilitate review of past accomplishments, revision of statements of departmental/program intentions, or adjustment of operational activities to better accomplish current intentions.

Unfortunately, taking advantage of the beginning of the academic year as the period for assessment feedback across the institution means that a great deal of information must be conveyed in a short period. For this task to be accomplished, sets of feedback presentation data must be prepared before the beginning of the academic year, and for several weeks those involved with presenting departmental/program assessment seminars must conduct several such seminars each day. Regardless of the effort involved, there is no more crucial portion of the assessment process than successful feedback of the results.

Expectations for Initial Implementation

What is reasonable to expect from the institution's initial operational implementation of institutional effectiveness, and particularly its assessment plan, in this third year? Anything less than chaos should be considered a substantial success. It must be borne in mind that what should be taking place is perhaps the most pervasive and comprehensive change in the institution's means of doing business in many years and that this initial implementation is simply going to be a bit bumpy.

On many campuses incomplete implementation may be the rule rather than the exception. However, during this initial implementation, evidence of a good-faith effort to implement the assessment plan is as important, if not more so, than the comprehensiveness or precision of this initial implementation, which should be viewed as a pilot test of the assessment and feedback procedures designed.

As the third year of implementation of institutional effectiveness (and the first year of operational implementation) draws to a close, the institution should accentuate the positive through press releases concerning the most successful aspects of the "Trial Assessment Procedures Implementation." It should also emphasize concrete examples of the benefits that the campus and students can expect to gain through "Initiation of the Annual Institutional Assessment Cycle" during the fourth year of implementation. In addition, the institution should treat generously those who have contributed most to successful implementation as an incentive to others to act in a similar manner as the annual cycle is implemented in the following year.

CHAPTER SIX

Establishment of the Annual Institutional Effectiveness Cycle

The work of the three previous years will have resulted in substantive planning/operational and assessment/evaluation accomplishments. Among the planning/operational accomplishments will be "Establishment of an Expanded Statement of Institutional Purpose"; "Identification of Intended Educational, Research, and Public Service Outcomes"; "Establishment of Administrative Objectives"; and "Implementation of Departmental/Program Activities to Accomplish Outcomes/Objectives Identified" (see Figure 4, p. 25). Assessment/evaluation activities during the first three years can best be summarized as the design and initial implementation of a comprehensive program of evaluation and assessment of the extent to which institutional intentions—expressed in the expanded statement of purpose—are being fulfilled through departmental/program actions.

Just as the third year has drawn to a close, feedback from the initial implementation of assessment/evaluation activities will be forwarded to the institutional level as well as to the department/program level. The receipt and consideration of this information initiate the series of events that will be repeated each year and that become the basis for practical implementation of the Institutional Effectiveness Paradigm shown in Figure 2 and further illustrated in Figure 13 as the **Annual Institutional Effectiveness Cycle (AIEC)**.

The establishment of the Annual Institutional Effectiveness Cycle is paramount on the campus. Institutions tend to operate on an annual cycle of events conditioned by the academic year and the annual budgetary process. If implementation of institutional effectiveness is

Figure 13

Final Year of a Four-Year Plan for Implementation of Institutional Effectiveness and Assessment Activities on a Campus

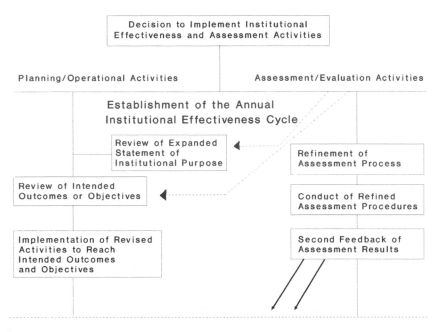

REPEAT FOURTH-YEAR ACTIVITIES--CONDUCT COMPREHENSIVE
INSTITUTIONAL AND PROCESS EVALUATION IN EIGHTH YEAR

to become part of the institution's normal or routine method of doing business, then it must become a part of the yearly sequence of events expected at the institution.

Initiation of the Annual Institutional Effectiveness Cycle must be based upon the accomplisments (planning/operational and assessment/evaluation) made during the first 3 years of implementation. The AIEC turns what probably had been on some campuses episodic and discontinuous efforts toward assessment for instructional improvement into an ongoing program of institutional improvement. It is simply unreasonable to expect that an institution can divert sufficient resources (time of current employees and additional out-of-pocket expenditures) in a single year to accomplish effectively all of the necessary tasks among the planning/operational and assessment/

evaluation activities described earlier. Even if sufficient resources were provided, the campuswide political ramifications of such an effort could easily preclude its success. In order to consider institutional effectiveness annually and to integrate it into the routine of campus operations, these accomplishments must be firmly established so that they can be *reviewed, adjusted,* and *evaluated* as part of the Annual Institutional Effectiveness Cycle.

On many campuses, excellent programs of instructional assessment and evaluation have flourished. Unfortunately, very few of these programs have been comprehensive or long-lived. There are many explanations for the limited scope and relatively short life of many of these programs. Too often the most common explanations relate to the establishment of such programs in response to the interests of an individual, who may subsequently change positions, or the requirements of a professional or regional accreditating body, whose periodic program reviews, once completed, often are quickly forgotten. Establishment of the Annual Institutional Effectiveness Cycle replaces transient personnel and external motivation with the systematic review, adjustment, and evaluation of institutional operations as part of the ongoing institutional process.

As the institution approaches implementation of the Annual Institutional Effectiveness Cycle in the fourth year of implementation activities, a certain amount of remotivation must take place. Although the institution's reward systems should have demonstrated not only the need for but also the wisdom in departmental program implementation during the first 3 years, a summary type of document regarding current status (accomplishments during the past 3 years) and components of the Annual Institutional Effectiveness Cycle to be undertaken in each of the coming years should be prepared and widely distributed. The role of the CEO in solid support of institutional effectiveness implementation should be visible to all as he or she leads the review of the Expanded Statement of Institutional Purpose, directs resource allocation in support of institutional goals, and administers his or her office's objectives. The components of the Annual Institutional Effectiveness Cycle are as shown in Figure 13 and described in the following paragraphs.

Planning/Operational Activities and the Annual Institutional Effectiveness Cycle

The primary planning/operational activities conducted each year as part of the Annual Institutional Effectiveness Cycle relate to the review and, if needed, revision of institutional and departmental statements of intentions. At both levels, these actions are initiated at the earliest part of the annual cycle (July through August) by receipt of assessment results from the previous year's cycle.

At the institutional level, activity is centered around review and revision of the Expanded Statement of Institutional Purpose. Based upon analysis of the results of the previous year's assessment (as generalized and focused at the institutional level), a decision should be reached annually regarding the general feasibility of the current Expanded Statement of Institutional Purpose and its goals statements in particular. Should analysis of the assessment results emanating from the previous year indicate substantially less accomplishment than intended, then a value judgment must be made concerning either adjustment downward of institutional expectations or renewal of efforts to accomplish potentially unrealistic institutional aspirations. Although the decision to renew efforts may be more politically palatable and defensible over the short run, the institution's intentions eventually should be aligned with its accomplishments as revealed through assessment results reported annually.

Review of the Expanded Statement of Institutional Purpose should be conducted relatively quickly and with input from external data sources. Each year, the review should be conducted within the first several weeks of the AIEC by a relatively small representative group headed by the institution's CEO. There is no reason to replicate the effort that went into establishing the Expanded Statement of Institutional Purpose. Rather, the focus should be upon review and adjustment of the statement based upon assessment results and, at those institutions practicing strategic planning, information concerning environmental fit, or the relationship of the institution to its external environment.

The result of review and adjustment of the Expanded Statement of Institutional Purpose will be the establishment of such a statement validated for the then current Annual Institutional Effectiveness Cycle. This statement should be distributed widely on the campus within the first several weeks of the cycle as the basis for further activities.

At the departmental/program level, the Annual Institutional Effectiveness Cycle is initiated based upon receipt of the previous year's assessment results and the current cycle's Expanded Statement of Institutional Purpose. Each department/program is initially called upon to compare the results of the previous year's assessment with the intended outcomes or objectives for that period. Undoubtedly, assessment results will reveal outcomes or objectives that are being overrealized as well as ones that are not being completely achieved or for which the results are inconclusive.

In the case of overrealization, departments/programs will probably adjust their statements of intended outcomes or objectives upward to match their accomplishments. In the case of those intended outcomes or objectives whose assessment indicates that they are not being met, departments/programs should determine whether to lower their expectations or revise their procedures or activities designed to accomplish their intentions. It is vitally important—particularly in the institution's academic departments—that consideration of the previous year's assessment results and the adjustment of departmental statements of intentions (as just described) be undertaken by the department/program as a whole, with emphasis upon input from all faculty or staff involved and their ultimate identification with the decision reached.

An important part of this departmental/program consideration of the previous year's assessment results is the evaluation of those results themselves. Particularly in those cases in which assessment results appear incomplete or contradictory regarding an intended outcome or objective, departments should review carefully the adequacy, validity, and completeness of the assessment results provided. The results of this review should be reported to those individuals responsible for conducting the institution's assessment/evaluation activities so that the problems identified can be corrected in the following AIEC.

In addition to reviewing the results of assessment related to its departmental/program intentions, each unit should carefully review the then current Expanded Statement of Institutional Purpose and compare it with the previous year's purpose statement. Such a review may provide the basis and impetus for revision of departmental/program statements of intentions, which must remain linked to the current institutional statement of intentions.

The results of departmental/program review and any revisions will be a current set of intended outcomes or objectives for this Annual Institutional Effectiveness Cycle. This set of departmental/program statements should be finalized by the beginning of the fall semester each year. As future iterations of the AIEC take place, progressively fewer adjustments to such statements should be expected.

The balance of the planning/operational activities (roughly September through July) will focus upon departmental/program activities designed to accomplish the refined departmental/program statements of intended outcomes or objectives. Departments should bear in mind that it may take several iterations of the Annual Institutional Effectiveness Cycle for changes in departmental policies, actions, curricula, and so forth to be reflected fully in assessment results.

In summary, planning/operational activities during the Annual Institutional Effectiveness Cycle are loaded into the first several months of each cycle with review of assessment results and revision, if needed, of institutional and departmental/program statements of intention. The balance of the year is devoted to normal institutional and departmental operations aimed toward accomplishment of the statement of purpose and of intended outcomes/objectives.

Assessment/Evaluation Activities in the Annual Institutional Effectiveness Cycle

Each year the assessment/evaluation activities associated with the Annual Institutional Effectiveness Cycle will be comprised of three actions: (a) review of the previous year's assessment activities and "Refinement of Assessment Process," (b) "Conduct of Refined Assessment Procedures," and (c) the "Feedback of Assessment Results" to the departmental/program and institutional levels as the basis for the next year's cycle (see Figure 13).

Although the bulk of actual assessment/evaluation work each year will take place in the last 4 to 5 months of the annual cycle, a critical review of the previous year's assessment/evaluation activities and refinement of such procedures should take place within the first several months of each year's cycle. Information concerning the previous year's assessment/evaluation activities will come from the departments/programs being serviced and from those individuals coordinating the assessment/evaluation program. As part of the feedback mechanism, departments/programs should be submitting reports concerning both gaps in assessment/evaluation coverage of their statements of intentions and seemingly contradictory results that require further technical review. Additionally, those charged with coordinating and conducting the assessment/evaluation activities will, doubtlessly, have a list of problems encountered during the previous year which they do not wish to repeat. Typically, this problem list will be fairly extensive in the initial AIEC iterations but will be shortened with successive refinements of the procedures.

In addition to a review of recent assessment/evaluation efforts, assessment procedures will need to be updated in light of both campus and external changes. On campus, those charged with coordination of assessment/evaluation activities will need to ensure that changes to departmental/program statements of intentions are incorporated into the assessment plan and that adequate coverage is provided. Additionally, changes in and additions to assessment/evaluation technology (standardized testing instruments, licensure examinations, survey instruments and techniques, etc.) should be considered for incorporation into the institution's refined assessment/evaluation procedures.

The results of the review and updating of institutional assessment/ evaluation procedures should be a refined assessment/evaluation plan for implementation during the second half of the Annual Institutional Effectiveness Cycle. During early iterations of the cycle, implementation of the assessment/evaluation plan can be expected to focus upon smoothing implementation mechanics, filling gaps in coverage of assessment/evaluation procedures, and increasing the efficiency of the process.

With any operation as large and complex as the process of implementing assessment/evaluation activities on a campus there are bound to be a substantial number of "bumps," "stumbles," and apparent failures in initial implementation. There will be simply too many unforeseen and uncontrollable variables for which to plan initially. Once the process has been implemented on a trial basis, these problems will surface and will take several iterations to reduce to a manageable level—although a comprehensive institutional assessment/evaluation inevitably involves a degree of discomfort

Likewise, initial implementation of the assessment/evaluation plan can be expected to leave considerable gaps in coverage of departmental/program intentions. These gaps will exist for numerous reasons, and over the years most will be filled by one or more assessment/ evaluation techniques.

Once active implementation begins, one of the greatest possible improvements in assessment/evaluation techniques may occur: increased efficiency in conducting the process. A considerable portion of the initial year's implementation time will result from the inherent inefficiency in starting most processes. As the years progress, expenditures for assessment/evaluation should remain relatively constant; however, efficiency gained in implementation should be expected to offset (partially or completely) cost escalations and expansion of the process to fill gaps. The final assessment/evaluation activity conducted each year as a portion of the Annual Institutional Effectiveness

Figure 14

Annual Institutional Effectiveness Cycle Applied to an Academic Year Sequence (Early Semester)

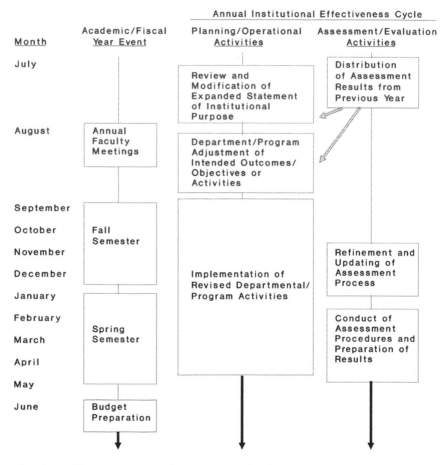

Cycle is the provision of assessment/evaluation results—otherwise known as feedback—which acts as the stimulus for the next year's cycle. Although this activity will transpire in the last several weeks of the cycle, review of reactions by the departments/programs to the feedback techniques used in the previous year should be gathered early in the cycle with departmental/program reactions to the assessment/evaluation results.

Two important improvements in early feedback procedures should be possible in succeeding years. First, by accumulation of results over several years, the limited number, or N, of results concerning certain programs should be mitigated and greater confidence established in the combined results of several years. Second, refinements in techniques should lead to increased utilization of graphic and narrative forms of feedback and the gradual deemphasizing of tabular data presentation.

Implementing Institutional Effectiveness at Two-Year Colleges

While the four-year plan for implementation described in Figure 4 is adaptable to various types of institutions, it is important to note that institutional circumstances and characteristics markedly affect implementation processes. Such impacts on the implementation of institutional effectiveness and outcomes assessment in two-year colleges are described in the resource section beginning on page 228.

Summary

Shown as Figure 14 is a month-by-month representation of the Annual Institutional Effectiveness Cycle which might be typical of those institutions operating on an "early semester" calendar and a June 30 to July 1 fiscal year. This timing would necessarily need to be modified at those institutions with significantly different academic and fiscal cycles.

The establishment of the Annual Institutional Effectiveness Cycle and the continuing program of institutional study/assessment/evaluation which it represents is the final process-oriented result of the implementation process. However, the final actual result is an institution taking purposeful actions toward its intended ends, assessing/evaluating its results to date, and adjusting its future actions to be more successful.

Implementing Institutional Effectiveness at Two-Year Colleges

Harriott Calhoun

The term *two-year college* is applied to colleges that differ among themselves as much as they differ from other segments of higher education. The category includes technical colleges, technical community colleges, comprehensive community colleges, junior colleges, two-year campuses of university systems, and other colleges that, regardless of their names, fulfill some combination of the functions that are generally associated with two-year community colleges.

Although the institutional effectiveness paradigm and the implementation plan presented in this *Handbook* are applicable for all types and sizes of institutions, there are some factors of particular concern to two-year institutions in demonstrating institutional effectiveness. First, many two-year colleges (particularly comprehensive community colleges) have broad and diverse missions that include the traditional freshman- and sophomore-level college coursework, career/ vocational programs, job training/retraining, developmental education, continuing education programs, and a variety of individual and community enrichment activities.

A second factor is a student population that is increasingly diverse in terms of age, race, socioeconomic background, academic preparation, and purpose for enrollment. Additionally, two-year college students tend to use the curricula and services of the college for pursuing their educational objectives in their own time frames. They are most often commuters who attend part-time, for a variety of purposes, for one term or over a very extended period of time. Palmer (1990, p. 23) has described two-year college students as having "ad hoc attendance and course-taking patterns that often do not follow established curricular paths."

These factors and others provide unique problems both in defining appropriate indicators of institutional effectiveness and in collecting appropriate data for assessing effectiveness. The institutional effectiveness assessment model adopted by two-year institutions must address this diversity in institutional purpose, student population, and student purpose for enrollment.

Expanded Statement of Institutional Purpose

Since the purposes of two-year colleges are often misconstrued by the public and by other segments of postsecondary education, it is critical for each college to articulate clearly what kind of institution it is and what it is trying to accomplish. A carefully worded statement of purpose is essential, both for communication with those outside the institution and as a practical first step in assessing institutional effectiveness.

The "Expanded Statement of Institutional Purpose for Your Community College," provided in Appendix B, is not intended as an expression of what all two-year colleges should be, but rather illustrates an effectively worded statement of purpose for one hypothetical community college. Some elements of the purpose for Your Community College may be inappropriate for a technical college or a traditional junior college. Also, a particular college may give more weight or attention to some functions than others, depending on the needs of its constituents and the programs provided within the service area by other agencies and institutions. Whatever the particular functions of the institution, detailed design at the departmental level must clearly relate institutional effectiveness measures to the college's Expanded Statement of Institutional Purpose.

Detailed Design at the Departmental Level/Identification of Intended Student Outcomes and Administrative Objectives

As on any campus, winning the commitment and support of faculty and administrative personnel at the department/unit level is one of the most difficult tasks in implementing institutional effectiveness. At two-year colleges, developing outcomes or objectives and the strategies for assessing their achievement involves additional tasks for people who have heavy work loads and may feel considerable skepticism about the benefits of such a substantial undertaking. The president and chief academic officer must demonstrate their commitment by providing resources and released time to the extent that institutional constraints permit. To ensure a process that will ultimately strengthen the institution, commitment by the leadership must be as strong a motivator as are external requirements from an accredting agency, a governing board, or a coordinating board.

The following general suggestions are offered:

1. Focus on the total institution so that all functions are addressed (credit instruction, continuing education, training for business and industry, support services, etc.).
2. Add minimally to the already heavy work load by stressing those things that are essential and that will facilitate decisions that the institution is prepared to make.
3. Be sensitive to the implications of assessment. Insensitivity in the reporting of some measures can be harmful to minority and non-traditional students who are already underrepresented in higher education. Internally, results of assessment should be seen as formative, not punitive.
4. Allow for flexibility, because "responsiveness" is part of the distinctiveness of the two-year colleges.
5. Identify responsibility at the department/unit level and coordinate centrally at the institutional level to ensure that attention to institutional effectiveness efforts is not lost in the pressure to carry out the process functions of the institution.
6. Involve the total campus community in the process. Faculty, administrators, professional staff, and students must experience involvement if the results are to be meaningful.
7. Tie the budgeting process to the entire institutional effectiveness process. There is a strong incentive to participate in planning activities when college personnel can see that goals and objectives established at the unit level affect budget decisions.

Each academic and administrative unit of the college should identify appropriate outcomes or objectives, carefully linked to the Expanded Statement of Institutional Purpose, and the means through which their results will be assessed. Some community colleges have expressed instructional outcomes in the form of competencies that students will possess at the completion of a course or an educational program. Specific competencies may be developed for special functions within the curriculum, such as general education or developmental education, as well as for each degree and certificate program.

Provided in Appendix C are examples of the linkage between the Expanded Statement of Institutional Purpose, Program Intended Outcomes/Objectives, and Assessment Criteria and Procedures for a transfer program and an occupational/technical program at Your Community College. In support or service units, intended results may take the form of administrative objectives, but these too should be linked to the Expanded Statement of Institutional Purpose.

Assessment/Evaluation

Since two-year colleges face some special problems in assessing institutional effectiveness because of broad diversity in institutional purpose, in student population, and in student intent/purpose for enrollment, accurate assessment requires multiple and realistic measures that address these issues. Consequently, some definitions and effectiveness measures that are appropriate for four-year colleges may be inappropriate for two-year colleges.

Student tracking presents particular difficulties at two-year colleges because of the large number of students who move rapidly in and out of the institution and the extended period of time usually required by nontraditional students for program completion. Further, students enrolling in one or two courses for personal enrichment, specific job skills, or transfer will require different assessment measures than those who intend to obtain an associate degree. Kreider and Walleri (1900) persuasively make the case that two-year colleges should "seize the agenda" in assessment by utilizing a student-success approach that is tied to student intentions.

As a prerequisite to any tracking efforts, students should be identified as to their educational intent/purpose for enrollment. To ensure data collection on student intent, Prince George's Community College, Maryland, has required two pertinent questions in their computerized registration process (Clagett, 1989). One question asks for the student's immediate educational goal (to obtain a degree, to obtain a certificate, or to take courses only), and the other asks for the student's primary reason for attending the college (prepare for new job/career; update skills for current job/career; prepare for transfer; explore academic or occupational areas; or pursue personal enrichment).

Jefferson State Community College, Alabama, requests purpose for enrollment on the application for admission and affirms/changes the student's purpose as part of the advising process prior to each registration. Students are asked to select one of the following purposes: (1) to obtain an Associate Transfer degree—AA or AS; (2) to obtain an Associate Career degree—AAS; (3) to obtain a certificate; (4) to take a few courses before transfer; (5) to take courses for self-improvement or personal enrichment; (6) to take job-related courses; or (7) no definite purpose in mind.

Because of the centrality of student intent to any assessment of institutional effectiveness, each institution should identify the appropriate question(s) and establish procedures that capture this information at initial enrollment and verify it in subsequent terms of enrollment. Even the graduation rate, which is a rather straightforward calculation at some types of institutions, cannot be calculated appropriately at two-year colleges without knowing which students entered the institution with the intention of obtaining the associate degree.

Assessing Instruction and Instructional Outcomes

Course Performance. Student performance in individual courses is a fundamental learning outcome and is particularly important for colleges where a large portion of students enroll for the purpose of taking only one or a few selected courses. Faculty do the assessing and should individually or collectively determine the criteria. Regular analysis of course grade distribution is useful for determining high-risk courses where special strategies of instruction or tutorial/learning assistance programs are needed.

General Education. Many two-year colleges have designated a core curriculum of general education for every degree or certificate, with the largest number of general education units required for the AA/AS degrees and significantly fewer for the AAS (Associate in Applied Science). Certificate programs may require no more than one course in English composition and one in mathematics. Although the use of a nationally normed, standardized test may seem attractive as a measure of general knowledge at the end of a degree program, relatively few published tests are available, and their appropriateness for two-year-college graduates, particularly those obtaining the AAS, has been questioned.

Two-year colleges may find a criterion-referenced examination more appropriate and useful than a norm-referenced test. An advantage to using a criterion-referenced test is that the performance of completers of any particular program, as measured against the established criteria, can be evaluated in terms of the degree to which the curriculum of that program addresses each of the specified criteria.

Assuming that an appropriate test is identified, the institution must also determine which students should take the test and motivate those students to participate. For those two-year-college students who are simultaneously coping with job, family, and school responsibilities, a lengthy test as a condition for graduation may be a strong disincentive to graduation.

The Institutional Matrix Form of College BASE (a criterion-referenced achievement examination described on pp. 83) is appealing in part because it requires only 40 minutes of testing time. Using a matrix sampling design, the entire test battery (covering English, mathematics, science, and social studies; three cross-disciplinary reasoning skills; and a writing sample) is distributed among the students being tested. If sufficient numbers of students are tested, institutional data may be reported for subgroups that have varying requirements in general education, such as those receiving the AA, AS, and AAS degrees that have varying requirements in general education. One should note that the Institutional Matrix Form of College BASE yields aggregate data appropriate for institutional program review but does not produce individual student scores (*Presenting College BASE*, 1989).

An additional or alternative approach to assessing the outcomes of general education utilizes institutionally developed measures that are incorporated into the exit examinations of required general education courses. Departmentally approved final examinations in specified courses can be assessed once for purposes of assigning student grades and a second time to determine institutional-level results that are useful in program review.

A measure sometimes overlooked is students' self-assessment of the contribution of general education to their development. Johnson County Community College, Kansas, has incorporated this measure into several routine student follow-up surveys (see Seybert, 1990a, 1990b).

Assessment in the Major. Two-year colleges often have certificate or applied degree programs that directly prepare students to take licensure or certification examinations. These examinations are nationally or regionally normed and can serve as an important measure of program effectiveness. The following examples illustrate the type of reports available.

The *National Council Licensure Examination for Registered Nurses*

(NCLEX-RN), published by the National Council of State Boards of Nursing (625 North Michigan Avenue, Suite 1544, Chicago, Illinois 60611) is a criterion-reference test for which results are reported as pass/fail. Summary reports include number of candidates writing the exam for the first time, number repeating the exam, and percentage of each category passing, for the institution and for other member (accredited) programs within the institution's state jurisdiction. An institution may also subscribe to NCLEX Summary Profiles (CTB/ McGraw-Hill, 2500 Garden Road, Monterey, California 93940), which reports examination performance of the institution's graduates in the context of several theoretical/curriculum categories and gives the program's rank (based on examination results) within its jurisdiction and among all member jurisdictions.

The institutional reports from some certification boards provide scaled scores and subtest scores as well as pass/fail rates. The Medical Laboratory Technician Examination is a national certification examination given by the Board of Registry of the American Society of Clinical Pathologists (ASCP, P.O. Box 12270, Chicago, Illinois 60612-0270). The Program Performance Summary, provided by ASCP to each institution whose graduates take the examination, includes five parts: (1) individual student scaled scores; (2) program and national scaled score comparisons; (3) national distribution of examinee scaled scores; (4) national distribution of program scaled scores; and (5) program and national subtest and item p-score comparisons.

The Summary Report to Educational Programs: Certification Examination in Radiologic Technology (American Registry of Radiologic Technologists, 1255 Northland Drive, Mendota Heights, Minnesota 55120) reports the average scaled score for the total test and content sections within the test for each administration of the examination. Both institutional and national data are provided that enable program faculty to compare a given score to the scores obtained by other examinees and to interpret individual and group scores in terms of the degree of mastery of the material. The conference of Funeral Service Examining Boards (15 Third Street N.E., Washington, Indiana 47501) provides the institution with individual student scores for its program graduates and a national mean score for comparison.

In fields where no certification is required, a capstone course or end-of-sequence examination is an appropriate indicator of student learning in the major field. Also, employment related to the major, salary/wages earned, and evaluation of occupational preparation can be obtained in surveys of career program graduates and their employers.

Transfer Data. Academic education for those preparing for transfer to baccalaureate-granting institutions is one of the functions for many, though not all, two-year institutions. Among those for which it is a specified function, assessment of transfer effectiveness poses difficult conceptual and methodological problems. The most common indicators of transfer effectiveness include (1) transferability of courses, which involves course articulation with the receiving institutions; (2) rate of transfer, which is calculated in various ways; (3) student success after transfer, which is often measured by GPA and persistence to graduation; (4) and student satisfaction with preparation for transfer, which is obtained in routine student follow-up surveys.

The "transfer rate" is the measure that has recently drawn the most public attention and is probably the most difficult for institutions to obtain accurately. Entirely different rates are derived, depending on the definitions and algorithms used. Once definitions are established, institutions must have the pertinent data and the ability to access it so that the pool of potential transfer students can be identified, and they must receive complete and comparative data from the institutions to which their students transfer (Bers, Seybert, & Friedel, 1990).

Defining the denominator used in calculating transfer rates is basically a question of identifying those who are expected to transfer. Although some measures of transfer effectiveness presume that all students should/could/might transfer, this presumption is naive and inappropriate when one considers the missions of two-year colleges and the characteristics, behaviors, and purposes for enrollment of their students.

The most restrictive definition would hold that the denominator should be based on the graduates who receive the transfer degree (AA or AS), as these are the students for whom the institution is accountable in preparing them for transfer. In reality, however, these are not the only students who transfer (Calhoun, 1985; Clagett, 1989). Many students transfer without completing their associate degree and should perhaps be included in the pool used to determine the transfer rate. One approach is to include in the denominator all those who express the intent to transfer and achieve at least 12 semester hours of transferable credits.

The numerator in the calculation of transfer rate is most often defined as attendance at a senior institution. Cohen (1990) adds a time factor to his definition by specifying that the transfer student must "take one or more classes at the university within four years" (of initial enrollment at the community college). Given the extended time frame usual for nontraditional students, this would seem to be a low minimum.

Varying definitions and data methods used by receiving institutions and undercounting due to institutions that do not report back to the sending institutions are major problems in establishing the numerator. Routine, statewide cooperative efforts among both public and private institutions are necessary if two-year colleges are to answer even the most basic questions about how many students transfer and how well they perform after transfer.

Program Review

Many two-year colleges assess a broad range of institutional functions under the rubric of program review. These include credit and noncredit instruction, developmental studies, student services, administrative services, and support services. In addition to the usual productivity and quality measures that can be derived from existing institutional data systems, two-year colleges make extensive use of student follow- up surveys, "user" surveys, and advisory committees as important elements in program development and evaluation. For example, some institutions evaluate all courses and customized programs offered for business and industry by surveying both program participants and company managers. An example of a comprehensive educational program review is found in the *Manual for Evaluating Occupational/Technical Programs* (rev. ed., 1990) developed at J. Sargent Reynolds Community College.

Summary

Although two-year colleges address the same basic issues in providing quality educational programs and assessing their effectiveness that are addressed by other segments of higher education, the special mission of these institutions in serving their communities and the diverse and transient nature of their student populations present unique problems. Two-year colleges have historically emphasized the teaching function, and they have taken the lead for the last three decades in educating nontraditional students. As Losak (1986) has said of community college students, "Stopping out of college is more prevalent, part-time enrollment is increasing, and most students have objectives that are not synonymous with earning a baccalaureate degree within four years."

Because two-year institutions are often misunderstood by the general public and by other segments of higher education, these colleges must be assertive in developing appropriate measures for assessing effectiveness. The nature of these institutions and the educational goals of their students require quite different definitions of success than those appropriate for other colleges and universities.

Resources are always limited. At two-year colleges, faculty have heavy teaching loads, administrators carry out multiple job functions, and support staff is at a minimum. A meaningful program of assessment of institutional effectiveness must make effective use of time and personnel, which are basic resources. The following suggestions are offered.

1. Use existing data as much as possible.
2. Incorporate assessment procedures into routine operations of the functional units.
3. Coordinate surveying efforts.
4. Use a cycle of assessment so that everything is assessed within a 3- to 5-year period.
5. Develop definitions (for transfer rate, graduation rate, student success, etc.) that are appropriate to the mission of the college.
6. Collect only information that will be used.
7. Establish baseline information and set targets so that expectations of results are realistic.

Assessment is not new to two-year colleges. Not only assessment for placement but also advisory committees and student follow-up studies for program development and evaluation have been employed for decades. Once institutions recognize and utilize the assessment measures that are already in place, many may find that only a few additional measures are needed. Institutions that assess themselves with appropriate and realistic measures not only have information vital for improvement but also the means with which to demonstrate institutional effectiveness to others.

Note: Appreciation is extended to the following members of the Association for Institutional Research who sent material and assisted in identifying the special issues involved in institutional assessment at two-year colleges: Bob Alexander, North Hennepin Community College (C.C.), MN; D. L. Anderson, Mississippi Gulf Coast C.C., MS; Felix Acquino, Dallas County C.C.

District, TX; Richard Bailey, San Jacinto College District, TX; Trudy Bers, Oakton C.C., IL; Kathleen Bigby, Centre for Curriculum & Professional Development, British Columbia Council of College and Institute Principals, Vancouver, BC; Randy Braswell, Gordan College, GA; Craig Clagett, Prince George's C.C., MD; Thomas Hawk, C.C. of Philadelphia, PA; Lucy Hinson, Greenville Tech. College, SC; Laurel M. Kilbeck, Cuyahoga C.C., OH; Arthur Kramer, Passaic County C.C., NJ; Mark Oromaner, Hudson County C.C., NJ; John Quinley, Central Piedmont C.C., NC; K. Rajasekhara, Dundalk C.C., MD; Estelle Resnik, Cumberland County College, NJ; Jeffrey Seybert, Johnson County C.C., KS; Jeffrey Stuckman, Florida C.C. at Jacksonville, FL; Janice Van Dyke, State Tech. Institute at Memphis, TN; Dan Walleri, Mt. Hood C.C., OR; and Faith Willis, Brunswick College, GA. Appreciation is also extended to James W. Firnberg, President Emeritus of LSU Alexandria, LA, and to Cathryn A. McDonald, Tammie Brown, and Ellen F. Peak, my colleagues at Jefferson State, AL, who offered suggestions on this section.

References: Cited and Recommended

Bers, T. H., Seybert, J. A., & Friedel, J. (1990). *Measuring the effectiveness of the transfer function.* Paper presented at the Institute for Institutional Effectiveness and Student Success in the Community College, Toronto.

Calhoun, H. D. (1985). The transfer process. Office of Institutional Research Report, Jefferson State Community College, Birmingham, AL.

Clagett, C. A. (1989). Student goal analysis for accountability and marketing. *Community College Review, 16*(4), 38–41.

Cohen, A. M. (1990). Counting the transfers: Pick a number. *The Community, Technical, and Junior College Times, 2*(9), 2, 8.

Kreider, P. E., & Walleri, R. D. (1988). Seizing the agenda: Institutional effectiveness and student outcomes for community colleges. *Community College Review, 16*(2), 44–50.

Losak, J. (1986). What constitutes student success in the community college? *Community College Journal for Research and Planning, 5*(2).

Manual for Evaluating Occupational/Technical Programs. (1990). Richmond, VA: J. Sargent Reynolds Community College.

Palmer, J. (1990, June/July). Is vocationalism to blame? *Community, Technical, and Junior College Journal, 60*(6), 21–23, 25.

Presenting College BASE. (1989). Chicago, IL: Riverside.

Seybert, J. A. (1990a). A transfer study. Overland Park, KS: Office of Institutional Research, Johnson County Community College.

Seybert, J. A. (1990b). Assessment of institutional effectiveness at Johnson County Community College. Overland Park, KS: Office of Institutional Research, Johnson County Community College.

Walleri, R. D. (1990). Tracking and follow-up for community college students: Institutional and statewide initiatives. *Community/Junior College Quarterly of Research and Practice, 14*(1), 21–34.

CHAPTER SEVEN

Maintaining Institutional Effectiveness Operations Over an Extended Period of Time

The initial work to implement institutional effectiveness on a campus may have appeared to be an almost "insurmountable opportunity," as Pogo might say, but the maintenance of institutional effectiveness operations over an extended period of time represents an even greater challenge. Assuming that an institution has put into place the Annual Institutional Effectiveness Cycle described in the previous chapter and that it wishes to continue such operations, there are further developmental phases that can be expected and forces that will affect successful continuation.

During the fourth through approximately the seventh years of implementation, the campus should repeat the Annual Institutional Effectiveness Cycle. In addition to the smoothing-out process inherent in the cycle, several other adjustments should take place during this period.

First, and most important, each year minor adjustments should be made in the Expanded Statement of Institutional Purpose in reaction to the generalized assessment findings of the previous cycle and changes in the institution's external environment. Additionally, relatively substantial changes should take place in departmental/program statements of intentions during the first several years of cycle implementation as a result of the detailed assessment/evaluation results provided. If either institutional or departmental/program statements of intention remain static from year to year, institutional effectiveness is not being taken seriously and will ultimately be discontinued at the institution as a pointless exercise.

During the fourth through the seventh years of implementation, a task almost as important as institutional adjustments of statements of intentions is the gradual expansion of the assessment plan to address service gaps in initial coverage and utilize assessment/evaluation methods developed to date. Without doubt, gaps in coverage and inconsistent results will emerge from the assessment/evaluation activities undertaken during the first several years of implementation of the Annual Institutional Effectiveness Cycle. As problems are resolved, major adjustments in and expansion of assessment/evaluation activities as well as implementation of newly developed means of assessment should occur each year.

Finally, during the period of Annual Institutional Effectiveness Cycle implementation in years 4 through 7 of implementation, substantive improvement can be expected in feedback procedures and in the extent to which departments/programs understand the results. Part of this improvement in communication and understanding of the results can be attributed to both increasing familiarity with the assessment/evaluation results provided to departments/programs each year and the improvement in feedback mechanisms.

Comprehensive Review of Institutional Effectiveness Operations

The basic philosophy behind institutional effectiveness is that of stating an institution's intentions, conducting activities, and assessing/evaluating the extent to which the institution's intentions have been accomplished. This same philosophy must also guide institutional effectiveness operations themselves. In approximately the eighth year of implementation (after four complete repetitions of the AIEC) a thorough assessment of institutional effectiveness operations should take place.

Such a comprehensive assessment should probably have both procedural and substantive components. Each of the components (activities) during the Annual Institutional Effectiveness Cycle should be reviewed regarding its internal merits and the manner in which that element is functioning as a portion of the annual cycle. From the substantive perspective, the institution should conduct a thorough review and updating of its Expanded Statement of Institutional Purpose as well as its departmental/programmatic statements of intended outcomes/administrative objectives. Although adjustments and refinements to these statements should be expected annually, these actions cannot take the place of a periodically conducted thoughtful and extended reconsideration of the institution's and departments'/ programs' basic purposes or intentions.

The comprehensive review of institutional effectiveness operations envisioned should take the better portion of a year. Hence, it is suggested that the Annual Institutional Effectiveness Cycle be discontinued during the year in which the comprehensive review takes place and resumed the following year, using the changes suggested from the review.

Forces Impeding Continuation of Institutional Effectiveness Operations

A number of natural and understandable forces that impede long-term continuation of institutional effectiveness operations on a campus can be expected to come into play. These same forces tend to thwart long-term continuation of all except absolutely essential (registration, budgeting, etc.) activities.

The first of these forces is what can be characterized as institutional exhaustion or loss of interest. Frankly, institutional effectiveness operations are not absolutely essential to maintaining an institution (registering students, holding classes, conducting research, etc.)—only to leading an institution toward accomplishment of its stated intentions. After the period of additional effort required to implement the Annual Institutional Effectiveness Cycle, many individuals will tend to consider the matter accomplished and want to return to maintaining the institution in the manner in which it had been functioning earlier.

Naturally complementing this tendency toward regression to previous methods of operations may well be the departure from the institution of those individuals most responsible for institutional effectiveness implementation. Normal personnel turbulence during the period of time between initial implementation and comprehensive review of the process will result in the loss of a number of personnel instrumental in institutional effectiveness implementation and personally identified with such operations. There is also some likelihood that a disproportionately heavy share of turnover among faculty and key staff will be among those most responsible for institutional effectiveness implementation as their progressive ideas and actions are recognized and they are selected for positions of greater responsibility. Such action may leave those less supportive of institutional effectiveness to greet the replacements. It should be observed that these replacements will probably not be personally identified with institutional effectiveness to the extent that their predecessors were and that these replacements may well be less enthusiastic about continuation of institutional effectiveness operations as they seek to make their own mark on the institution.

Both institutional exhaustion and personnel turnover can be described as passive impediments to continued institutional effectiveness operations. Some members of the campus community, however, may actively resist continuation. This active resistance is likely to arise from individuals who are philosophically opposed to institutional effectiveness or whose personal interests are not best met by the process. Even following successful implementation of the Annual Institutional Effectiveness Cycle, some members of the campus community will remain unalterably opposed philosophically to institutional effectiveness because they do not believe the results of the educational process are assessable. On the other (more pragmatic) hand, some individuals will continue to see their own personal ends as better served through a less objective (and frequently more political) decision-making process. These people will oppose continuation on grounds more publicly acceptable than vested self-interest, but with a single aim in mind. Active opposition to continuation of institutional effectiveness operations can be expected to increase from both of these groups as the proponents of institutional effectiveness depart, their less committed replacements arrive, and institutional commitment becomes less apparent.

Marshaling Forces to Encourage Continuation of Institutional Effectiveness Operations

Without the long-term existence on a campus of a "true believer" in institutional effectiveness or a senior member of the administrative staff closely identified with the concept, there is an excellent chance that institutional effectiveness operations will gradually diminish. There must be an individual to champion the cause of continuation, and that person must have the active and visible support of the CEO. If such a person exists and is supported by the CEO, he or she can call into play a number of forces that will facilitate continuation of institutional effectiveness operations.

From a philosophical standpoint, proponents of institutional effectiveness can argue the intrinsic value of the process and support this assertion with examples of institutional and departmental/program improvements that have been brought about through institutional effectiveness. This is potentially one of the strongest inducements toward continued support by a substantial segment of the campus community, but this argument will have little impact on those actively opposed to continuation.

Another strong motivation toward continued implementation of institutional effectiveness operations may be external pressure in the form of regional and professional accreditation requirements. With implementation of the current national movement toward increased emphasis on assessment of student learning outcomes as part of accreditation requirements, institutions will be required to document their activities in institutional effectiveness and outcomes assessment by an increasing number of accrediting bodies. Such activities are obviously not easily initiated in a short period of time, and institutions desiring to have their various professional and specific regional accreditations reaffirmed will find it far easier to continue their existing institutional effectiveness operations than to reinitiate such operations in response to the demands of various external accrediting bodies.

For public institutions, external pressure from accrediting agencies may not be the only form of pressure being exerted from beyond the campus. As stated earlier, the vast majority of central governing boards and state legislatures are currently requiring information regarding institutional practices concerning outcomes assessment or institutional effectiveness. Thus, pressure from the agencies that provide funding to public institutions can be a significant factor in the continuation of institutional effectiveness operations.

Both the intrinsic value of institutional effectiveness and potential external pressure should serve to foster continuation of institutional effectiveness operations, but the best motivation to that end is the incorporation of these operations into the recurring annual series of events at the institution. Just as naturally as fall semester registration is expected to take place in the last week of August, review of the Expanded Statement of Institutional Purpose and departmental/program statements of intentions should be anticipated during the first 3 weeks in August. Just as operational budgets are expected to become effective July 1 each year, assessment findings or results should arrive in the institution's departments during the last week in July. Before students take part in graduation exercises each spring, they are expected to have completed cognitive or performance testing in their major and to have returned their graduating student questionnaire. Institutional effectiveness operations should become the norm or expectation, and breaking that momentum should become just as difficult as was breaking the inertia of institutional resistance when such operations were initiated.

Despite significant forces operating to impede long-term continuation of institutional effectiveness operations, sufficient incentives, motivation, and means exist to support successful long-term institutional effectiveness practices for the welfare of the institution and those whom it would serve.

Our University Expanded Statement of Institutional Purpose

OUR UNIVERSITY STATEMENT
OF INSTITUTIONAL MISSION

Our University is an independent, nonsectarian, coeducational institution, in the tradition of the liberal arts and sciences. Seeking to be faithful to the ideals of its heritage, Our University is committed, in all of its policies and practices, to the unrestricted and rigorous pursuit of truth, to the centrality of values in human life, and to a respect for differing points of view.

Our mission is to provide an outstanding education for a relatively small number of talented and highly motivated students from a diversity of geographic, ethnic, and socioeconomic backgrounds. To achieve this end, we recruit and retain outstanding faculty members who are dedicated to the art of teaching and advising; to the search for and dissemination of truth through scholarship, research, and creative endeavor; and to service to the university and the larger community. We also seek to provide a supportive and challenging environment in which students can realize the full potential of their abilities and come to understand their responsibility of service in the human community.

The principal focus of Our University's curricular programs is undergraduate education in the liberal arts and sciences, combined with a number of directly career-related and preprofessional fields. Relations between the liberal arts and the career related and preprofessional fields are carefully nurtured to provide mutually reinforcing intellectual experiences for students and faculty. Our University also offers master's and doctoral degree programs in selected professional areas that will prepare individuals for positions of leadership in their chosen careers. In addition, recognizing its responsibility to the larger community, Our University provides a variety of carefully selected programs of continuing education and cultural enrichment. Finally, Our University recognizes its responsibility in maintaining a position of excellence and leadership in research.

In its recruitment and retention of members of the University community, Our University, consistent with its academic and institutional heritage, maintains an openness to all qualified persons.

OUR UNIVERSITY STATEMENT OF
INSTITUTIONAL GOALS

I. INTRODUCTION

The "Statement of Institutional Mission" on the preceding page expresses a vision of what our institution intends to be and do. The purpose of the present document is to set forth specific goals for each major area of the university for the next 5 years, with the conviction that the achievement of these goals will lead to the fulfillment of Our University's stated mission.

It must be recognized that such achievement is contingent upon a number of circumstances, including the availability of adequate financial and other resources. Indeed, decisions regarding essentially academic matters must sometimes be based, at least in part, on factors that are themselves not specifically academic in nature. What immediately follows in this introduction, therefore, is a summary of certain economic assumptions (i.e., matters over which the university has little or no control), planning parameters, and implications that are presupposed in the following sections of the document.

A. *Economic Assumptions*
  1. Inflation will remain approximately at 4% to 5% over the next 5 years.
  2. Financial support to private institutions and students by state and federal agencies will tend to be reduced in the next 5 years.
  3. The annual income from the current unrestricted endowment sources will remain relatively fixed over the next 5 years.

B. *Planning Parameters*
  1. The student–faculty ratio (FTE students to FTE faculty) will stabilize at 13 to 1 by 1994–95.
  2. The Education and General (E & G) Budget (the basic operating budget) will increase between 7% and 8% each year in the next 5 years and will reach approximately $50 million in the 1994–95 academic year.
  3. Annual giving will increase moderately between now and 1995.
  4. Adequate fiscal reserves should be created or enlarged to

allow for the timely renovation of campus buildings and other facilities.

   5. Annual tuition rate increases will be approximately 7% in each of the next 5 years.

C. *Implications*

   1. By the 1994–95 academic year, the total number of under-graduate students will stabilize at approximately 4,000.
   2. The number of entering freshmen will increase by approximately 30 per year and will reach a class size of approximately 1,200 by the 1994–95 academic year.
   3. Efforts will be made to increase the number of applications for admission each year so that we obtain 3,200 applications from highly qualified students by 1994–95.
   4. The proportion of the undergraduate students who attend on a full-time basis will increase by approximately 1% per year for the next 5 years.
   5. The attrition rate will be reduced by .5% per year for each of the next 5 years.
   6. The increasing number of undergraduate students will create the need for a new residence hall in the 1992–93 academic year.
   7. To accommodate more undergraduate students, funds should be dedicated to development of more playing/athletic fields.
   8. To accommodate the needs of our changing student body, we will need to renovate/add to the University Center.

II. ACADEMIC AFFAIRS

The goal of Our University is to be one of the leading independent liberal arts and sciences universities in the nation, as measured by the quality of its faculty, the strength of its curriculum and academic programs, the effectiveness of its support services, the excellence of its graduates, and the accomplishment of its intended outcomes. Significant steps already have been taken toward achievement of this goal through continued offering of both liberal arts programs designed to impart a depth of understanding in the major field and preprofessional programs preparing the graduate for employment upon graduation. Although the following goals do not represent the totality of intellectual and administrative activity within academic affairs, they do represent focal points for action in the near future.

A. *Curriculum and Academic Programs*

Our University is committed to offering all students a distinctive and challenging academic foundation in liberal studies in order to enhance their communication and analytic skills; to provide an understanding of their intellectual and cultural heritage; and to assist them in the development of self-awareness, responsible leadership, and the capacity to make reasoned moral judgments. Our University will continue to offer the range of disciplines basic to a liberal education and will maintain a balance in the undergraduate curriculum among the humanities, fine arts, behavioral sciences, natural sciences, and selected preprofessional programs. The following goals are of high priority:

1. Study the university's general education program to determine whether revisions are desirable.
2. Initiate more varied forms of instruction for entering students, such as freshman seminars.
3. Establish a process to identify systematically those academic programs that should be targeted for qualitative enhancement and/or numerical growth. The principal criteria to be employed in making these judgments should be centrality to our mission, quality of the existing program, demand, cost-effectiveness, and comparative advantage in offering the program.
4. Encourage new academic program initiatives, particularly of an interdisciplinary nature, that reflect emerging intellectual perspectives and that are appropriate to the mission of Our University.
5. Encourage the development of new minors and areas of concentration that complement existing degree programs and are responsive to student interests and societal needs.
6. Be responsive to the continuing education needs of local business and industry in areas in which Our University is academically strong.

B. *Graduate and Research Programs*

Although the primary academic thrust of Our University will continue to be its undergraduate program of instruction, graduate education and research will play an increasing role in support of the institution and its attraction and retention of outstanding students and faculty. Within this secondary academic role, Our University will seek during the next 5 years to

1. Develop a limited number of additional graduate-level programs in areas in which the institution maintains a strong undergraduate program, sufficient student demand is evi-

denced, and local or regional demand for graduates is identified.

2. Review current graduate programs to determine the academic and economic feasibility of their continuation.
3. Increase the level of organized or sponsored research expenditures by 5% per year for the next 5 years.
4. Focus the development of proposals for externally funded or organized research on subjects directly related to local/regional industries or those subjects of particular interest to foundations with which Our University has enjoyed a continuing relationship.

C. *Continuing Education/Public Service*

While maintaining primary commitments to teaching and research, Our University is also committed to helping to meet the continuing education and cultural enrichment needs of our surrounding community. In the next 5 years, Our University's goals are to

1. Offer noncredit instruction targeted to meet the continuing education needs of Our University's faculty, staff, and surrounding community. Such programs should not duplicate the efforts of two- and four-year postsecondary institutions within a 25-mile radius of Our University.
2. Provide cultural enrichment opportunities for the university and surrounding community through an artist/lecture/concert series.
3. Schedule in-service specialized short courses and seminars for local business and industry.

D. *Faculty*

Persons who combine a love of teaching with a continuing curiosity and a passion for learning, scholarship, research, and creativity are the most important resources of the university. Excellent teaching and advising are essential to the fulfillment of the mission of Our University, as is the conduct of both basic and applied research that contributes to the advancement of knowledge and to the consideration of important societal problems. Various steps have already been taken to develop and maintain an excellent faculty, and the following goals are particularly important:

1. Maintain salaries at highly competitive levels in order to attract a diverse faculty noted for its teaching excellence, scholarly achievements, and dedication to the highest standards of professional activity.

2. Continue to emphasize research and scholarly activity through research assistants' support, travel funds, library materials, adequate access to computer facilities, and other forms of faculty development such as academic leaves and summer stipends.

3. Continue to develop the emphasis placed on advising and working directly with individual students.

E. *Students*

Our University will remain an institution of modest size with a total enrollment of no more than 4,000 students. In the recruitment of all students, emphasis is placed on potential for the very highest in academic achievement; leadership, special talents and abilities; and diversity in geographic origin, ethnicity, and socio-economic status. Appropriate scholarships and need-based financial aid programs will be administered to facilitate recruitment and retention of these students, continuing the significant advances made in the 1980s.

1. Our University seeks to make it possible for each student to experience the academic and cultural diversity of the university, and the following academic goals for the composition of the student body directly address this commitment:

    a. Continue to increase the number of academically talented students attending Our University, achieve by 1995 an average SAT score for entering freshmen of 1200, and maintain this level as a minimum throughout the rest of the planning period.

    b. Continue to increase the number of out-of-state students attending Our University, so that this group will comprise 50% of the student body by 1995, and maintain this percentage as a minimum for the rest of the planning period.

    c. Give increased emphasis to recruitment of minority students (Hispanic, black, Asian, and Native American) and increase their representation in the overall student population.

    d. Strive to have an equal number of men and women in the student body.

2. Each graduate of Our University will be treated as an individual, and all graduates of baccalaureate-level programs at the university will have developed a depth of understanding in their major field and been afforded the opportunity to prepare for a career or profession following graduation. Additionally, they will be able to

   a. Express themselves clearly, correctly, and succinctly in writing.
   b. Make an effective verbal presentation of their ideas concerning a topic.
   c. Read and offer an analysis of periodical literature concerning a topic of interest.
   d. Complete accurately basic mathematical calculations.
   e. Demonstrate a sufficient level of computer literacy.
   f. Utilize basic scholarly modes of inquiry.
E. *Academic Support Services*
   Services in direct support of academic programs must be both effective and efficient in the accomplishment of their assigned activities. Our University will strive for excellence in the following goals:
   1. Continue to increase library acquisitions so that the number of bound volumes will reach 650,000 by 1995.
   2. Improve the quality of library materials supporting instruction by acquiring the most advanced audiovisual equipment and by judiciously purchasing periodicals applicable to a liberal arts and sciences curriculum, as well as the limited number of graduate programs offered.
   3. Increase accessibility of computer facilities at the university for both students and faculty through expansion of microcomputer laboratories and enhancement of computer support.
   4. Develop more systematic data concerning the outcome of each student's educational experiences.
   5. Plan and modify the existing classroom and laboratory space to meet the evolving needs of the new curriculum.

III. STUDENT AFFAIRS

The function of the Student Affairs Office is to establish an environment at Our University that supports and encourages students in their academic progress and to assist those students in their personal and social development. Student Affairs prepares Our University graduates for adult life by teaching them to appreciate quality, to develop values, to accept responsibility for their decisions and actions, and to know how and when to compromise.

To accomplish this mission, the following specific goals must receive continuing and expanded attention:

A. *Environment*
1. Provide a comfortable and secure living environment in the residence halls.
2. Encourage development of appropriate attitudes and conduct for a communal academic environment.
3. Expand and encourage supplemental cultural and intellectual enrichment opportunities outside the classroom.
4. Explore the possibility of offering more options in housing.
5. Provide opportunities in an informal atmosphere for interaction of faculty with students outside the classroom.
6. Include in the University Center, which is being redesigned, a bookstore offering excellent academic support materials and current literature, as well as appropriate notions, supplies, and services needed by students, faculty, and staff.
7. Provide a variety of options for nutritional meals in comfortable and attractive settings for resident as well as commuting students, faculty, staff, and guests.

B. *Development*
1. Offer opportunities for self-evaluation and self-knowledge through administration and interpretation of standardized tests.
2. Provide comprehensive career planning for all students and career counseling for seniors and graduate students, prepare students to conduct effective job searches, and coordinate employment interviews on the campus.

IV. FISCAL AFFAIRS

The purpose of the university's Fiscal Affairs operations is to provide an environment that enables faculty, staff, and students to concentrate on their appropriate tasks, which are essentially educational.

Fiscal Affairs has two major areas of responsibility: (1) the management of, and accounting for, financial resources (the handling of funds, endowments, investments, and expenditures for salaries and wages); and (2) the operation of support services (physical plant, purchasing, security, personnel, and other areas). These two essential areas provide a base upon which the institution can accomplish its mission.

A. *Financial Resources*
1. To achieve expansion and growth in financial assets, Our University will

    a. Manage the budget prudently.

    b. Encourage and assist its faculty in seeking university-administered grants and contracts from external sources.

    c. Price its auxiliary enterprise services so that they are self-sustaining and do not draw from other resources of the institution.

2. In allocating funds for its academic and economic needs, the university will emphasize the following goals:

    a. Maintaining a level of salaries that will attract and retain competent professionals.

    b. Providing adequate funding for scholarships to attract exceptional students.

    c. Purchasing and replacing equipment in support of the instruction and research needs of the university.

    d. Building adequate plant-fund reserves in order to protect against deferred maintenance.

B. *Support Services*

1. To achieve maximum utilization of its resources, the University will

    a. Use its personnel, equipment, structures, and funds efficiently and effectively to provide a safe and comfortable environment for all faculty, staff, and students.

    b. Fund support services at a level that provides for the most efficient operation consistent with a scholarly environment.

2. In personnel matters, the university will

    a. Improve communications between support services and all employees to ensure that applicable fiscal and personnel procedures are understood.

    b. Maintain a vigorous affirmative action program that will include specific goals and a systematic review of procedures and progress.

V. UNIVERSITY RELATIONS AND DEVELOPMENT

The University Relations and Development function manages the closely related areas of fund raising, alumni activities, and public relations. Most of the activities and programs take place for the ultimate purpose of increasing gift income for the university and attracting qualified students and faculty to the university.

Within this context, the University Relations and Development function has established the following integrated goals:

A. *Fund Raising*
   1. Build a permanent university endowment of $150 million to $155 million by 1995.
   2. Achieve a level of annual giving (unrestricted annual fund) of at least $750,000 per year by 1995.
   3. Achieve 35% participation among alumni in the annual giving program.

B. *Alumni Activities*
   1. Have 5% of all alumni return to campus for various programs such as Alumni Weekend, Alumni College, class reunions, etc.
   2. Develop an active national alumni association with chapters in all cities where 100 or more alumni reside.

C. *Public Relations*
   1. Achieve a national image of the university as a high-quality, selective-admissions liberal arts and sciences institution that is among the best of its type in the nation.
   2. Maintain a positive relationship with the community in which the institution is located.

Example Expanded Statement of Institutional Purpose for Your Community College

YOUR COMMUNITY COLLEGE MISSION

Your Community College is an open-admission, community-based comprehensive college designed to provide inexpensive, quality educational opportunities to residents of a five-county service area in the central portion of the Magnolia State. The college was formed early in 1971 by the joint action of the Smith, Lawrence, Karnes, Neuceuss, and Willow county governments and recognized by the legislature and the State Board of Community Colleges later in that year. The college replaced a former branch of Magnolia State University and has developed an educational mission characterized by diversification, growth, and community orientation.

Your Community College operates in the belief that all individuals should be

1. Treated with dignity and respect,
2. Afforded equal opportunity to acquire a complete educational experience,
3. Given an opportunity to discover and develop their special aptitudes and insights,
4. Provided an opportunity to equip themselves for a fulfilling life and responsible citizenship in a world characterized by change.

Finally, the college functions as an integral part of the five-county area that it serves and has a responsibility to provide educational and cultural leadership to this constituency.

INSTITUTIONAL GOALS

Your Community College seeks to
1. Serve students in the first 2 years of instruction leading to a bachelor's degree.
   a. Recipients of the Associate of Arts (AA) or Associate of Science (AS) degree will be readily accepted at all public universities in the Magnolia State.
   b. The majority of graduates with the AA or AS degree attending four-year institutions on a full-time basis will complete

their bachelor's degrees within 3 years of enrollment at the four-year institution.

   c. Courses offered at the college as a foundation or prerequisite for courses at public four-year colleges will be fully accepted for that purpose.

2. Serve persons of all ages in preparing for job entry and careers in a variety of fields.

   a. Recipients of an Associate of Applied Science (AAS) degree will be well prepared for their first or entry-level position in a career field.

   b. The great majority of AAS graduates will find employment in the five-county service area.

   c. College AAS programs will be focused on career-related opportunities for graduates in the five-county area.

3. Insure that all recipients of an associate (AA/AS or AAS) degree will be able to

   a. Express their thoughts clearly and correctly in writing.

   b. Read and understand literature and current event articles commonly found in the print media.

   c. Perform the basic mathematical calculations required to function in society.

4. Assist students in overcoming deficiencies and acquiring skills fundamental to further academic and career achievement.

   a. Prior to entry into AA/AS or AAS degree programs, all students will hold a high school diploma or GED certificate.

   b. The college will provide a noncredit college preparatory curriculum for students seeking to receive their GED certificate.

   c. Students completing noncredit occupational/technical training programs will be offered assistance with obtaining their GED certificate if they have not completed high school.

5. Provide a broad range of student services, including counseling, career planning, placement, and financial assistance.

   a. Counseling and career planning services will support both transfer (AA/AS) and career/technical (AAS) students.

   b. Placement services will be oriented toward the support of career/technical (AAS) graduates and focused in the five-county area.

   c. Every effort possible will be pursued to provide financial assistance for those in need of such support to attend the college.

6. Serve constituents who need additional training for advancement in their current field or retraining for employment in new fields.

    a. Continuing career education classes will be offered annually at night in each field in which the college offers an AAS.

    b. In conjunction with Magnolia State University, continuing professional education opportunities will be offered in business and other professional areas.

    c. Opportunities for retraining will be made available to all citizens of the five counties and intensified, should economic circumstances warrant.

7. Provide educational programs to meet the needs of employers in the five-county area.

8. Serve persons who want to take special classes and workshops, as well as regular credit classes for personal development or cultural enrichment.

9. Cooperate with community agencies in community development activities.

APPENDIX C

Examples of Linkage between Expanded Statement of Institutional Purpose, Departmental/Program Intended Outcomes/Objectives, and Assessment Criteria and Procedures

Accounting Degree Program

Example of Linkage between
Expanded Statement of Institutional Purpose,
Departmental/Program Intended Outcomes/Objectives, and
Assessment Criteria and Procedures at Our University

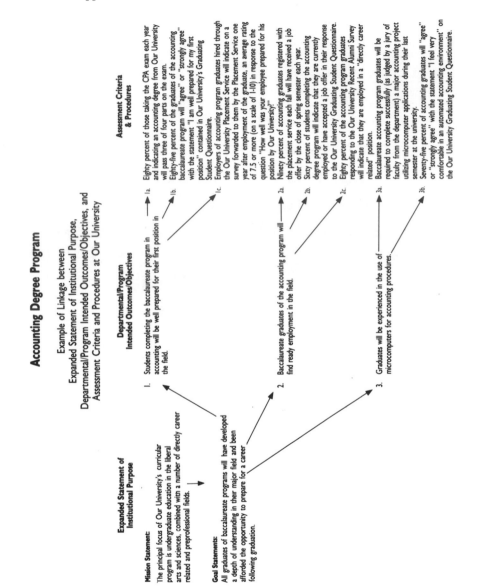

Expanded Statement of Institutional Purpose

Mission Statement:
The principal focus of Our University's curricular program is undergraduate education in the liberal arts and sciences, combined with a number of directly career related and preprofessional fields.

Goal Statements:
All graduates of baccalaureate programs will have developed a depth of understanding in their major field and been afforded the opportunity to prepare for a career following graduation.

Departmental/Program Intended Outcomes/Objectives

1. Students completing the baccalaureate program in accounting will be well prepared for their first position in the field.

2. Baccalaureate graduates of the accounting program will find ready employment in the field.

3. Graduates will be experienced in the use of microcomputers for accounting procedures.

Assessment Criteria & Procedures

1a. Eighty percent of those taking the CPA exam each year and indicating an accounting degree from Our University will pass three of four parts on the exam.

1b. Eighty-five percent of the graduates of the accounting baccalaureate program will "agree" or "strongly agree" with the statement "I am well prepared for my first position" contained in Our University's Graduating Student Questionnaire.

1c. Employers of accounting program graduates hired through the Our University Placement Service will indicate on a survey forwarded to them by the Placement Service one year after employment of the graduate, an average rating of 7.5 or more (on a scale of 1-10) in response to the question "How well was your employee prepared for his position by Our University?"

2a. Ninety percent of accounting graduates registered with the placement service each fall will have received a job offer by the close of spring semester each year.

2b. Sixty percent of students completing the accounting degree program will indicate that they are currently employed or have accepted a job offer in their response to the Our University Graduating Student Questionnaire.

2c. Eighty percent of the accounting program graduates responding to the Our University Recent Alumni Survey will indicate that they are employed in a "directly career related" position.

3a. Baccalaureate accounting program graduates will be required to complete successfully (as judged by a jury of faculty from the department) a major accounting project utilizing microcomputer applications during their last semester at the university.

3b. Seventy-five percent of accounting graduates will "agree" or "strongly agree" with the statement "I feel very comfortable in an automated accounting environment" on the Our University Graduating Student Questionnaire.

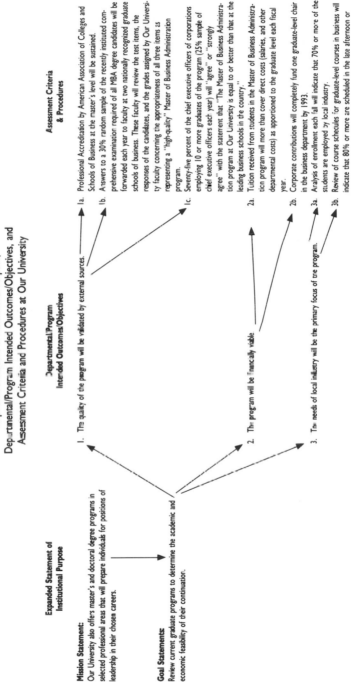

Master of Business Administration Degree Program

Example of Linkage between
Expanded Statement of Institutional Purpose,
Departmental/Program Intended Outcomes/Objectives, and
Assessment Criteria and Procedures at Our University

Expanded Statement of Institutional Purpose

Mission Statement:
Our University also offers master's and doctoral degree programs in selected professional areas that will prepare individuals for positions of leadership in their chosen careers.

Goal Statements:
Review current graduate programs to determine the academic and economic feasibility of their continuation.

Departmental/Program Intended Outcomes/Objectives

1. The quality of the program will be validated by external sources.

2. The program will be financially viable.

3. The needs of local industry will be the primary focus of the program.

Assessment Criteria & Procedures

1a. Professional Accreditation by American Association of Colleges and Schools of Business at the master's level will be sustained.

1b. Answers to a 30% random sample of the recently instituted comprehensive examination required of all MBA degree candidates will be forwarded each year to faculty at two nationally recognized graduate schools of business. These faculty will review the test items, the responses of the candidates, and the grades assigned by Our University faculty concerning the appropriateness of all three items as representing a "high-quality" Master of Business Administration program.

1c. Seventy-five percent of the chief executive officers of corporations employing 10 or more graduates of the program (25% sample of chief executive officers each year) will "agree" or "strongly agree" with the statement that: "The Master of Business Administration program at Our University is equal to or better than that at the leading business schools in the country."

2a. Tuition received from students in the Master of Business Administration program will more than cover direct costs (salaries, and other departmental costs) as apportioned to the graduate level each fiscal year.

2b. Corporate contributions will completely fund one graduate-level chair in the business department by 1993.

3a. Analysis of enrollment each fall will indicate that 70% or more of the students are employed by local industry.

3b. Review of course schedules for graduate-level courses in business will indicate that 80% or more are scheduled in the late afternoon or evening, or on the weekend.

General Education Program

Example of Linkage between
Expanded Statement of Institutional Purpose,
Departmental/Program Intended Outcomes/Objectives, and
Assessment Criteria and Procedures at Our University

Expanded Statement of Institutional Purpose

Mission Statement:
The principal focus of Our University's curricular program is undergraduate education in the liberal arts and sciences.

Goal Statements:
(related to baccalaureate graduates):
Additionally, they will be able to

a. Express themselves clearly, correctly, and succinctly in a written manner.

Departmental/Program Intended Outcomes/Objectives

1. Prior to graduation each student will demonstrate general expository writing with correct grammar, punctuation, and spelling.

2. Graduates will have demonstrated their ability to organize and effectively express their thoughts in writing concerning a major issue of then current interest in their chosen field of study.

Assessment Criteria & Procedures

1a. By the end of their junior year, all students will have placed on file in the Office of Career and Life Planning within the Our University Placement Service a 500-word essay outlining their career plans related to their courses of study. During each summer, the Director of the Freshman Writing Program will review these documents to determine whether they meet the standards of students completing the Freshman Writing Program. Those students whose career essays are judged unacceptable will be required to complete a one-semester Senior Writing Clinic during their next semester in enrollment, following which they will be required to submit another career essay for evaluation.

2a. During the first semester of their senior year, each student will (separate from any course requirement) be required to submit to the appropriate academic department a minimum 5,000-word research/ argumentative paper putting forward their position regarding a then current issue or problem in their primary field of study. Departmental juries of faculty will be convened to review each paper for its organization and assess the student's writing ability and knowledge in the field. Students will not be permitted to receive a degree until the appropriate department has certified acceptance of their research/argumentative paper.

Library in General Education

Example of Linkage between
Expanded Statement of Institutional Purpose,
Departmental/Program Intended Outcomes/Objectives,
and Assessment Criteria and Procedures
at Our University

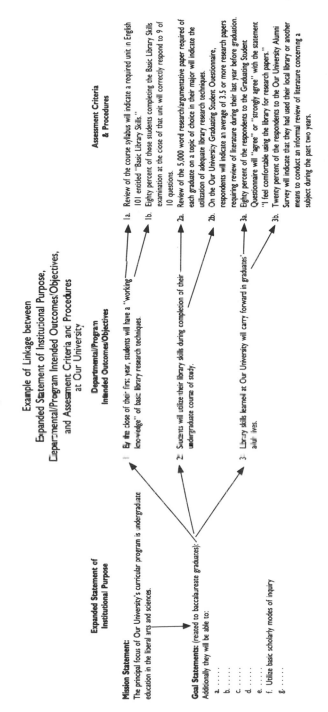

Expanded Statement of Institutional Purpose

Mission Statement:
The principal focus of Our University's curricular program is undergraduate education in the liberal arts and sciences.

Goal Statements: (related to baccalaureate graduates):
Additionally they will be able to:
a. . . . . . .
b. . . . . . .
c. . . . . . .
d. . . . . . .
e. . . . . . .
f. Utilize basic scholarly modes of inquiry
g. . . . . . .

Departmental/Program
Intended Outcomes/Objectives

1. By the close of their first year, students will have a "working knowledge" of basic library research techniques.

2. Students will utilize their library skills during completion of their undergraduate course of study.

3. Library skills learned at Our University will carry forward in graduates' adult lives.

Assessment Criteria
& Procedures

1a. Review of the course syllabus will indicate a required unit in English 101 entitled "Basic Library Skills."

1b. Eighty percent of those students completing the Basic Library Skills examination at the close of that unit will correctly respond to 9 of 10 questions.

2a. Review of the 5,000 word research/argumentative paper required of each graduate on a topic of choice in their major will indicate the utilization of adequate library research techniques.

2b. On the Our University Graduating Student Questionnaire, respondents will indicate an average of 3.5 or more research papers requiring review of literature during their last year before graduation.

3a. Eighty percent of the respondents to the Graduating Student Questionnaire will "agree" or "strongly agree" with the statement "I feel comfortable using the library for research papers."

3b. Twenty percent of the respondents to the Our University Alumni Survey will indicate that they had used their local library or another means to conduct an informal review of literature concerning a subject during the past two years.

Department of Continuing Education

Example of Linkage between
Expanded Statement of Institutional Purpose,
Departmental/Program Intended Outcomes/Objectives, and
Assessment Criteria and Procedures at Our University

Expanded Statement of Institutional Purpose	Departmental/Program Intended Outcomes/Objectives	Assessment Criteria & Procedures
Mission Statement: In addition, recognizing its responsibility to the larger community, Our University provides a variety of carefully selected programs of continuing education and cultural enrichment.	1. Identify the continuing education needs of local businesses and industries.	1a. During academic year 1991-92, the Our University Department of Continuing Education will have conducted a needs survey of local businesses and industries to identify unmet needs for continuing education support. 1b. By the close of academic year 1991-92, the results of the needs survey will have been utilized to identify a limited number of opportunities for continuing education activities servicing local businesses and industries.
Goal Statements: Be responsive to the continuing education needs of local businesses and industries in areas in which Our University is academically strong.	2. Offer credit and noncredit programs on-site at various industries in the local area as well as on campus.	2a. In academic year 1992-93 and each year thereafter, the Department of Continuing Education will be able to identify a minimum of 25 continuing education programs (credit or noncredit) during that year conducted on-site at various local businesses and industries. 2b. In academic year 1992-93 and each year thereafter, the Our University Chief Academic Officer will be able to identify a minimum of 10 on-campus courses (during the fall and spring semesters combined) that have been scheduled during the late afternoon, evening, or on Saturday in response to needs expressed by local businesses and industries for continuing professional education for their employees.
	3. Conduct the continuing education program so as to meet its own costs or generate excess revenue.	3a. Annual comparison of expenditures for the Department of Continuing Education with revenue from all sources generated by that unit will indicate at least a break-even relationship each fiscal year.

Student Services

Example of Linkage between
Expanded Statement of Institutional Purpose,
Departmental/Program Intended Outcomes/Objectives, and
Assessment Criteria and Procedures at Our University

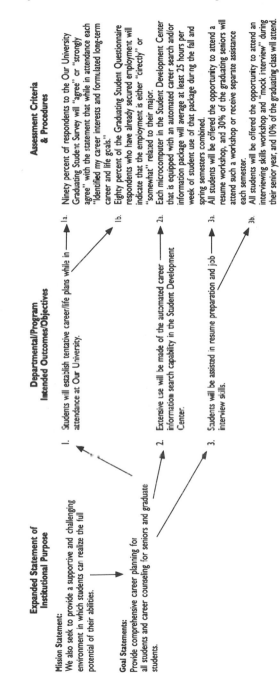

Expanded Statement of Institutional Purpose

Mission Statement:
We also seek to provide a supportive and challenging environment in which students can realize the full potential of their abilities.

Goal Statements:
Provide comprehensive career planning for all students and career counseling for seniors and graduate students.

Departmental/Program Intended Outcomes/Objectives

1. Students will establish tentative career/life plans while in attendance at Our University.

2. Extensive use will be made of the automated career information search capability in the Student Development Center.

3. Students will be assisted in resume preparation and job interview skills.

Assessment Criteria & Procedures

1a. Ninety percent of respondents to the Our University Graduating Student Survey will "agree" or "strongly agree" with the statement that while in attendance each "identified my career interests and formulated long-term career and life goals."

1b. Eighty percent of the Graduating Student Questionnaire respondents who have already secured employment will indicate that the employment is either "directly" or "somewhat" related to their major.

2a. Each microcomputer in the Student Development Center that is equipped with an automated career search and/or information package will average at least 25 hours per week of student use of that package during the fall and spring semesters combined.

3a. All students will be offered the opportunity to attend a resume workshop, and 30% of the graduating seniors will attend such a workshop or receive separate assistance each semester.

3b. All students will be offered the opportunity to attend an interviewing skills workshop and "mock interview" during their senior year, and 10% of the graduating class will attend.

Admissions Office

Example of Linkage between
Expanded Statement of Institutional Purpose,
Departmental/Program Intended Outcomes/Objectives, and
Assessment Criteria and Procedures at Our University

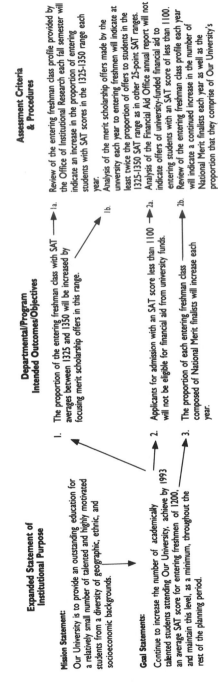

**Expanded Statement of
Institutional Purpose**

Mission Statement:

Our University is to provide an outstanding education for
a relatively small number of talented and highly motivated
students from a diversity of geographic, ethnic, and
socioeconomic backgrounds.

Goal Statements:

Continue to increase the number of academically
talented students attending Our University, achieve by 1993
an average SAT score for entering freshmen of 1200,
and maintain this level, as a minimum, throughout the
rest of the planning period.

**Departmental/Program
Intended Outcomes/Objectives**

1. The proportion of the entering freshman class with SAT
averages between 1325 and 1350 will be increased by
focusing merit scholarship offers in this range.

2. Applicants for admission with an SAT score less than 1100
will not be eligible for financial aid from university funds.

3. The proportion of each entering freshman class
composed of National Merit finalists will increase each
year.

**Assessment Criteria
& Procedures**

1a. Review of the entering freshman class profile provided by
the Office of Institutional Research each fall semester will
indicate an increase in the proportion of entering
students with SAT scores in the 1325-1350 range each
year.

1b. Analysis of the merit scholarship offers made by the
university each year to entering freshmen will indicate at
least twice the proportion of offers to students in the
1325-1350 SAT range as in other 25-point SAT ranges.

2a. Analysis of the Financial Aid Office annual report will not
indicate offers of university-funded financial aid to
entering students with an SAT score of less than 1100.

2b. Review of the entering freshman class profile each year
will indicate a continued increase in the number of
National Merit finalists each year as well as the
proportion that they comprise of Our University's
entering freshman class.

Sponsored Research

Example of Linkage between Expanded Statement of Institutional Purpose, Departmental/Program Intended Outcomes/Objectives, and Assessment Criteria and Procedures at Our University

Expanded Statement of Institutional Purpose	Departmental/Program Intended Outcomes/Objectives	Assessment Criteria & Procedures
Mission Statement: Our University recognizes its responsibility in maintaining a position of excellence and leadership in research. **Goal Statements:** Our University will seek during the next five years to 1. . . 3 4. Focus the development of proposals for externally funded or organized research on subjects directly related to local/regional industries or those subjects of particular interest to foundations with which Our University has enjoyed a continuing relationship.	1. The majority of the research proposals for external funding forwarded through the Office of the Associate Vice Chancellor for Research and Dean of the Graduate School will be directly linked to local or regional (within this state) industries. 2. The proportion of those proposals for external funding that are directly linked to local or regional industries and are funded will substantially exceed all other such proposals submitted. 3. Local industries will be aware of Our University's efforts to seek funding in research areas related to their fields.	1a. Each proposal for externally funded research will be accompanied by a one-page transmittal sheet explaining if and how the proposal relates to a local or regional industry. At the end of the fiscal year, the transmittal sheets will be reviewed, and 50% or more will be judged as directly linked to local or regional industries by the Our University Research Board. 2a. Following annual identification of those research grant proposals directly linked with local or regional industries, analysis of actual funding will reveal that twice the proportion of such proposals, compared to all proposals submitted, receive funding. 3a. Of those proposals for external funding identified as being directly linked with local or regional industries, half or more will include a letter of support, endorsement, or cooperation from the appropriate local or regional industry. 3b. Half of those CEOs of major local industries responding to a letter from Our University's CEO (25% sample each year) will be able to identify research performed by Our University that has been directly related to their products.

Physical Plant

Example of Linkage between
Expanded Statement of Institutional Purpose,
Departmental/Program Intended Outcomes/Objectives, and
Assessment Criteria and Procedures at Our University

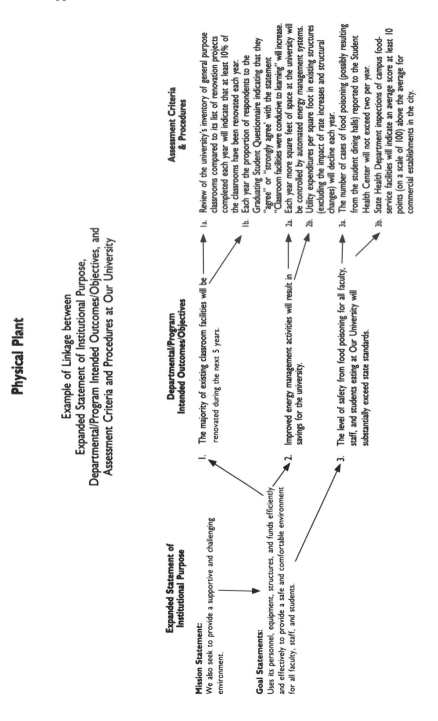

Expanded Statement of Institutional Purpose

Mission Statement:
We also seek to provide a supportive and challenging environment.

Goal Statements:
Uses its personnel, equipment, structures, and funds efficiently and effectively to provide a safe and comfortable environment for all faculty, staff, and students.

Departmental/Program Intended Outcomes/Objectives

1. The majority of existing classroom facilities will be renovated during the next 5 years.

2. Improved energy management activities will result in savings for the university.

3. The level of safety from food poisoning for all faculty, staff, and students eating at Our University will substantially exceed state standards.

Assessment Criteria & Procedures

1a. Review of the university's inventory of general purpose classrooms compared to its list of renovation projects completed each year will indicate that at least 10% of the classrooms have been renovated each year.

1b. Each year the proportion of respondents to the Graduating Student Questionnaire indicating that they "agree" or "strongly agree" with the statement "Classroom facilities were conducive to learning" will increase.

2a. Each year more square feet of space at the university will be controlled by automated energy management systems.

2b. Utility expenditures per square foot in existing structures (excluding the impact of rate increases and structural changes) will decline each year.

3a. The number of cases of food poisoning (possibly resulting from the student dining halls) reported to the Student Health Center will not exceed two per year.

3b. State Health Department inspections of campus food-service facilities will indicate an average score at least 10 points (on a scale of 100) above the average for commercial establishments in the city.

Computer Center

Example of Linkage between
Expanded Statement of Institutional Purpose,
Departmental/Program Intended Outcomes/Objectives, and
Assessment Criteria and Procedures at Our University

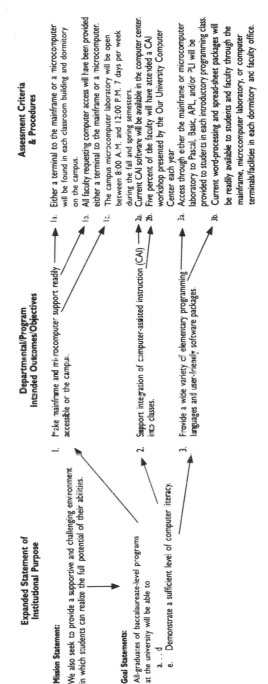

Expanded Statement of Institutional Purpose

Mission Statement:

We also seek to provide a supportive and challenging environment in which students can realize the full potential of their abilities.

Goal Statements:

All graduates of baccalaureate-level programs at the university will be able to

a. . . d

e.   Demonstrate a sufficient level of computer literacy.

Departmental/Program Intended Outcomes/Objectives

1.   Make mainframe and microcomputer support readily accessible on the campus.

2.   Support integration of computer-assisted instruction (CAI) into classes.

3.   Provide a wide variety of elementary programming languages and user-friendly software packages.

Assessment Criteria & Procedures

1a.   Either a terminal to the mainframe or a microcomputer will be found in each classroom building and dormitory on the campus.

1b.   All faculty requesting computer access will have been provided either a terminal to the mainframe or a microcomputer.

1c.   The campus microcomputer laboratory will be open between 8:00 A.M. and 12:00 P.M. 7 days per week during the fall and spring semesters.

2a.   Current CAI software will be available in the computer center.

2b.   Five percent of the faculty will have attended a CAI workshop presented by the Our University Computer Center each year

3a.   Access through either the mainframe or microcomputer laboratory to Pascal, Basic, APL, and/or PLI will be provided to students in each introductory programming class.

3b.   Current word-processing and spread-sheet packages will be readily available to students and faculty through the mainframe, microcomputer laboratory, or computer terminals/facilities in each dormitory and faculty office.

Your Community College
Business Transfer Program

Example of Linkage between
Expanded Statement of Institutional Purpose,
Departmental/Program Intended Outcomes/Objectives,
and Assessment Criteria and Procedures

Expanded Statement of Institutional Purpose

Mission Statement:
Your Community College is an open-admission, community-based, comprehensive college designed to provide inexpensive, quality educational opportunities (college transfer, career/technical and continuing education) to residents of a five-county service area in the central portion of the Magnolia State.

Goal Statements:
Serve traditional students seeking the first two years of instruction leading to a bachelor's degree.

a. Recipients of the Associate of Arts (AA) or the Associate of Science (AS) degree will be readily accepted at all public universities in the Magnolia State.

b. Graduates with the AA/AS degree will complete their bachelor's degrees at almost the same rate and in about as much time as students completing their entire degree at four-year institutions in the state.

c. Courses offered at the College as a foundation or prerequisite for courses at four-year colleges will be fully accepted for that purpose.

Departmental/Program Intended Outcomes/Objectives

1. Students transferring to a four-year college in the field of accounting will find their Accounting 101-102 at Your Community College fully accepted as the basis for Accounting 201-202 at a four-year institution.

2. Most of the students completing Accounting 101-102 at Your Community College who major in business at a four-year college will successfully (grade "C" or better) pass Accounting 201-202 at their four-year institution.

3. Students completing the two-year course of study leading toward transfer to a four-year college as a full-time student in the field of business will complete their baccalaureate degree at almost the same rate as those students originally enrolling at the four-year college.

Assessment Criteria & Procedures

1a. Ninety percent of those business students responding to a follow-up survey one year after transfer to a four-year institution will respond that their Accounting 101-102 courses taken at Your Community College were fully accepted by the four-year college.

1b. An annual spot check of 25% of Your Community College's primary transfer institutions will reveal that they indicate full acceptance of Accounting 101-102 taken at Your Community College as a prerequisite for Accounting 201-202 at their institution.

2a. Analysis of data received by Your Community College concerning grades in specific courses made by its graduates at each four-year institution will indicate that greater than 70% of its graduates who took Accounting 101-102 at Your Community College and majored in a business-related field at the four-year college made a grade of "C" or higher at the four-year college in Accounting 201-202.

2b. More than 70% of Your Community College transfer graduates who are majoring in business at a four-year institution will report making a grade of "C" or higher in Accounting 201-202.

3a. Analysis of data received by Your Community College concerning its transfer students will reveal graduation rates in the field of business by its full-time transfer students at 85% or higher of the rate for full-time students originally admitted at four-year institutions.

Your Community College
Automotive Technology Program

Example of Linkage between
Expanded Statement of Institutional Purpose
Departmental/Program Intended Outcomes/Objectives,
and Assessment Criteria and Procedures

Expanded Statement of Institutional Purpose

Mission Statement:

Your Community College is an open-admission, community-based, comprehensive college designed to provide inexpensive, quality educational opportunities (college transfer, career/technical and continuing education) to residents of a five-county service area in the central portion of the Magnolia State.

Goal Statements:

Serve persons of all ages in preparing for job entry and careers in a variety of fields.

a. Recipients of an Associate of Applied Science (AAS) degree will be well-prepared for first or entry-level positions in a career field.

b. College AAS programs will be focused on career-related opportunities for graduates in the five-county area.

c. The majority of AAS graduates will find employment in the five-county service area.

Departmental/Program Intended Outcomes/Objectives

1. Graduates of the Automotive Technology Program will be successfully employed in the field.

2. Graduates of the Automotive Technology Program will be technically proficient.

3. Employers of the Automotive Technology Program graduates in the five-county service area will be pleased with the education received by their employees.

Assessment Criteria & Procedures

1a. Fifty percent of the graduates of the Automotive Technology Program will report employment in the field on the Graduating Student Survey administered at the time of program completion.

1b. Eighty percent of the graduates of the Automotive Technology Program will report employment in the field on the Recent Alumni Survey distributed one year after graduation.

2a. At the close of their final term, 90% of the graduates will be able to identify and correct within a given period of time all of the mechanical problems in five test cars that have been "prepared" for the students by Automotive Technology Program faculty.

2b. Eighty percent of the Automotive Technology Program graduates will pass the National Automotive Test.

3a. Eighty percent of the automotive respondents to an Employer Survey conducted every 3 years by the college will respond that they would be pleased to employ future graduates of the Automotive Technology Program.

3b. Fifty percent of the automotive employers registered with the College Placement Service will make at least one offer to a graduate of the Automotive Technology Program each year.

Your Community College
Basic Academic Skills
Noncredit Program

Example of Linkage between
Expanded Statement of Institutional Purpose,
Departmental/Program Intended Outcomes/Objectives,
and Assessment Criteria and Procedures

Expanded Statement of Institutional Purpose

Mission Statement:
Your Community College operates in the belief that all individuals should be:

a. Treated with dignity and respect.
b. Afforded an equal opportunity to acquire a complete educational experience.
c. Given an opportunity to discover and develop their special aptitudes and insights.
d. Provided an opportunity to equip themselves for a fulfilling life and responsible citizenship in a world characterized by change.

Goal Statements:
Assist students in overcoming deficiencies and acquiring skills fundamental to further academic and career achievement.

a. Prior to entry into AA/AS or AAS degree programs, all students will hold a high school diploma or GED certificate.
b. The college will provide a noncredit college preparatory curriculum for students seeking to receive their GED certificate.
c. Students completing noncredit occupational/technical training programs will be offered assistance with obtaining their GED certificate if they have not completed high school.

Departmental/Program Intended Outcomes/Objectives

1. Students admitted to the AA/AS and AAS programs will hold a high school diploma or a GED certificate.

2. Each year the college will conduct noncredit GED preparatory classes in both the fall and spring semesters and the majority of students enrolled in these classes will pass the GED.

3. More than half of the students completing noncredit training programs who do not at the time hold a high school diploma or GED certificate will receive one within one year.

Assessment Criteria & Procedures

1a. A random sample of 10% of the students enrolled in AA or AAS programs each fall will reveal that all students in the sample hold a high school diploma or a GED certificate.

2a. Review of the college course schedule each year will verify the offering of noncredit GED preparatory classes in each semester.

2b. By the close of the academic year, 50% or more of the people identified on course rosters for the noncredit classes will have passed the GED test.

3a. Review of the educational attainment of those students completing noncredit occupational/technical training programs will identify those not holding high school diplomas or GED certificates.

3b. Review of Your Community College records will indicate that within one year 50% of the students identified above have successfully completed the GED.

3c. Half or more of the respondents to the Your Community College Recent Alumni Survey who indicated neither high school diplomas nor GED certificates at the end of their noncredit program at the college will further indicate receipt of the GED certificate within a year of completion of their program at Your Community College.

Outline of Twelve-Month Sequence of Events for Preparation of Expanded Statement of Institutional Purpose

OUTLINE OF TWELVE-MONTH SEQUENCE OF EVENTS FOR PREPARATION OF EXPANDED STATEMENT OF INSTITUTIONAL PURPOSE

I. Doing the Homework (September through December)
   A. Appoint Broad-Based Constituent Group—The group should be composed of faculty (probably the majority), administrators, student leaders, and representatives of the governing board. The purpose of the group is to serve as the overall steering committee that will review and discuss important issues related to the mission or purpose of the institution. This group may become somewhat large due to the need to involve various constituencies; however, most of the work done will be accomplished by several staff members appointed to support this work of the representative group.
   B. Review Current Statement of Purpose—The current statement of purpose should be reviewed for several reasons. First, it represents the official policy of the institution as of the beginning of the process. Second, from a political standpoint, it may be that this existing statement cannot be entirely discarded due to legal ramifications or other circumstances and will need to be incorporated into the ESIP or circumvented.
   C. Gather Input from Constituents—The attempt to involve the greater campus community in consideration of the ESIP should involve a broad canvassing of faculty, administrators, student leaders, and the governing board members for their opinions concerning the future development of the institution. The Institutional Goals Inventory from the Educational Testing Service has proven to be a useful tool for this purpose and is a relatively easy way to gain maximum participation with minimum effort and cost.
   D. Determine External Opportunities and Constraints—The term *environmental scanning* conjures up massive efforts by substantial staffs to describe every detail of the environment in which the institution operates. On the contrary, an abbreviated environmental scan can not only be a valuable source of relatively easily obtained information but also provide an opportunity for participation by faculty experts in the differ-

ent areas. It is possible to conduct an abbreviated environmental scan within 2 to 3 months and to present to the institution a summary of the political, economic, educational, and social issues forming the context within which it operates.

E. Consider Analysis of Internal Strengths/Weaknesses—It is highly unlikely (though possible) that the institution has the "intestinal fortitude" necessary to identify its weaknesses on paper. In most instances, institutions can go about the task of identifying those areas widely regarded on the campus as strengths. In this case, areas not identified as strengths should be considered as either generally acceptable or as weaknesses of the institution.

II. Conducting Meaningful Deliberations (January through April)

A. Establish Issues to Be Addressed

1. Identify Key Issues/Topics—The product of "Doing the Homework" should suggest a number of issues or topics (clientele, programs, research, etc.) that need to be addressed in the ESIP. It is important both to identify these topics as early as possible and to leave time for further topics to be developed during this second portion of the process.

2. Determine Relative Priorities—Some of the topics identified initially will obviously be of greater importance to the institution than others. As early as possible, these topics should be identified and sequenced for consideration, leaving several periods of time open for consideration of topics developed during this second phase.

B. Follow the Sequence of Deliberations

1. Schedule Meetings with Topics—The number of topics identified will determine, to a great extent, the number and frequency of meetings to be scheduled. It is important, however, that these meetings be scheduled in advance so that members will know what topic is to be considered at which meetings and, accordingly, can arrange their calendars well in advance.

2. Assign Responsibilities for Drafting Component of Mission and Goals Statements—Each topic to be discussed should have a "floor manager" appointed to consider the information provided during the "Doing the Homework"

phase and to frame initial components of the ESIP consideration by the group.

3. Target Draft Completion by March 31—Preparation of the draft ESIP in the 3 months from January 1 to March 31 will doubtlessly require a number of meetings to discuss the topics identified and the original draft of the ESIP. The staff members supporting the broad-based constituent group can be expected to bear primary responsibility for logistical aspects of the completion of the initial draft.

C. Distribute Draft ESIP on Campus for Review/Comment and Hold Open Meeting—During early April, the draft ESIP prepared should be widely distributed on the campus for comment and review by faculty, administrators, student leaders, and members of the governing board. An open meeting will need to be held, at which widely differing viewpoints will no doubt be aired.

D. Complete Revised Draft of ESIP by End of April—By the end of April, a revised ESIP should be forwarded to the chief executive officer for his or her review and potential modification.

III. Seek Approval and Complete Publication (May through August)

A. Have Final Review/Modification by Chief Executive Officer—The constituent groups' proposed ESIP should not come as a surprise to the CEO, since he or she should have been kept informed of progress throughout their deliberations. The CEO should have the authority to adjust and refine the statement presented to him or her; however, major or substantive changes of the proposed ESIP should be discussed with the broad-based constituent group prior to forwarding them to the governing board.

B. Gain Approval of Governing Board—Ultimately, the governing board of the institution should approve the ESIP. Chief executive officers who have accomplished this indicate that it is not among the most "comfortable" experiences they have "enjoyed." As members of the governing board, many for the first time, they are asked to play a meaningful role in charting the course of the future of their institution. However, following discussion, modification, and approval of the ESIP, the governing board should be more supportive of the

CEO's implementation of the concepts contained as representative of their collective will.

C. Publish Statement in Catalog—At least the mission component of the ESIP should be published in the college catalog. In addition, the complete ESIP should be widely disseminated on the campus so that faculty, administrators, and student leaders are knowledgeable concerning the directions for future growth of the institution.

D. Present Document to the Institution as the Basis for Institutional Effectiveness Implementation/Self-Study—Finally, the ESIP should be presented to the faculty at the beginning of the following academic year as the basis for implementation of outcomes assessment, institutional effectiveness, and, in many cases, the self-study process.

Executive Summary
Academic and Administrative
Program Review Procedures
Northwestern University

EXECUTIVE SUMMARY ACADEMIC AND
ADMINISTRATIVE PROGRAM REVIEW PROCEDURES
NORTHWESTERN UNIVERSITY

Background

For several years, the Policy Advisory Committee (PAC) of the faculty had recommended the initiation of a procedure of academic and administrative program review at Northwestern. In early 1985, at the urging of PAC, the administration agreed to introduce such a review process and in concert with PAC and various administrative representatives developed a set of procedures to govern that review. These procedures were reviewed initially by PAC, the General Faculty Council (GFC), the deans, department chairs, and administrative officers. They have subsequently been revised by the Program Review Council based on the experience of the initial four years. During the four years of this process (academic years 1985–86 through 1988–89), 58 individual or unit groups have been reviewed, including 48 academic units and 10 administrative entities. (Actually, ninety-three individual departments, centers or administrative units have been reviewed to date. Since some of the reviews included multiple units, e.g., the review of English included the department and the Comparative Literature Program, the Writing Program, the *Triquarterly*, and the Program in the Major in Drama, the total count is higher.)

Summary of Process and Schedule

Coverage and Duration

Review of approximately 15 units per year; all academic and administrative units reviewed every seven years.

Program Review Council

Appointment of Program Review Council by President composed of senior faculty and senior administrators based on nominees from the Committee on Committees, the deans and other administrative officers. The size of this council will mirror the number of units being reviewed in any given year. At least two-thirds of the members of the PRC will be faculty representatives. Members shall serve for non-renewable staggered three-year terms. The chair will be appointed by the President. The Vice President for Administration and Planning also serves as a member of PRC and as vice-chair to provide administrative coordination and support. (Completion by September 20 each year.)

Initiation of Review

Units scheduled for review are notified in the spring prior to their review in the following academic year and a meeting is convened by the Vice President for Administration and Planning to discuss the process and clarify expectations. In the fall, a PRC subcommittee from within the university is designated to work with each unit in the review. External reviewers are nominated by the units and selected by the PRC and scheduled by the Office of the Vice President for Administration and Planning as soon as possible. Units prepare calendars of availability for external reviewer visit. (Nominations of individuals as external reviewers and calendars of availability are due from the unit no later than October 31st.)

Unit Self-Study

Each review unit prepares a self-study report which describes the unit's history and identifies program strengths, weaknesses and opportunities in the context of the University's mission. Specific recommendations for improvement should be included. (Completion by January 1.)

Review Activities of PRC Subcommittees

PRC subcommittee members and chief administrative officer (dean or administrative officer) will review the unit self-study report. The PRC subcommittee will meet with the members of the unit (faculty or administrative personnel), students, and other related parties such as school visiting committee to discuss the report and the status and future directions of the unit. (Ongoing throughout the process.)

External Review

An external review will be conducted through an on-campus visit (two days) by leading experts (generally two individuals) in the area under review. The unit self-study report and program review guidelines will be provided to external reviewers at least three weeks before their visit. (Completion by May 1.)

PRC Subcommittee Draft Report

Summary written report (approximately 5 10 pages) by each PRC subcommittee to PRC. This report is developed based on the unit self-study report, the visits and discussions of the PRC subcommittee, and the report of the external reviewers. It should identify the major strengths and weaknesses of the unit and opportunities for improvement for the unit in concert with overall University objectives. Specific and concrete recommendations for improvement should be included. (Completion by May 31.)

PRC Final Report and Distribution

PRC meetings with each subcommittee and development of final reports by PRC. Provision of final reports to the President, Provost, Vice President for Administration and Planning, appropriate officers, as well as head of the unit reviewed (faculty and administrative personnel as appropriate). For academic program reviews, "officers" includes the Dean and the Vice President for Research and Dean of the Graduate School. For administrative reviews, it is the responsible line Vice President(s). Individual members of the unit (faculty and administrative personnel as appropriate) receive a letter of notification that the report is available for reading in the unit head's office. (Completion by July 1.)

Option for Unit Comment on the Review

After the distribution of the reports, the members of each unit will have an opportunity for a formal response or comment about the external reviewers' report and/or that of the PRC subcommittee. The Unit reviewed may choose through their chair or director to provide comment or rejoinder. (Completion by July 15.)

Central Administrative Meetings

The President, Provost, Vice President for Administration and Planning, and Dean of the Graduate School/Vice President for Research (in the review of academic units) meet with the dean/line vice president to discuss the results of program review. Following that meeting, the Provost, Vice President for Administration and Planning, and Dean of the Graduate School/Vice President for Research (in the review of academic units) meet with the dean/line vice president and the unit head to discuss the results of program review and agree on implementation steps. (Completion by September 30.)

Unit Meeting

Unit meeting with the dean and the department chair (or vice president and unit head) to discuss results of the review and anticipated changes. The dean/line vice president will schedule the meeting with the members of the unit and notify the Office of Administration and Planning when it has occurred. (Completion by November 1.)

Agreement on Implementation Plan

Agreement on steps to be taken as a result of the review following unit's meeting with dean and department chair (or vice president and unit head). Unit, with the dean/vice president's concurrence, prepares a written plan of steps and timetable to implement the recommendations from program review. Dean/line vice president transmits plan to the Provost and Vice President for administration and Planning. (Completion within 6 months of the end of the review.)

Two-Year Follow-Up on Implementation

Second year and fourth year reports by unit head on progress in implementing recommendations stemming from program review.

Reports should: briefly reiterate the changes that were called for in the program review report and implementation plan, including timetables; discuss steps and progress in implementing these recommendations, including any which have not yet been acted upon; and indicate future steps anticipated along with timetables for pursuing the objectives established during the program review. (Reports are due by October 15 following the second year and fourth year after review.)

Summary Report by PRC

There will be an annual Summary Report to the President by the PRC. This summary report will be an integrative report rather than a recapitulation of the individual reports. The overall purposes of the report are: to identify cross-unit and general issues uncovered by the reviews; to identify opportunities for improvement, growth, and interdisciplinary cooperation within the institution; and to identify external problems and opportunities. Suggestions for improving the program review process should also be included. (Completion by September 30 at the start of the next academic year.)

Summary Report by Vice President for Administration and Planning

Following annual discussions with each dean/line vice president, the Vice President for Administration and Planning will report to central administration and the PRC units' progress in implementing program review recommendations. (Completion by September 30.)

Report by the President

The President may provide reports to the Trustees on major findings and directions. (Ongoing throughout the process.)

Revisions to the Process

Revisions to the program review process based on each year's experience are coordinated and issued by the Program Review Council. (Completion by September 30.)

Index

Academic advising 59, 182–183, 194
Academic Profile test 83
Academic support services 14, 188–208, 252
(*See also* Educational support services)
Access to data 166, 170
Accreditation
agencies 2, 5, 7–10, 151, 176, 221, 230, 243
common components 8
policy 5
process 2, 7–10, 12–13, 99
requirements 7 8, 221, 230, 243
ACT. *See* American College Testing Program
Administrative objectives, nonacademic units 14, 25–26, 33, 151–154, 188–208, 231, 241
Adult Learner Needs Assessment 57
Advisory group 21, 31
Alumni followup 36, 57–58, 60, 72, 117–118, 136, 143, 165, 181, 214
Alverno College 96–97, 99, 121
American Assembly of Collegiate Schools of Business 89–90
American Chemical Society 90–91
American College Testing Program (ACT) 56–60, 63, 79–81, 86, 181
assessment 79–80
College Outcome Measure Program (COMP) 79–81, 86

Evaluation/Survey Service (ESS) 56–60, 63
American Institute of Certified Public Accountants 90
Annual Institutional Effectiveness Cycle (AIEC) 25–27, 218–227, 239–242
(*See also* Implementation plan, fourth year)
Assessment 9–12, 15
activities 9, 35–37
for administrative objectives 14, 25–26, 33, 151–154, 188–208, 231, 241
of behavioral change and performance 104–129
community and junior colleges 117–118, 144, 194, 227–238
connection to teaching and learning 169, 177–178, 188
of critical thinking 93–96
data systems 36, 130–147, 214
department level 155–167, 168–187, 188–207
existing activities 35–37
general knowledge 78–87, 177–179
interviews 120, 177, 182
of knowledge and general skills 76–103, 173
logistical support 20, 66, 73, 161, 165–166
methodology 154
national movement 4–7, 243

procedures 35, 159–162, 212
published resources 178–179
for research outcomes 25–26, 33,
    131, 150, 152, 189–193
for service outcomes 25–26, 33,
    131, 150, 152, 189–193
specialized knowledge 87–93,
    178–179
subjective measures 111, 161,
    201–202
unobtrusive measures 106, 111,
    177, 182
Assessment center 121, 180, 185
Assessment instruments
    local 36, 64–68, 84–87, 91–93
    standardized 79–84, 86–91,
        93–96, 177–180
Assessment methodology 154
    two–year institutions 117–118,
        194, 235
Assessment process design 24–26,
    155–167
Assessment results
    assembly and processing 215
    review 224–226
Assessment/evaluation activities
    210, 212–215, 224–227, 231–236
Assessment support person 20
Attitudinal instruments 35, 37,
    55–75, 165, 181–183, 214

Behavioral change 36, 104–129,
    184–185
Behavioral constructs 106–111
Budget planning 22, 164

Case study 111, 122
Chief Executive Officer (CEO) 2, 21,
    23, 72, 151, 164, 210, 221–222,
    230, 242
Classroom research 114, 123–124
Cognitive assessment 36, 76–103,
    177–180, 212–214, 232–234
    (*See also* Knowledge measures)
Collegiate Assessment of Academic
    Proficiency (CAAP) 81
College Board 56, 60, 63, 83, 88–89
College Outcomes Measures Project
    (COMP) 79–81, 86
College Student Experiences
    Questionnaire (CSEQ) 119, 181

College Student Needs Assessment
    57
Common components
    clear statement of institutional
        purpose 10–11
    intended departmental outcomes
        10–11
    means of outcomes assessment
        11–12
    utilization of assessment results
        11– 12
Community and junior colleges
    117–118, 144, 194, 227–238
    (*See also* Two–year institutions)
Constituent advisory group 21, 31
    55, 198
Consultants 63–64, 180
Continuing education 43, 192, 228,
    250, 260
Contracted services 63–64
Cooperative Institutional Research
    Program (CIRP) 56, 63
Coordination 19–21, 31, 151,
    166–167, 224–225, 230
Costs 22–23, 28, 64–65, 68, 111–112,
    165, 205, 220–221, 225
Council for the Advancement of
    Standards (CAS) 194
Council on Postsecondary
    Accreditation (COPA) 5, 7–8,
    10, 12, 194
Curriculum and instructional
    improvement 169, 220
Curriculum review 171

Data systems 130–147
    (*See also* Institutional data
        systems)
    academic progress elements
        139–140
    course–taking patterns 139, 143,
        176, 228
    decision support 36, 133–134
    existing 36, 130–134
    interinstitutional cooperation 144,
        202
    limitations 136–137
    longitudinal 137–138
    operational support 132–133
    student elements 138–139

student tracking 112–113,
139–140, 231
utilization 140–144
Department implementation
facilitator 20, 22
Department-level assessment 3,
13–14, 25–26, 149–154,
155–167, 168–187, 222–225,
229–231, 233–234, 239
(*See also* Implementation plan,
second year)
Departmental/program objectives
elements 151, 158–159
formats and outcomes 159–160
Direct observation 106, 111, 119–
120, 177
Dissemination of survey results 67,
71–72

Educational support services 14,
188–208, 252
(*See also* Academic support
services)
Educational Testing Service (ETS)
36, 56, 60–63, 83, 88–89, 99,
181
Employers of graduates 69, 98, 118,
120, 175, 214, 234
Entering student surveys 58, 60, 65
Entrance examinations 36
Environment 125–126, 181, 253
Evaluation of results 156, 215–217,
221–227
Evaluation standards 194–195,
202–203
Existing data 35–36, 130–145, 160,
165, 176, 189, 191, 236–237
reports 134–136, 160, 189, 191
(*See also* Reports)
Expanded Statement of Institutional
Purpose (ESIP) 3, 13–15, 23–25,
33–35, 37, 39–54, 152–153,
155–158, 167, 189, 216, 222–223,
229–231, 239, 241, 243, 276–279
(*See also* Statement of purpose;
Goals; Mission)
Expanded Statement of Institutional
Purpose
Our University 245–255
preparation 276–279

review 221–224, 240–241
Your Community College 257–260
External pressures 2–7, 151, 243

Faculty 27–28, 46–48, 52, 64, 67, 69,
87, 112, 120, 123, 163–165,
168–185, 190, 212, 223,
229–230, 232, 241
Federal government 2, 5–6,
134–135, 176, 189
Federal policy 5–6
Feedback mechanisms 163, 212, 224,
240
Feedback of assessment results 15,
27, 37, 53, 210, 216–217,
226–227
Funding 16, 19, 22–24, 28, 166, 180

General education 78–87, 174,
232–233
Goals 33–35, 39, 47–54, 152–153,
156, 189, 222
(*See also* Expanded Statement of
Institutional Purpose)
Governing and coordinating boards
7, 176, 188, 230, 243
Governors 6–7
Graduate Program Self Assessment
Service (GPSAS) 61–62
Graduate Record Examination
(GRE) 82–83, 86, 88–89
Graduating student surveys 60
Graduation rates 136, 141–142, 176,
232, 237
Grants and contracts 191–192

Implementation
of department/program plans
25–26, 149–154
obstacles 28–29, 149–150, 240–242
problems 28–29, 224, 240
team 20–21
Implementation plan 19–27, 33, 35
assumptions 19–24
first year 24–25, 31–38
(*See also* Institutional foundation)
fourth year 25–27, 218–227
(*See also* Annual Institutional
Effectiveness Cycle)
second year 25–26, 149–154

(*See also* Department-level
    assessment)
third year 25–26, 209–218
(*See also* Initial implementation)
In-house surveys 64–68, 84–87,
    91–93
    (*See also* Locally developed tests
    and surveys)
Incentives 23–24, 218, 230
Information users 69–70
Initial implementation 25–26,
    209–218
    (*See also* Implementation plan,
    third year)
Institutional accreditation, common
    components 8
Institutional data systems 36,
    130–147, 214
    (*See also* Data systems)
Institutional effectiveness 3, 9–16,
    240–244
    Annual Cycle (AIEC) 25–27,
    218–227, 239–242
    common components 8, 10, 12,
    15
    comprehensive review 240–241
    forces favoring 242–244
    forces impeding 241–242
    foundation 24–25, 31–38
    (*See also* Implementation plan,
    first year)
    implementation 1, 15–16, 24–29
    implementation team 20–21
    paradigm 10–16, 22, 33
    roles 20
Institutional foundation 24–25,
    31–38
    (*See also* Implementation plan,
    first year)
Institutional Functioning Inventory
    56, 62
Institutional goals 3, 11–12, 14,
    155–165, 241
    (*See also* Statement of intended
    outcomes)
Institutional Goals Inventories (IGI)
    56, 61
Institutional mission statement
    13–15, 33–35, 39–48, 155–158,
    188–189, 228, 235, 237

Institutional Performance Survey
    (IPS) 64
Institutional planner 20
Institutional Research Program for
    Higher Education 61–63
Institutional review of outcomes
    163–165
Institutional support 19
Instruments
    evaluation criteria 178–179
    unpublished 179
Intended educational outcomes
    25–26, 33, 131, 150, 152–154,
    168–187, 189–193, 211
    two-year institutions 229–236
Intended research and public
    service outcomes 25–26, 33,
    131, 150, 152, 189–193
Interviews 120, 177, 182
Inventory of Assessment
    Procedures 35, 37

Knowledge measures 36, 76–103,
    177–180, 212–214, 232–234
    (*See also* Cognitive assessment)

Library services 14, 119, 192–193,
    252
Licensure examinations 5, 36, 91,
    111, 136, 172, 233–234
Life competencies 184–185
Linkages 22, 34, 53, 135, 152–153,
    155–157, 164, 167, 230–231,
    262–274
    bottom–to–top 53, 156–157
    top–to–bottom 52–53, 156–157
Localized instruments 36, 64–68,
    84–87, 91–93
    advantages 65–66, 86
    development 66–68
    disadvantages 65–66, 87
    general knowledge 84–87
    specialized knowledge 91–93
Locally developed tests and
    surveys 64–68, 84–87,
    91–93
    (*See also* In–house surveys)
Logistical support 20, 66, 73, 161,
    165–166
Longitudinal studies 137–138, 190

Maintaining institutional
   effectiveness 239–244
Maintenance of data 166
Mission 13–15, 33–35, 39–48,
   152–153, 155–158, 188–189,
   228–229, 235, 237
   (*See also* Expanded Statement of
   Institutional Purpose)
Momentum 28–29, 244
Motivation 210, 213 214, 218, 221,
   230, 233, 243
Multiple Assessment Procedures 99,
   121, 154, 161–162, 176, 178, 183,
   231

National Center for Higher
   Education Management
   Systems (NCHEMS) 56, 60,
   63–64
National Teachers Exam (NTE) 91,
   111
Naturalistic approach 110–111,
   122–123, 177, 182–183
   (*See also* Qualitative approach)
Nonacademic units 188–208
Northeast Missouri State University
   66, 99, 164

Objectives 14, 25–26, 33, 151–154,
   188–208, 231, 241
   (*See also* Administrative
   objectives)
Office of institutional research 20,
   22, 64, 159, 176, 200
Outcomes
   continuing education 43, 192, 228,
      250, 260
   faculty development 171, 175,
      195, 251
   public service 25–26, 33, 131, 150,
      152, 189–193
   research 25–26, 33, 131, 150, 152,
      189–193, 250
Outcomes assessment 9–10
   departmental 3, 13–14, 25–26,
      149–154, 155–167, 168–187,
      222–225, 229–231, 233–234,
      239
   student data elements 138–139
Ownership 46, 65–67

Panel studies 137–138
Participation in implementation 15,
   20–22, 31, 230
   constituent 15, 21 31, 55
   faculty 24, 168–187
Performance examinations 36,
   107–111, 115, 174–175, 184
Philosophy 35, 39–48
   (*See also* Expanded Statement of
   Institutional Purpose)
Planning and budgeting processes
   16, 19, 22, 164, 168, 219, 230
Planning/operational activities
   151–153, 210–212, 221–224
Portfolios 5, 96–99, 177, 184
Presentation of results 67, 73, 163,
   217, 227
Professional licensure examinations
   5, 36, 91, 111, 136, 172,
   233–234
Professional standards 191–192
Program review 236
Program Self-Assessment Service
   56, 61
Psychomotor skills 105, 107–111,
   113 115, 173 174, 177, 183–185

Qualitative approach 110–111,
   122–123, 177, 182–183
   (*See also* Naturalistic approach)

Raters 120
Rational planning model 12
Referents 202–203
Refinement of assessment process
   27, 220, 224, 239–240
Regional accreditation 8–10, 13, 243
Reporting systems 131, 134–136
Reports 131, 134–136, 160
   (*See also* Existing data, reports)
   federal 131, 134–135, 176, 189
   internal 131, 136
   state 131, 135–136, 176, 189
Research and public service
   outcomes 25–26, 33, 131, 150,
      152, 189–193, 250
   administrative practice 191
   attitudinal measures 190
   data system indicators 190–191
   direct measures 189–190

Results, departmental analysis
    215–217
Retention rates 136, 141–142, 176,
    214
Revision of intended outcomes 13,
    27, 163–165, 222–226
Revision of standards 162–163
Reward system 24, 169, 221
Rhode Island College 65

Second year, planning/operational
    activities 151–153, 210–212,
    221–
    224
Self report 106, 111, 116–117, 183,
    233
Self-study 196–206
Southern Association of Colleges
    and Schools (SACS) 6, 9,
    155–156, 159
Standardized instruments 79–84,
    86–91, 93–96, 177–180
    advantages 86
    American College Testing
        Program 56–60, 63, 79–81, 86,
        181
    disadvantages 86
    Educational Testing Service 36,
        56, 60–63, 83, 88–89, 99, 181
    general knowledge 78–84, 86,
        177–179, 233
    specialized knowledge 87–93
Standardized testing 5, 36, 79–84,
    86–91, 93–96, 177–186, 212–214,
    233
State legislatures 7, 243
Statement of institutional goals
    Our University 172, 174, 247–255
    Your Community College 258–260
Statement of institutional mission
    Our University 246
    Your Community College 258
Statement of intended objectives,
    administrative 14, 25–26, 33,
    151–154, 188–208, 231, 241
Statement of intended outcomes 3,
    11–12, 14, 156–165, 229–231,
    241
    departmental 13–14, 155–165,
    167, 168–175, 229–231, 241

educational/instructional 11–12,
    14, 150–153, 168–185, 232–236
educational support services
    11–12, 14, 150–152, 192–203,
    252
research 11–12, 14, 150–152,
    189–192, 250
service 11–12, 14, 150–152,
    189–1924
Statement of mission 13–15, 32–35,
    39–48, 152–153, 155–158,
    188–189, 228–229, 235, 237
Statement of purpose 3, 13–15,
    23–25, 33–35, 37, 39–54,
    130–132, 152–153, 155–158, 167,
    216, 222–223, 228–231, 239, 241,
    243
    (*See also* Expanded Statement of
    Institutional Purpose)
Strategic planning 44–46, 222
Student compliance 213–214, 233
Student Instructional Report (SIR)
    62
Student outcomes
    affective 181–183
    behavioral 104–111
    cognitive 177–180, 232–236
    performance skills 104–111,
    183–185
Student Outcomes Information
    Service (SOIS) 56, 60
Student reactions to college 56, 62
Student tracking 112–113, 139–140,
    231
Support services 14, 188–208, 252
Subjective measures 111, 161,
    201–202
Survey implementation 70–71
Survey instruments, commercial
    56–63
Survey populations 68–70
Surveys 55–75
    attitudinal 55–75
    commercial 56–63, 165
    contracted 63–64
    in-house 64–68
    information characteristics 68

Transfer student performance 171,
    214, 235

Trial Implementation of Assessment
    Procedures 25–26, 210–212
Two-year institutions 117–118, 144,
    194, 227–238
    (*See also* Community and junior
    colleges)
    assessment instruments 232–234
    expected educational outcomes
    229–234
    link with senior institutions 118,
    236
    transfer data 118, 235

U.S. Department of Education 6
University of Maryland at College
    Park 195–206

University of Tennessee at
    Knoxville 92, 99, 164, 179
University System of Georgia 85
Unobtrusive measures 106, 111,
    177, 182
Unpublished assessment
    instruments 179
Utilization of assessment results
    131, 156, 159–160, 170, 240

Value-added education 142

Withdrawing/nonreturning student
    survey 59–60, 143
Writing 85, 97, 119, 177, 184, 233

NOTES

NOTES

NOTES